FORWARD PASS

Chicago 32 Northwestern 0

FORWARD PASS

THE PLAY THAT SAVED FOOTBALL

Philip L. Brooks

WESTHOLME
Yardley

PHOTO BY

Title page: The University of Chicago defeated Northwestern 32 - 0 on
October 22, 1904, in front of twenty-seven thousand fans. Note the
carriage used to carry players to the game. (*University of Chicago
Archives*)

First Westholme Paperback September 2014
Copyright ©2008 Philip L. Brooks

Westholme Publishing, LLC
904 Edgewood Road
Yardley, Pennsylvania 19067
Visit our Web site at www.westholmepublishing.com

ISBN: 978-1-59416-216-9
Also available as an eBook

Printed in the United States of America.

For my wife and best friend, Rose;
You are my hope, my lifelong inspiration,
and my eternal love

Contents

Preface   ix

Diagram Key   xiii

A Note about Football Scoring   xiii

1   Before the Forward Pass   1

2   A Bold Concept   21

3   The Mentor   35

4   A Perfect Spiral   63

5   A Rookie Coach   85

6   South to Wabash   111

7   A Change of Plans   137

8   Blue and Gold   153

9   Creating a Modern Team   171

10   The Rebirth of Intercollegiate Football   191

Legacy   217

Notes   223

Bibliography   241

Index   249

Acknowledgments   255

Preface

RETIREMENT AFTER 45 YEARS OF COACHING FOOTBALL AND teaching was agreeable and relaxing for the first few months, but I missed the spontaneity, challenges, and rewards. I decided to keep in touch with the game by exploring the way football was played in its first few decades and to learn through the voices of the early groundbreakers how football was tranformed into the modern sport. Visiting libraries and university archives, I began to read books and manuscripts written by pioneer football coaches and players. I soon discovered fascinating but conflicting stories on how the game changed, especially the forward pass.

Sports historians are quite aware of the precarious status of football in the early twentieth century, but others might not realize just how close football came to being banned as a college sport across the country. Drawing on numerous years of college football coaching experience and extensive research, I wrote this book in an effort to honor the young coaches and athletes that not only advanced the game but quite possibly preserved the profession for coaches like me to enter some 50 to 100 years later. I hope that this book will provide a better appreciation and understanding of the colossal challenges that football coaches and players faced during the introduction of the forward pass, a rule change designed to save the game of football.

I examined thousands of early 1900s resources including historical football books, coaches' daily notes, letters, original playbooks, action pictures of individuals and groups of players in
practice and games, football contracts and telegrams, university
yearbooks, college student newspapers, archives from *The New
York Times, Boston Globe, Chicago Daily Tribune*, and newspaper archives from numerous college towns.

During my research I consulted notable documents, includ-
ng some that had never before been examined for their historical
significance, such as the venerable Amos Alonzo Stagg's forward
passing playbook from 1906 and photos of his University of
Chicago Maroons performing modern receiving and throwing
skills still used today. It is apparent that Stagg was well ahead of
his time in understanding the way individual football forward-
passing skills were to be coached and how throwing the ball
would advance the game.

I was also amazed to read about John Heisman's refusal to
succumb to those who were resisting change to the game. He
never wavered from his keen recognition of the impact the forward pass could have on the way football might be played.

And there is the generally forgotten Edward B. Cochems,
who coached against Heisman, and when the forward pass was
finally legalized in 1906 approached passing the football with an
investigative process comparable to that of a scientist. His willingness to take risks and his development of plays and frequent
use of the forward pass while coaching at St. Louis University
established a new benchmark for football.

The next innovator, Jesse C. Harper, played for and studied
under Stagg. He got his first head coaching job at the age twen-
ty-two at Alma College in Alma, Michigan. Harper quickly mod-
ernized football practice, promoted off-season conditioning, and
created a contemporary offensive philosophy by combining the

forward pass with a punishing ground game in order to maintain ball possession. His most notable accomplishment using this strategy was transforming Notre Dame from an unremarkable regional team to a national football power.

To help the reader visualize how the game was played in 1906 to 1913, I have included diagrams of offensive pass plays and defensive formations designed and employed by early coaches. These charts reveal how comparatively contemporary the game was more than 100 years ago. I have also included photographs of Lake Michigan Catholic players reenacting some of these formations to give an idea of what an early twentieth-century team would have looked like.

Diagram Key

C = Corner

DE = Defensive End

DT = Defensive Tackle

FS = Free Safety

LB = Linebacker

NT = Nose Tackle

QB = Quarterback

SS = Strong Safety

Black Circle = Offensive Center

White Circle = Offensive Player

——————| = Blocking route

— — — — = Pass direction

——————▶ = Run and pass route direction

A Note About Football Scoring

From 1904 to 1908, the following point totals were used:

Touchdown = 5 points

Point After Touchdown = 1 point

Field Goal = 4 points

From 1909 to 1911, the following point totals were used:

Touchdown = 5 points

Point After Touchdown = 1 point

Field Goal = 3 points

From 1912 to today, the following point totals have been used:

Touchdown = 6 points

Point After Touchdown = 1 point (after 1958, if kicked; 2 points if run or passed)

Field Goal = 3 points

Chicago playing Michigan in 1902. (*The Chicago History Museum SDN-001076*)

1

Before the Forward Pass

IN 1905, DESPITE MANY COLLEGES EXPERIENCING OUTSTANDING success, the sport of intercollegiate football had arrived at a moment of truth. Since the 1880s, football had evolved into a hard-hitting, ball-carrying and kicking battle with players running, pulling, pushing, and tackling. Bleeding, bruising, and broken bones were commonplace, and although it would startle a modern fan, game fatalities were common, and the 1905 season would see nineteen lives lost. But 1905 started out as years past with the usual excitement and positive anticipation for alumni and football fans across the nation. Attendance for the season set a record pace with over a million people gathering each Saturday to support and cheer their favorite college team.

At the University of Chicago's Marshall Field that Thanksgiving Day, the clouds hung low with the thermometer barely registering ten degrees. Misty breath from twenty-seven thousand fans rose and circled above the stadium. A slight breeze swept the ground but did not affect the crucial contest between the two mighty giants, University of Michigan and Chicago, that would determine the Western Conference championship.

Fielding Yost, Michigan's head football coach, felt a sense of pride leading his team onto the field amidst approval from thousands of frenzied Wolverine football fans. A large entourage from Ann Arbor, Michigan, arriving by train, was supported by alumni living and working in the Chicago area. Others were Wolverine fans because of Michigan's overwhelming success. And why not?

Since Yost's arrival in 1901, and through the previous week's 75–0 victory over Oberlin College, his Michigan teams remained unbeaten for fifty-six consecutive games. Only a 6–6 tie at Minnesota in 1903 blemished an undefeated streak. During his five-year tenure, Yost's teams had amassed 2,821 total points while allowing only 40.[1] Not to be outdone, coming into the Chicago game, his 1905 Wolverines had scored 495 points while his stingy defense shut out all twelve opponents.[2]

A hands-on take-charge coach, Yost had to be concerned about this particular Thanksgiving Day contest. Michigan's starting eleven had hardly broken a sweat in last week's romp, and with only four days' practice to learn the University of Chicago offense and defense, his Wolverines faced the biggest challenge of the season with the unbeaten Maroons.

The University of Chicago Maroons, not to be outdone, had scored 246 points while posting eight shutout victories. Indiana was the only team to cross Chicago's goal line scoring a mere 5 points.[3]

Chicago Maroons head coach Amos Alonzo Stagg waited for the Wolverines to clear the field entrance and gather at their bench before leading his team out onto the field and center stage. Prior to this mighty Michigan challenge, the Maroons' last test was twelve days ago, on Saturday, November 18, when they defeated the University of Illinois 44–0.[4] The team was well rested and prepared.

The game was a defensive struggle for nearly the entire 70 minutes. In front of a record-breaking crowd, punts filled the air. The ball, however, remained in Michigan's territory most of the afternoon, thanks to the brilliant punting of Chicago's talented quarterback, Walter Eckersall.[5] The outcome of the scoreless game hung in doubt until the final few minutes. Eckersall punted from midfield driving the ball deep behind the Wolverine's goal line where halfback William Clark tried to make something magical happen for Michigan's uncharacteristically struggling offense. With Clark attempting to run the ball out from behind the goal, Chicago's tackle Art Badenoch and captain Mark Catlin stalked him down as the clock ticked down. Both Maroons smashed into Clark, driving him back for a safety and Michigan's defeat, its first in five years. The glorious Thanksgiving Day victory provided Chicago the Midwestern championship and an undefeated season with a brilliant 10-0-0 record.[6] As *The New York Times* headlines rang out: "Chicago's Notable Victory, Michigan's First Defeat."

In the East at Philadelphia's Franklin Field on that same November Thursday, a combined twenty-thousand football fans braved a strong, bitter, cold wind, producing a single-digit chill index to witness the annual Pennsylvania–Cornell season finale. The Pennsylvania Quakers entered the 1905 game with eleven wins, no losses, and one tie with Lafayette.[7] Entering the holiday contest, Cornell had recorded a respectable season of six wins and three losses.

After completing a frustrating and scoreless first half, Penn continued to hold on despite their numerous fumbles and poor play. The Cornell Big Red gained 125 yards rushing in the first half while yielding 72 yards to their stumbling Quaker opponent.[8]

In the second half, after 10 minutes of exchanging punts, Penn gained possession on their own 10-yard line but fumbled the opportunity away on their first down. Cornell recovered the ball on Penn's 8-yard line. A Quaker 5-yard offside penalty moved the ball to the Penn 3-yard line. Cornell's offense scored on their second line plunge just inside the corner of the goal at the sideline. The Big Reds elected to "punt out" to gain better field position for their point-after try with a fair catch, but the short punt struck the ground.* The intended Cornell player picked up the ball and attempted to run it over but was tackled short of the goal line. The score now read Cornell 5, Penn 0.[9]

The Quaker enthusiasts believed Penn would rally in the second half, but Penn continued to fumble, playing with an apparent lack of genuine effort. *The New York Times* described Penn's predicament: "It looked as though the fruits of that hard season were to be thrown away at the end as gloom settled over the

---

*A team scoring a touchdown in 1905 was allowed to attempt a kick after goal (a point-after touchdown — PAT — in today's football) with a choice of an immediate placekick at any depth on the field parallel to the sideline at the point where the ball crossed the goal line or, if the ball crossed the goal line close to the sideline, the scoring team could set up a better kicking position by first attempting a punt-out. In a punt-out, the scoring team would punt the ball from behind the goal line (there was no end zone in 1905) at the point of the touchdown and the PAT was then attempted where the ball was caught. The opponents were allowed to line up anywhere on the goal line except within a space of 15 feet on either side of the punter's mark. The defense was not allowed to interfere with the punter standing behind the goal line. However, because the defending team was onside, as soon as the ball was put into play, they were allowed to charge in and attempt to block the kick or run out and interfere with the catch. If the catch was muffed, the offensive team could recover the ball and try to run it across the goal line for the point; otherwise, if the play was unsuccessful, as was the case with Cornell, the ball was dead and out of play, with no PAT. (see Fielding Harris Yost, *Football for Player and Spectator*. Ann Arbor, Mich.: University Publishing Company, 1905, 280, 298.)

Pennsylvania stands. But the mighty west wind was still doing its work helping Penn's punter drive the ball 15 to 20 yards further than Cornell's backs could return it. Finally Penn received her chance gaining possession on Cornell's 35-yard line."[10]

The Quakers were not to be denied as they advanced the ball closer and closer to the goal line. Cornell's only hope was another fumble, but this was not to be as Penn held onto the ball and scored crashing over the goal line. The game was tied at 5 points each. Penn, not electing a punt-out, lined up for a placekick from scrimmage. The kick was good with the Quakers winning 6–5.

As these two games demonstrate, by 1905, coaches had developed an offensive game plan based on the principle of moving the football through two distinct means in roughly equal measure. The first advanced the football with the running game. The second, and just as important, was the use of a tactical kicking game. Depending on the prevailing weather conditions, it was common for a team to average close to thirty punts a game.[11] As an example, the University of Michigan crushed Stanford in the 1902 Rose Bowl 49-0. Despite the Wolverines gaining 527 yards rushing and twenty-seven first downs to Stanford's 67 yards and five first downs, Michigan still punted twenty-one times in the game.

According to Fielding Yost, "The team goal was to develop an outstanding punter capable of driving the opponent deep into their own territory until such time when his team, reaching the so-called 'scoring distance,' unleashed the full complement of the running attack upon the defense."[12] Most games that resulted in punting duels found the team possessing the best punter usually advancing as the victor.

Michigan's offensive strategy under Fielding Yost dissected the football playing field into three areas. In general, he established the concept to help his quarterback's play selection. The first area was the portion of the field between one's own goal line and the 35-yard line. Yost's teams were instructed to always kick. He believed if the opponents' backs had a difficult time fielding kicks, a team must punt frequently.[13]

When punting near the sideline, the punter was instructed to direct the ball toward the width of the field, but not too far, because protecting the open field was difficult. Losing player leverage and allowing long returns during punting were a concern for Yost.

Yost's second field area was between a team's own 35-yard line and the opponents' 35-yard line. The quarterback was instructed to call an array of running plays including end sweeps, off-tackle slants, plunges, reverses, and double reverses. Yost's philosophy was to maintain possession by attempting to gain first downs by running, but to punt on third down unless gaining the necessary yardage for a first down was a sure bet. (In 1905, there were three downs allowed to gain the 5 yards necessary for a first down.) The third field segment was the opponent's 35-yard line to their goal line. This offensive area is analogous to what today we call the "red zone." A team in scoring territory was expected to attempt a field goal, if unable to score a touchdown.[14]

When the Intercollegiate Football Rules Committee (IFC) implemented "down and distance" in 1882, they also approved a rule permitting the offensive team to call signals aloud. Coaching or calling the plays from the sidelines was prohibited because the IFC wanted to keep the game under the players' control. At the conclusion of each play, the captain or quarterback made sure his team was ready to listen to his commands.[15]

The "quarterback" has an interesting history. In the early days of football, the center either rolled the ball back or stood at the line of scrimmage holding the ball with one hand while kicking

Michigan coach Fielding Yost divided the football field into three areas to assist his quarterback with his offensive game plan. The first (1) was from his goal line to the 35-yard line, the second (2) was to his opponent's 35-yard line, and the third (3) was to the opponent's goal line, analagous to the modern "red zone." At this time, a point after a touchdown was kicked along a line perpendicular to the point where the ball was declared down. A team had the option, if the ball were too near the sideline, to attempt a punt and fair catch, and if successul, the point after could be attempted from the spot of the fair catch. Note the 5-yard grid on the field, a marking system in early football that provided the term "grid iron." (*Library of Congress*)

the ball back with his opposite foot to a player who was standing a quarter of the way back from the 5-yard grid, thus the name "quarterback." The name of the position stuck, but it was not until 1893, when John Heisman introduced the concept of the center handing the ball off between his legs to the quarterback that the modern idea of the position was born.

Fielding Yost had three requirements for the quarterback: make the call plain, simple, and rapid. The quarterback was instructed to call the signal out clear and only one time. Yost's system called a new play immediately following the completion of the preceding play.[16]

Most early coaches believed the quarterback's ability to apply football knowledge could not be learned from an established set of rigid standards. They recognized many new variables confronted a team from one week to the next. A quarterback's field decision needed to be based on knowledge learned about the strength or weakness of the opponent, such as the kicking game, or offense and defense. Inclement weather conditions played a major role with excessive wind, rain, cold, or heat interfering with the ability to play good, consistent football.

Teams did not use the huddle at this time, so the quarterback called plays rapidly at the line of scrimmage. "Speed was intended to wear down an opponent so the players in the best physical condition would clean up in the second half," Stagg recalled.[17] With the teams quickly reassembling after every running or kicking play, no player was allowed to remain on the ground and recover. A 45-minute half allowed two teams to run well over one hundred plays per half by averaging one play every twenty-seven seconds.* Covering and returning punts demanded high player physical conditioning levels. Numerous serious injuries resulted because of the nature of the game—high punting frequency, accelerated pace, an excessive number of high-speed collisions, and the lack of time for a player to fully recover before the ensuing play.

I t was clear that by 1905, football play had advanced beyond many of the archaic rules established years earlier, creating a risk and a lack of adequate safety. The first rule contributing to potential injuries was how a down was defined. When a ball carrier's momentum was stopped by an opponent or the ball carrier went out of bounds, the referee blew the ball dead at that spot. The rules, however, permitted a runner carrying the ball to be pushed or pulled by teammates as long as he maintained forward

---

*Through the 1893 season each half was 45 minutes long. In 1894, each half was shortened to 35 minutes, and in 1906 each half was further reduced to its current 30 minutes.

progress. The ball was not declared dead by officials until the runner verbally declared himself "down." Assisting the runner resulted in multiple physical collisions and increased the risk for injury.[18]

A touchdown declaration rule permitted extended physical contact after a player had crossed the opponent's goal line. There was no end zone, so a ball carrier could be chased or tackled behind the line until he physically touched the ball to the ground resulting in a dead ball and a touchdown.

The out-of-bound rule stated that when a player carrying the ball was on or outside the sidelines or when the ball touched the ground on or outside the sideline, the down was over. A ball carrier being tackled was instructed to carry the ball out of bounds. There were no hash marks in 1905; therefore, the offensive team then had a choice of moving the ball back on the field either 5 or 15 yards out from the sideline where the ball was declared out of bounds for the next scrimmage play. This rule led to extended physical contact with an opponent attempting to keep a ball carrier in bounds to run the clock and his teammates fighting to knock him out of bounds.

The rules for players' equipment required no head gear, so wearing a leather-padded helmet was optional. Felt or rubber pads were sewn or placed under the jersey to pad the shoulders. Some players wore shin guards over their legs, but most thought they were heavy and impeded movement. The uniform consisted of a jersey and canvas pant. Players wore long socks to cover their lower legs and leather shoes with leather cleats. Metal cleats were illegal. The game was rugged, hard hitting, and fast and demanded improved and safer equipment for the participants.

The substitution rule allowed a player to be replaced at any time during the game. The substitute entering the game was to report directly to the referee before taking a position. The player being replaced was prohibited from reentering the remainder of the game. This last restriction placed a burden on the starting eleven, as they were expected to play the entire contest. Individuals played through pain, fatigue, and injury to remain on the field. A free-substitution rule might have reduced the numerous muscle compression injuries and tired players sustaining various injuries.

The tackling technique was a formula for disaster. Players were instructed to aim at the point between the hips and knees. The tackler led with his head and shoulders and on contact attempted to slide the head to one side or the other to avoid the runner's legs. He wrapped his arms around the legs of the ball carrier with a firm grasp and with heavy momentum attempted to drive the runner backward and off his feet. The head and body were exposed to gang tackling and vicious attacks of punching, piling-on, and pummeling, let alone the bone-cracking potential of a knee to the head. This form of tackling led to serious head, neck, and spinal injuries. Regardless if one was wearing a helmet or not, the use of this tackling technique was poorly devised and dangerous to use. Brutality designed to intentionally injure was common.

Offensive coaches taught blocking by leading with the head and shoulder, and offensive linemen were legally allowed to use their hands to block, push, and pull defenders. Shoulder blocking without a helmet combined with the use of hands and arms on both sides of the ball permitted each player to smash the face, head, or neck of the opposing player. The result was numerous cuts, bruises, broken noses and jaws, and other injuries.

Mass formations led to plays featuring tackle interference and backs or ends trailing the play offering assistance to the ball carrier, thus creating unnecessary physical contact. Interference (blocking) directed at the defensive tackle or end was intended

Two University of Nebraska defensive players leading with their heads while attempting to tackle a University of Chicago receiver who has caught a forward pass from quarterback Walter Eckersall in 1906. (*University of Chicago Archives*)

to overwhelm the defender at the point of attack. Four players blocked at the point of attack, with an offensive end assigned to follow the play and assist the runner from behind. The repeated physical beating sustained by the defensive tackle or end often resulted in injury and sometimes, tragically, even death.

Despite the roughness and brutality, by 1905, American intercollegiate football had grown so popular that over 250 college teams competed throughout the United States. Harvard University's football stadium was constructed in 1903 with a state-of-the-art capacity to seat up to forty-three thousand spectators. Most football facilities were not constructed large enough to accommodate the enormous number of fans desiring to support their alma mater. Many universities resolved the issue by leasing playing fields located in large metropolitan areas. This created a madhouse of fanatics pouring into the cities to enjoy the weekend's social event.

Football was quickly becoming the dominant spectator sport, and increased newspaper circulation to the middle class helped to expand the campus football craze. Public interest and support intensified with fans attending games in greater numbers. College presidents struggled with the concept of institutional support because of their concerns with game's violence, its distraction from academic pursuits, and the carnival atmosphere surrounding many games.

In addition to the championship between Michigan and Chicago and the great Penn–Cornell rivalry, in 1905 other great games occurred. The week before Thanksgiving, in what many sports fans considered as the eastern game of the year, Yale defeated Harvard in a hard-fought contest 6–0 before a sell-out crowd. Yale stormed through the year undefeated with a 10-0-0 record and was the only eastern college to win every contest. The Naval Academy recorded the finest season in its twenty-six years of football with ten wins, one loss, and a 6-6 tie with archrival Army in the season finale on December 2, 1905. President Roosevelt, his family, cabinet members of his administration, admirals, generals, diplomats, the French Ambassador, and the German Ambassador were in attendance at the game played at Princeton's field before an estimated twenty-thousand fans. The game, however, was terminated before the official time limit because of darkness.[19]

In the Western Independent Conference, Nebraska won the championship with an overall record of eight wins and two losses. The University of Colorado finished second with an 8-1 record, losing to Nebraska 18–0. The University of Kansas had an outstanding season winning ten games while losing only to Colorado 15–0.[20]

In the far west, Stanford was undefeated with a 8-0-0 record.

Vanderbilt was crowned champion of the Southern Independent Conference with a conference record of five wins and no losses, and an overall record of seven wins and one loss.

Virginia Tech finished second winning the only two conference games scheduled and completed the season with an impressive record of nine wins and one loss.[21]

The evils of football described by university presidents were not the sole responsibility of the players and coaches because much of the blame rested on their own shoulders.[22] Despite the outcry of many calling for reform, the campus administrators expended little energy developing and maintaining control over athletics programs.

Student-athletes were interested in a rough-and-tumble sport featuring competitive running, kicking a ball, and scoring. In the formation years of football, college administrations failed to recognize the potential for the sport's popularity and fan interest. A lack of vision played into the hands of special interest groups allowing the development of independent student football associations on college campuses. They controlled and managed the financial budgets, hired coaches, scheduled games, contracted officials, and basically orchestrated all necessary activities to conduct a successful football program. College leaders tolerated these activities and regarded them necessary for college spirit.

However, the colleges' failure to assume control of football programs permitted the creation of a two-headed monster. Institutional leaders' omission of responsibility and lack of supervision opened the door for coaches and inexperienced student representatives to assume control over the powerful Intercollegiate Football Association (IFA) and the Intercollegiate Football Rules Committee (IFRC). These governing organizations met annually to evaluate, discuss, and revise the adopted game rules. Football evolved through the decision making of players, captains, and coaches representing a limited number of eastern colleges. College administrators did not publicly appear concerned about the inadequate control they had over the game.

The lack of standardized college eligibility rules allowed players to register in a different college year after year. It was discovered by one university that seven of their starting eleven players weren't actually enrolled in school. Players moved from college to college so they could play football for six to eight consecutive years.

In late November, the *Chicago Record Herald* and *Chicago Tribune* portrayed the 1905 season as one of the bloodiest and deadliest in football's history. Media accounts recorded nineteen deaths directly attributed to playing football. Most of the deaths were a result of spinal, neck, or head trauma from high-impact tackling or blocking. Fractures continued to lead the number of serious injuries, with broken phalanges, arms, collar bones, and legs being reported. The same newspapers that helped create football's popularity were now calling for reform of the game. Deaths highlighted that year included nineteen-year-old Union College of Schenectady halfback William Moore, who died after being tackled and piled on by numerous players in a game against New York University, and a freshman at Swarthmore College who sustained a fatal brain hemorrhage after a hard hit during football practice. Facing strong public pressure, state governments deliberated on rendering football on college campuses illegal.[23]

The death toll in 1905 caused some leading journalists and academic leaders to question the validity of continuing such a brutal and vicious game. College presidents and university chancellors threatened to ban the sport. Many college leaders vocalized great concern with a unifying call for direction, leadership, and accountability from the football rules committee.

In additions, serious allegations of corruption and fraud in college football's environment involving players, coaches, football associations, and college admissions departments were made public. In response, the college leaders called for immediate reforms and blamed the old football rules committee for its failure to heed previous warnings of the dangers football incurred. College presidents also did not have confidence in the Committee's ability or integrity to change the special interest in the game that student organizations had created.

President Theodore Roosevelt, who loved the game of football, and did not want it abandoned, strongly called for modification of its rules.[24] The president charged colleges to study the sport of football and demanded leaders to adopt new safety measures or he would mandate executive orders to ban the game altogether. The president also commissioned college leaders to devise a universal system of intercollegiate regulation and supervision over the game.[25]

On December 4, 1905, a meeting took place at the White House between President Roosevelt, Harvard's head coach Dr. William Reid, Jr., and Herbert White, also from Harvard, for the purpose of reviewing the preceding football season's serious problems and its reformation. It was believed Roosevelt suggested remedies for its moral correction but left the technical revision in the hands of the coaches and players.

The president's intervention may have been too late. The game was in serious jeopardy as college presidents and their respective board of trustees across the country began buckling to the intense public pressure to bury the popular sport. Boston College, Duke, Temple, Columbia, Dartmouth, Georgetown, MIT, University of Virginia, State University of New York at Brockport, Trinity, and Union College in the East all banned football on their campuses. In the West, similar abolition of football occurred as Stanford University and the University of California replaced football with rugby, while Arizona, Arizona

State, San Jose State, and Tulsa banned football completely. In the Midwest, Northwestern, Central Michigan, and Cincinnati followed suit. In the South, Wake Forest, Baylor, and Southwestern Louisiana also barred the playing of football.[26]

H enry M. McCracken, chancellor of New York University, invited nineteen eastern Atlantic coastal colleges to initiate a discussion on football reforms. Thirteen colleges accepted—Syracuse, Rutgers, Stevens, Trinity, Fordham, Wesleyan, Columbia, Army, Rochester, Lafayette, Haverford, Union, and New York University—and the representatives convened at the Murray Hill Hotel in New York on December 8, 1905.[27]

President Wilson of Princeton University responded that he was not prepared to take part in such a conference. His concern was the leaders taking a hasty action in reaction to the public's antagonistic attitude. Harvard University, Amherst College, and Hamilton College also refused to send representatives. Harvard's president Charles Eliot refused to send a representative because of his disgust for Walter Camp—who was perhaps the person most responsible for popularizing the sport that Eliot loathed, let alone being from rival Yale—and because of his lack of faith in the college presidents' ability to effect the necessary positive change in reforming football.[28]

One of the first actions taken by the council was adopting the name of the Intercollegiate Athletic Association of the United States or IAAUS. For the colleges to assume greater control and responsibility over the reformation of football, resolutions were adopted that an IAAUS college representative could not be a player, coach, umpire, or referee but must be an active member of the faculty.

The university presidents' discussion centered on three central questions: Ought the present game of football be abolished?;

if not abolished, what changes should be made in the game to remedy its defects; and, if abolished, what sport should take its place? After heated discourse and dialogue representing contradicting views, a resolution stating, "The game of football played under existing rules should be abolished" was put to the vote. *The New York Times* reported five colleges including Columbia voted "aye," and eight voted "nay," resulting in defeat of the resolution. Therefore, reform not abolition was favored by a majority of the voting institutions.[29]

The IAAUS next established a fact-finding committee for exploring and recommending rule changes to eliminate football's dangerous play. Henry McCracken, Palmer Pierce of West Point, and Francis Bangs of Columbia were appointed to head the committee to meet in Philadelphia.

The thirteen colleges scheduled a follow-up national convention for later that December, resolving that the nation's more than two-hundred colleges sponsoring football should be invited to attend.[30] The purpose of this gathering was clearly stated: "Answers for making football safe and less brutal made by leading universities will be awaited with great interest and anticipation." It also mentioned that a separate committee had convened at Harvard and, according to William Reid, "The Harvard committee would make even more dramatic recommendations than announced at Philadelphia on Saturday and only radical changes can avail, if the game is to be continued at Harvard."[31]

The football rules committee agreed to wait on Harvard's plan until mid-December. Members of the Intercollegiate Football Rules Committee were free to make public statements regarding their recommendations discussed at the previous rules meeting in Philadelphia.

On Thursday, December 28, 1905, a second meeting of the IAAUS was held in New York City, where sixty-two colleges

debated the future of football. They determined the game needed direction and broader control by the universities. They also
reiterated that the IAAUS (later to be renamed the National
Collegiate Athletic Association in 1910) must find ways to
reduce the risk of injury, even if it meant changing the nature of
the game.[32]

It appeared as if no decision or compromise would be
reached because delegates still held strongly opposing views.
After heated debate, the practical men in the conference managed to convince the others that recognition of the present
Intercollegiate Football Rules Committee at least was necessary.
If any effective reforms were to be made in revising the code,
they needed to work together.

Emerging from a stormy 9-hour session, the delegates presented their plan. A committee of seven was appointed to revise
the football rules. They were charged to seek an amalgamation
with the old Intercollegiate Football Rules Committee. If they
failed, they were to independently formulate a second set of football rules. The third directive was to develop an open game,
eliminating rough and brutal play, along with effective enforcement of the playing rules.[33]

The newly formed rules committee traveled the next day,
December 29, to Philadelphia to meet with the old football
IFRC's committee with an agenda to realign the committees into
one. The football convention preferred one rule code, not two.

The next item on the agenda was the governance of football.
The IAAUS developed a resolution placing the responsibility for
the reform of football directly on the shoulders of the universities' academic authorities as follows: "Hereby, Resolved that this
conference recommends the academic authorities of the colleges and universities throughout the country hold themselves as

ultimately responsible for the conduct of athletes and coaches within their respective institutions."[34]

In late December 1905, Washburn College and Fairmount College played an experimental game in Wichita, Kansas, to field test the proposal of extending the distance to be gained to 10 yards for a first down. It was thought that the increased distance would force teams to open their offenses with more end runs and reverses. *The New York Times* described the contest as a complete failure. The two teams compiled a total of seven first downs. Six weeks earlier, these same two opponents met under the old rules of three downs to gain 5 yards and totaled eighteen first downs. "Except through punts, neither team was able to get within striking distance of their opponent's goal line. The game was played almost entirely in the center of the field."[35] Unfortunately, the model game lacked the key ingredient to an open-style offense: the forward pass.

Observers, including football coaches and fans were highly disappointed in the outcome of the model game. Pessimism circulated throughout the coaching ranks and subsequent football rules committee meetings about the new rule. Punting on third down for gaining 10 yards in two attempts seemed like an impossible task. Something had to change. Walter Camp, chair of the subcommittee for opening the game, proposed a four-down plan, but the idea gained very limited support. The final verdict, however, was for the distance to be gained to remain at 10 yards and the number of downs at three.

With football now under the charge of college administrators and a committee set up to reduce the violence in the game, there was speculation about just what an "open game" would look like and how it would change the nature of football.

One of Amos Alonzo Stagg's quarterbacks demonstrating an overhead spiral forward pass in 1906. (*The Chicago History Museum SDN-05451I*)

2

A Bold Concept

ACCORDING TO A REPORT BY LOUIS HENRY BAKER in his 1945 book, *Football: Facts and Figures*, a successful forward pass was inadvertently thrown as early as November 30, 1876.[1] Walter Camp, a freshman running the ball for Yale, was being tackled by a Princeton player when he suddenly threw the ball forward. Oliver Thompson, a Yale teammate, caught the advancing ball and outran the opposition for a touchdown. After Princeton's vociferous protest declaring the play illegal, the referee C. B. Bushnell, a Yale undergraduate, decided to use a coin toss to determine the fate of the play.[2] Yale won the toss affirming the touchdown, thus sanctioning football's first forward pass.

Reading newspaper game summaries in the late 1880s often causes confusion as the term "pass" is frequently noted in the story line. The words "lateral" and "pass" were used interchangeably during recorded game accounts. A published article reporting the November 24, 1883, Princeton versus Yale game played on Manhattan Field in New York, however, is explicit: "A pass by

Yale's quarterback Twombley to halfback E.L. Richards was overthrown so far that he had to run forward to catch it."[3] It just so happens that one of the spectators of the game was a young high-school graduate visiting potential colleges, Amos Alonzo Stagg. In his 1927 book, *Touchdown*, he describes the play as a long lateral that overshot the receiver, forcing the Yale split end to catch the ball on the run, where he "went for a long gain before being tackled by Princeton's defensive fullback."[4] This was Stagg's first brush with the forward pass, and he would not forget its significance.

Twelve years later, on October 26, 1895, rookie coach Glen "Pop" Warner, who was destined to become one of the greatest coaches of the age, stood on the sidelines watching North Carolina's punter line up on the goal line preparing to kick the ball to his Georgia team.

The Bulldog defense had just stopped the Tar Heels on their 13-yard line. Warner anticipated his team would obtain good field position with an opportunity to score. The ball was snapped, and a heavy rush overwhelmed the punter. Expecting a blocked kick, the punter wittingly sidestepped the rush and threw a sidearm end-over-end 17-yard forward pass toward left halfback George Stephens, who was heading downfield covering the punt. The ball landed in the hands of a startled Stephens. Still in stride, he scampered another 80 yards for a touchdown.

Pop Warner and the Georgia team were astounded. They protested the forward pass was illegal and argued it should be nullified. The referee denied seeing the play and awarded North Carolina the winning touchdown.[5] The final score read North Carolina 6, Georgia 0.

Just as Stagg was fortunate enough to witness the Yale forward pass, another future football legend, John Heisman, happened to see this unusual play. Heisman, who played football and earned a law degree from the University of Pennsylvania in 1892, accepted the head football coach position at Oberlin College after graduation instead of practicing law. He soon moved on to Akron before assuming the helm of Auburn's football program in 1895. Heisman was scouting the Georgia–North Carolina game in preparation for Auburn's November 28 contest with Georgia. Stephens's touchdown catch and run left an overwhelming impression on Heisman. He realized that the forward pass was exactly what was needed to open up football's brutal constricted play and as a result create a safer game. Heisman would talk about this spectacular pass play for years to come.

In 1903, with critics beginning to question the way football was played, Heisman wrote to Walter Camp, now secretary of the Intercollegiate Football Rules Committee, presenting the advantages of the forward-pass concept. But the communication fell on deaf ears, and no action was taken. Heisman addressed Camp again in 1904, illuminating the importance of studying the legalization of the forward pass.[6]

Bearing the conscience of football, the persistent Heisman would not back away from his conviction concerning the importance of transforming the game with the forward pass. Realizing more advocates were needed, Heisman approached Navy's Lt. Paul Dashiell, the football rules committee chair, convincing him of the value of legitimatizing the forward pass. Together, Heisman and Dashiell achieved the support of numerous newspaper sports editors and writers as well as John C. Bell, Philadelphia's district attorney and fellow football rules committee member.

Bell and Dashiell were persistent in their quest for legalizing the forward pass. Support for the innovative concept also came from William Reid, Harvard's head coach. The University of Chicago's representative Amos Alonzo Stagg, a strong forward-pass advocate, was recuperating from an illness and unable to attend the critical January meetings. Walter Camp was opposed to the proposition of a forward pass being introduced into the game but strongly supported extending the distance to be gained to 10 yards instead of 5 yards for a first down.[7]

After public outcry for reform following the disastrous 1905 football season, on January 12, 1906, a joint meeting between the old football rules committee and the newly appointed authority was held. The newly assembled fourteen-member football rules body became known as the American Intercollegiate Football Rules Committee (AFRC). It included six members of the old rules committee: Navy's Lt. Paul Dashiell, Walter Camp of Yale, Harvard's Dr. William T. Reid, J. B. Fine, a Princeton professor, district attorney of Philadelphia John C. Bell of the University of Pennsylvania, the University of Chicago's professor and head football coach Amos Alonzo Stagg, and eight newly appointed members: Cornell professor L. M. Dennis, Henry L. Williams, Minnesota's head football coach and a converted forward-pass advocate, F. Homer Curtis of Texas, West Point's Lt. Charles D. Daly, Dr. James. A. Babbitt of Haverford, professor C. W. Savage of Oberlin, professor James T. Lees of Nebraska, and E. K. Hall of Dartmouth.[8]

The new committee created four subcommittees to study and make specific recommendations on eliminating brutality and foul play, opening the game, experimenting with test games to try out innovations, and centralization of the officials.[9] These fourteen men would be responsible for charting a new direction for the game.

Walter Camp, E. K. Hall, and William Reid were responsible for studying and recommending alternative proposals for opening the game. Camp and Hall were nonsupporters of the forward pass, so their subcommittee had numerous heated and conflicting discussions about opening up the game. They finally agreed on a written compromise by incorporating the forward pass and 10-yard concept.[10]

In late January, they presented their controversial proposal to the whole body. Not everyone agreed on a single solution, but after three months of debate, a compromise plan was finalized and adopted for what the coaches believed would save intercollegiate football. The final wording of the innovative forward-pass legislation was endorsed on April 14, 1906.

The American Football Rules Committee approved twenty-six rule revisions to make the game safer for future years of competition. Five crucial modifications for opening up the constricted play were adopted:

1. The forward pass.
2. The onside kick.
3. A minimum of six offensive players on the line of scrimmage.
4. A prohibition on the use of the hands while blocking.
5. The establishment of a neutral zone to prevent encroachment.

For the first time in over twenty years, colleges and universities agreed to formulate major changes in the game of football. These five new rules would ultimately open up the game, thereby making it safer and less brutal, but they also were the last major components in the creation of a distinctive American sport.[11] Modern football had arrived. But you would not know it from the coaches and players.

These new rules were not a blueprint for success. Coaches and players alike had no previous experience with the forward pass. Coaches had only four months to learn, understand, and develop tactical football passing and receiving techniques before the start of the 1906 season. No one possessed the knowledge of pass routes or protection blocking. There were no forward-passing books or secret formulas for implementing successful strategies for this newly created game-changing variable. Another problem was, simply, that a majority of the college football coaches did not desire or welcome these dramatic changes.

Forward-pass architects were delving into uncharted territory. Even zealot advocates on the committee expressed serious concern when they announced the innovative rules. Because forward passing was such a newfangled concept, the committee members believed they had to be very cautious with its introduction. In discussing the proposed rule changes, they considered two major factors. First, that a suitable balance should be maintained between the offense and defense. The football committee members did not desire to create a rule that would weaken the defense and thus favor the offense. Preserving the integrity of the defense was one of their top priorities.

John Heisman, despite no appointment to the rules committee, strongly believed the defense would have to adjust to the forward-pass threat by deploying defenders off the line to cover the deep areas. The defense would then become more vulnerable to the ground game thereby creating a more equalized state between it and the offense. He also believed the balance would reduce mass play and save football by helping to prevent unnecessary deaths and multiple injuries.

The second concern was that the forward pass might actually cause additional injuries. The members' goal was to create and promote a safer game based on conservative and cautious modifications of the rules. The new forward-pass rules stated that: 1) The pass was required to cross the line at least 5 yards out from each side of the center, 2) The ball could not be caught in a 5-yard zone on either side of the center or within a rectangle 10 yards wide extending to the opponents goal line (This rule was implemented to prevent the ball from being caught in the congested middle of the formation over fear of injuries to the receiver. A severe penalty including the loss of possession at the spot of the pass was imposed for the ball not correctly crossing the line.), 3) The ball had to be touched by a player of either team before striking the ground or loss of possession occurred at the spot of the pass.[12] This latter rule had the unfortunate affect of paralyzing a team's decision to use the pass. Additionally, a forward pass 4) was limited to the field of play bounded by the side lines and the goal line. A ball could not be caught for a touchdown because a forward pass had to be completed within the field of play. When a pass went out of bounds, before crossing the opponent's goal line, ball possession changed where it intersected the sidelines. If, however, the ball struck any in-bounds player, and then passed out of bounds, possession remained with the offense. A ball caught by either team over the goal line was ruled a touchback and awarded to the opposition on their 25-yard line. The penalty for an untouched incomplete pass thrown from behind the goal line was considered a safety and awarded to the defense. The ball was then placed on the 25-yard line and kicked-off to the defenders.

Although the above rules were eventually discarded, four additional points in the original forward-pass legislation have never been rescinded: First, only the two end men on the line of scrimmage and those in the backfield were entitled to catch or touch a forward pass. (The tight end and eligible players were added later.) Second, only one forward pass was allowed during a scrimmage down. Third, only the team placing the ball into play was allowed to generate a forward pass, and fourth, forward passes could only be legally thrown from behind the line of scrimmage.[13]

Many early football resources incorrectly stated that 1906 passes were limited in length to fewer than 20 yards, but this rule would not be enacted until 1910. Prior to this time, a pass could be thrown any length as long as it was touched within the field of play.

Another major factor limiting the amount of passing was a defensive player's right to interfere with the receiver. There was no rule or penalty preventing the defender from pushing, pulling, or knocking down a receiver, and there was no official protection for the receiver. The defense held the advantage and was legally allowed to use any means to intercept or knock the ball away from the receiver.

The new forward-pass rules, however, did contain some favorable qualities. In contrast to the lateral or the backward pass, a forward pass was not required to be completed as long as it was touched by one of the two teams. The offensive team did not lose possession on an incomplete forward pass that was touched, with the result being only a loss of a down. A lateral, however, had to be caught because an errant or dropped one resulted in a live ball for either team to recover. The receiver's job was to retrieve the fumbled or wayward lateral; however, it generally meant loss of yards for the offensive team as well as the down.

The onside kick, which supplemented the forward pass, was a direct snap to a quarterback or halfback who immediately punted the ball across the line of scrimmage and toward a vacated spot in the defensive front, usually at a distance for a first down. The rule implied, because the kicking team was "onside" as soon as the ball touched the ground, they were eligible to recover a live ball. Prior to this rule the kicking team could not recover the ball unless it was first touched by an opposing player. The punter kicked the ball with a low trajectory, like a pooch punt, to hit at the moment when an end or halfback sprinting downfield arrived to recover the ball. In many ways, this play was as difficult to master as the forward pass.

A majority of football coaches, especially in the East, South, and West, found the new forward-pass rules extremely restrictive. Working with the quarterback to master the accuracy of throwing to a receiver required a great deal of practice time. Coaches were not willing to take the time or the risk of a poor passing performance with a high probability of turning the ball over to the opponents. Even the rules committee members were concerned that introducing the forward pass into football would totally change the game from that played in 1905.

P rior to the 1906 football season, there were rumors of general dissatisfaction with the new code and serious talk of holding another football rules convention in early October, but no meeting to consider revisions to the new legislation ever materialized.

August 26, 1906, *The New York Times* headline announcing that the "New Style Football will be Spectacular" brought smiles of optimism to many fans and coaches. West Point had agreed to take the lead in the creation of a field laboratory game with subcommittee chair Lt. Charles D. Daly and professors J. B. Fine and C. W. Savage evaluating the outcomes. The article featured West Point's spring practice experimentation with the newly created open football game finding it demonstrated great promise for success.[14]

One prominent West Point football man said, "I believe there will be marked changes in both the defense and offense, but I do not feel the forward pass brought the expected openness. I do not believe forward passing will achieve a prominent role in opening up the 1906 football play. The pass was too uncertain, required too much accuracy, and found too difficult to change from the old rules to make it of great value. The moral effect, in keeping the defense on the verge of expectancy watching for its use will be of greater value than the pass itself." He went on to elaborate more specifically on forward passing and its complex execution,

> If a forward pass was called, the pass had to be made to certain prescribed men, in certain prescribed directions, and cleanly handled or lost. The change which I regard as most important in opening up play was the on-side kick. When a kicked ball was free to be secured by either side it introduced the greatest possibilities imaginable. What a powerful factor is the quarterback's on-side kick. There was no necessity to remain on-side until the kick was made, as ends and halfbacks could run downfield to secure a ball kicked in front of them.
>
> The consequences of this and the forward pass threat was the spreading out of the tight closed defense of nine and ten men fronts. The result was weakening the defensive line and opening up the opportunity for a successful running play. I believe the ten yard rule would have been ruinous without these changes. Also the six-men front rule, and not allowing one of the five interior men to move into the backfield to lead interference, will eliminate the line bucking mass plays and reduce the chance for injury.
>
> Altogether, the sport is immensely benefited by the modification of the rules. I am not one who believes that the old grand game will die. I believe the virility and innate value will pull it through its serious sickness and that the coming season will see it restored to an all time popularity and power. I further believe the team that builds up the best defensive system will become the successful team, not the one with the strong offense.[15]

Left, DePaul's quarterback P.J. Barry throwing an end-over-end forward pass in 1908. Right, an unidentified college player demonstrating a forward pass cradle catch. (*The Chicago History Museum SDN-054528, left; SDN 061997, right*)

West Point found integrating the forward pass into their offensive scheme in spring drills very difficult. Their receivers and backs' only previous experience catching a football was fielding punts or kickoffs. The backs had practiced receiving a lateral on a running play or a direct snap from the center in their overshifted backfield alignment, but no college player had ever run a pass pattern and caught a purposely thrown forward pass.

According to Fielding Yost, good receivers were hard to find. His reasoning was that coaches had little practice time to devote to help a player become a proficient catcher or thrower. There was too much team preparation to cover to become game ready each week. He believed football was already full of passes (kicks and laterals); and each time the ball was passed (a lateral), it must be handled accurately or the play was destined to fail. So, consequently, players needed to be good receivers.[16]

Coaches taught that receiving a football was the same as catching a lateral, kick, or punt. The player faced the ball with his eyes focusing on the flight, while forming a pocket with his hands, arms, and body. The receiver caught the ball with cupped hands while bringing it into his body and cradling the ball with his arms.

The first pass plays coaches devised were very simple routes. A single receiver ran for an open field relying on sheer speed to outrun the defender. The passer heaved the ball downfield hoping his teammate would turn around, eye the ball, and catch it. A spot pass was throwing to a specific receiver in a distinctly weak area of the defense. The receiver ran into the open area, stopped, turned, and faced the passer. The ball needed to be delivered timely so the defender could not intercept, knock down, or push the receiver out of the way before the completion.

Throwing an accurate forward pass was even more challenging than catching the ball because the football at the time was "watermelon" shaped. The quarterback had some previous practice tossing laterals, so the natural coaching transition was to use the same basic method for the forward pass. Consequently, the elliptical shaped ball usually traveled end over end, rather than spiraling.

There were three techniques used for throwing a football. First, underhand passing allowed the quarterback to grasp the end of the ball with the palm and fingers. The ball's surface rested on the forearm just above the wrist. With the opposite leg extended from the throwing arm, the quarterback led by swinging the nonball arm forward and upward for balance and momentum. In sequence, the throwing hand and arm was swung forward as a pendulum. The ball was released from the fingers as the body weight transferred in completing the action.

The second method of passing was called a sidearm throw. The football was held in the palm with the fingers extended over the surface and end of the ball. The quarterback's body position was similar to the underhand pass, except the throwing arm was raised higher horizontally. In passing the ball, the quarterback rotated the body by shifting the weight from the back foot to the front foot while swinging the throwing arm in a sidearm motion. The lead arm was used for balance by extending and moving it forward. The ball was released from the palm and fingers with a pushing motion. In both methods, the quarterback's head was held high, his eyes fixed on the target for accurate throwing.

A few teams used a third method of throwing the football that was a two-hand basketball chest pass. The ball was held horizontal with the laces up or down in both hands with the fingers spread around each side of the ball and the thumbs supporting from behind. Stepping forward, the quarterback used a pushing motion with both arms from the chest resulting in the ball being released with a slow end-over-end rotation as the hands opened and thumbs rolled in and upward.

D espite their desire and public pressure to make the game safer, most college football coaches and teams decided not to adopt an open offense and change the nature of their running and kicking philosophies.[17] They refused to incorporate the forward pass because they did not fully understand the necessary working components and how to coach successful forward-passing techniques. They were also concerned over the high risk of losing possession by using an inadequately prepared passing game. Nonetheless, most coaches declared their offense did contain forward-pass plays. However, these plays were 30- to 40-yard bombs used only when their team was far behind in score or just before halftime.

It would take many years for college football coaches to fully accept the forward pass as a tactical means of moving the football for possession and scoring, but there was one man who did see the future.

Amos Alonzo Stagg in 1905. (*University of Chicago Archives*)

3

The Mentor

AMOS ALONZO STAGG WAS BORN ON AUGUST 16, 1862, IN WEST Orange, New Jersey, and is regarded as one of the most remarkable figures in the history of American football. His outstanding high school baseball-playing career began in 1879 and continued at Yale University from 1884 through the spring of 1890.[1] His brilliant pitching led the Bulldogs to five consecutive championships resulting in numerous professional contractual offers, all of which he rejected.

Stagg joined Yale's football team in 1888 and earned a starting position at left end. During his last season playing right end, he was selected to Walter Camp's first 1889 All-American Football Team.

Stagg's athletic playing career closely paralleled the transition of rugby into football, including establishing a line of scrimmage, the adoption of three downs and 5 yards to go, no huddle offense with quarterback signals, touchdowns counting more points than a field goal, tackling below the waist, the change from an open game into a fixed T-formation, and the ball snapped back by hand from the center instead of being kicked.[2]

Stagg was an extraordinary contributor to the game's evolution; he was an ingenious strategist and prolific innovator who helped mold the modern game. He introduced new formations, plays, tactical strategy, players' football technique, equipment, practice drills, in-season and off-season conditioning techniques, and while serving on the football rules committee, supported a new open-style game.[3] Stagg implemented several of football's surprise tactics including the quick kick and a handoff from the fake kick. He was also credited for numbering players, padding goal posts, developing a blocking sled, and padding tackling dummies. In 1896, he was the first to utilize the huddle and wind sprints in practice. Stagg developed line shifts in 1897, lateral passes in 1898, a man in motion in 1899, and an unbalanced offensive line in 1900. Stagg was also credited with being the first to install lights on the practice field in 1901 and, in 1903, perfected the backfield shift from the T-formation into the direct snap or the short punt formation.[4]

Stagg was a head football coach for fifty-seven years and is considered by many sports authorities as the most respected in the pantheon of coaching.[5] In 1890, he accepted his first head-coaching position and finally retired as a head coach in 1946 at the age of eighty-four.

Stagg's 330 victories place him fifth among Division I-A's all-time coaching leaders. He spent forty-one years at the University of Chicago where he produced undefeated seasons in 1899, 1905, 1908, and 1913, while winning seven Big Nine championships.[6]

Chicago had a mandatory retirement age of seventy so he was forced to resign after the 1932 season. The following year Stagg was named head football coach at the College of Pacific in

California and remained until 1946. For the next six years, he assisted his son Amos Alonzo Stagg, Jr. at Susquehanna College in Selinsgrove, Pennsylvania, until the age of ninety. He finished his coaching career at Stockton (Calif.) Junior College as an assistant and finally retired from coaching at the incredible age of ninety eight.[7]

Stagg set high standards for himself as well as his players. His daily routine contained personal physical conditioning, eating "good" plain food, and speaking a vocabulary void of profanity. He was a positive role model for his players. While his team rode a bus from the field to the gym after practice, Stagg jogged the mile and a quarter to the dressing quarters. Stagg believed in living right to feel right. He once said, "Cursing is an opiate and progressively increasing doses are necessary for effect. Too, cursing is likely to leave a permanent wound on the person, no matter how impersonally it is delivered."[8]

In 1890, Stagg abandoned Divinity School and theology as a career yet kept his interest in building character. Some historians point to Stagg's fear of his inability to deliver a moving sermon as the impetus for giving up the ministry to become a coach and a teacher. He decided he could deliver a better message to youth by working closely with them in athletics rather than as a preacher. Stagg's message was more than how to play the game; it was how to live and play by the Golden Rule, maintain self-respect, and realize full individual potential as a contributing citizen in life.[9]

Many felt if Stagg had become a preacher, it is doubtful he could have influenced more young people than he did through college athletics. To Stagg, football was a ministry and a manifestation of faith. He always led his team in prayer before each game but stated, "My prayer has not been for victory. Let each player do his best."[10]

Stagg believed great men made good things happen, emphasizing that no man was larger or more important than the team. He worked closely with his young men by taking a special interest in their lives outside of athletics. He developed a personal relationship with each of his players by having them visit his home and conversing in a relaxed environment.[11]

Stagg showed a sincere interest in their hopes and dreams. He worked to provide opportunities for his players after graduation by writing recommendations and making phone calls to potential employers on their behalf. To ensure their success, he demanded academic excellence and monitored every player's academic standings.

In 1890, at the age of twenty-eight, Stagg was named head football coach at YMCA's Springfield College, Massachusetts, with an enrollment of forty-two students.[12] He abandoned the regular T-formation learned while competing at Yale and introduced an innovative formation with the ends aligned off the ball. Playing as a college end, he found lining up off the line of scrimmage provided better angles for blocking and carrying the ball on sweeps.[13] Offensive football philosophy in the early 1890s had evolved into one of employing a punishing ground game with stronger players assigned to brutally beat up lesser opponents.

Stagg's Springfield team comprised fifteen young men with only two having previously played high school football. Stagg used heavy interference plays with his ends-back formation but also employed a variety of trick and misdirection plays including laterals, single, double, and triple reverses to make up for his team's inexperience.

Stagg not only coached but was obliged to play quarterback. One of his favorite plays was leading the defense into believing he was running around end when suddenly he would stop and throw a long lateral back across the field to a receiver on the opposite side of the field for a significant gain. Despite Springfield's lack of experience, during their second season in 1891, they won five, lost eight, and tied one. Two of their losses were to Harvard and one to undefeated Yale.[14]

In his pioneer formation, Stagg positioned both ends approximately 2 1/2 yards off the line of scrimmage and assigned them to become lead blockers or trailers for the ball carrier. They assisted the runner by pushing or pulling him along. This ends-back formation was the origin of the so-called mass momentum attack that featured blocking inertia with overwhelming brute strength.[15]

Stagg also used his ends as effective ball carriers for off-tackle and outside-sweep plays and used his ends-back formation for reverses and double reverses, the first of its kind used in an actual game (Figure 3.1).[16]

In 1892, Stagg was hired by the University of Chicago's first president Dr. William Rainey Harper, his former Bible professor at Yale. This newly created university was endowed by millionaire John D. Rockefeller and was still under construction. Stagg agreed to a contract for an annual salary of $2,500 dollars with an academic title of associate professor and granted tenure for life.[17]

He was assigned to teach at the university and the newly created Morgan Park Academy on the southwest side of Chicago. Founded as a military school in 1873, Morgan Park Academy also served as a preparatory school.[18] When Dr. Harper became Chicago's founding president, the university purchased the academy and developed it into a nonsectarian, integrated, and coeducational preparatory feeder system for the university.

Stagg directed Chicago's athletics program while coaching football, basketball, baseball, and track. In the formative years,

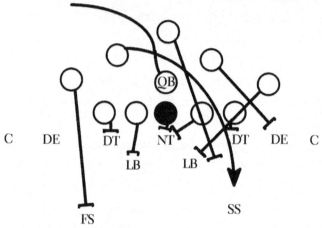

C   DE   DT   NT   DT   DE   C

LB   LB

FS   SS

FIGURE 3.1 Stagg developed the ends-back formation in 1890 at Springfield College, Massachusetts. The formation created mass interference at the point of attack, allowing the runner with the ball (arrow) to reach the defensive backfield. The formation was also used for the first reverse plays in football. (*Photo: John Madill*)

he coached football concurrently at Morgan Park Academy.[19] The dual role provided Stagg an excellent opportunity to not only coach academy athletes but also observe their competition. This advantage provided a superb recruiting tool. The academy had an excellent reputation throughout the Midwestern region and was competitive academically and athletically.

While coaching the University of Chicago Maroons in 1894, Stagg developed the innovative tackles-back formation. Both tackles moved from the line of scrimmage to a position of 2 to 3 yards deep and directly behind the offensive guards.[20] After the quarterback called the formation and the play to be run, the tackles moved back into tandem with the guards. In sync with the tackles' movement, the ends shifted to the inside and adjacent to the offensive guards. The tackles were used primarily as interference for the ball carrier. Most of the plays were designed as fullback plunges and slants inside the formation. An open-style play was featured with the halfback carrying the ball as the tackles and backs ran interference on end sweeps (Figure 3.2).

In 1900, Yale's Walter Camp converted Stagg's tackles-back formation into a single tackle-back formation. Camp found the formation's five-man offensive line unable to effectively block a hard rush from the defensive halfbacks when they were stationed outside the ends position. Camp designed a six-man line with one tackle positioned in the backfield.[21] The tackle-back formation relied on a more physical blocker leading the ball carrier yet still maintained the capability of running outside sweep plays and deceptive crisscross reverses. The tackle-back formation led to serious injuries to defensive players because of the mass interference developed at the point of attack (Figure 3.3). Chicago adopted the tackle-back offense in the early 1900s, and it quickly became Stagg's staple formation. He also added a wrinkle by using the tackle as a ball carrier as well as a lead blocker.[22]

Football historians credit Stagg as one of the first coaches to use the backfield shift. On the quarterback's command, all backs moved together establishing a new formation. The quarterback, normally aligned behind the center, moved 5 yards deeper in the backfield.

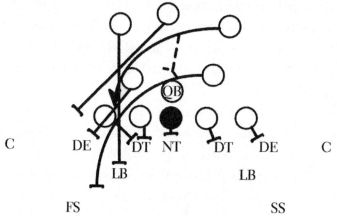

FIGURE 3.2 Stagg developed the tackles-back formation in 1892 at the University of Chicago. This play featured the halfback carrying the ball (arrow) with the tackles and backs running interference on end sweeps. (*Photo: John Madill*)

In 1894, Chicago played eighteen regular season games and four postseason contests in December and on New Years Day, 1895, of which three were in California—including the first-ever intersectional game when Chicago met Stanford University on Christmas Day—and one in Salt Lake City on the return trip. Stagg took pride in the fact Chicago was the first midwestern team to play colleges on the Pacific Coast. That season, his team won fourteen games, lost seven, and tied one.[23]

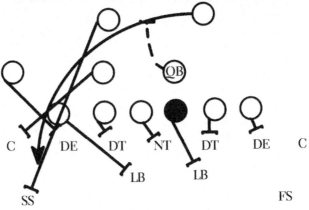

FIGURE 3.3 The tackle-back formation featured a six-man offensive line and allowed mass interference on the strong side featuring a single tackle set back from the line of scrimmage. This formation was a staple of the Chicago teams of the early 1900s. (*Photo: John Madill*)

One of Stagg's key plays in 1894 was the lateral (backward pass). His quarterback, F. E. Hering, could throw the football from the shoulder like a baseball pitcher. He used Hering as the deep receiver on the kickoff return team and had him handle the ball. After catching the kick and running up-field, he would stop and throw (laterally) the ball back to a receiver on the sidelines.[24] According to Stagg, Hering was the only man, before the forward-pass legalization, he ever saw throw a football with a spiral. The lateral pass remained in Chicago's playbook because one writer recorded that the first team to use it against Penn was Chicago in an 1898 game.[25]

In 1904, Stagg was appointed as a western representative on the Intercollegiate Football Rules Committee and reappointed in 1905. He was directly involved in the months of deliberation and study for developing safer football. He also participated in the decision-making process that dramatically changed the game. Stagg favored the open-style attack featuring the forward pass and wide runs. He never feared taking a risk. He had, after all, used the lateral pass in the old game, and he loved misdirection and finesse football.

In the few short months from the legalization of the pass in April until the season started in September, Stagg was working on creating a new open-style offense for Chicago. It was a natural transition because of his successful experience with the lateral, and a welcome challenge for this great football innovator.

In creating the open-style forward-passing offense, Stagg had to answer four questions. What constraints did the new forward-pass rules imply? How could Chicago adapt the forward pass into the present successful multiformation running game? What individual techniques did the players need to learn to attain forward-passing success? And how should daily practice be revised to successfully implement the forward pass?

In answer to the first question, a legal forward pass had to be thrown 5 yards outside the center on each side of the ball and could not be completed within a 10-yard rectangle down the length of the field. This rule required movement from the passer to throw the ball from outside the offensive tackle's position. Stagg advanced his forward-pass plays based on that premise. Every pass pattern he designed exploited the short, intermediate, and deep flat areas. He also developed crossing or throw-back patterns involving boot, reverse, and double-reverse run action.

Before the passing game was introduced, Stagg's team's success—and of football teams in general—centered on strong, well-conditioned, physical players capable of superior blocking and tackling. The offensive running backs' requirements were to be tough with great leg drive and good balance. They also had to absorb a great deal of physical punishment from multiple tacklers and teammates assisting by pushing or pulling. The game was very constricted and demanded tough, hard-nosed players for the close-knit brutal play. Players requiring special skills were the punter, kicker, short and long snapper, and the kick return men. Running backs worked on catching short tosses from the quarterback. The game was simple and easy to coach.

Now with the new forward-pass rules, most college coaches developed their teams' passing attack around the quarterback's old lateral-throwing techniques and the receivers turning or stopping to complete the cradle catch. These skills demanded less time to implement into their offense. The pass patterns were very elementary and generally involved only one or two receivers. These coaches did not intend to execute their offense around the passing game but simply added it as a supplementary threat or to use occasionally.

Stagg developed his offense using a different approach. He experimented by developing pass plays on paper, studied them, and made written notations stating that they either needed further work or were ready to teach in practice. Stagg's receivers were assigned specific routes and were expected to catch the ball in stride. They also ran a curl pattern 10 yards downfield, stopped, turned their face toward the quarterback, and caught the ball with their hands, not with their bodies.

Stagg's experience playing and coaching baseball gave him insight on how a football could be caught and thrown. Baseball players practiced receiving the ball with their hands away from the body and occasionally caught the ball over the shoulder. Baseball players threw the ball overhand. Stagg understood that baseball demanded more time for improving individual skills than for team play. Baseball coaches also recognized that improved individual techniques contributed to a stronger team performance. Practice always focused on upgrading a player's hitting, bunting, fielding, throwing, or base-running skills. He realized the team aspect of baseball, although important, did not require the same kind of demands as football's daily game preparation. But now, with the inception of football's newly created open-style play, the game changed from power to finesse and possession, requiring a smarter and better organized practice.

Knowing that his players lacked the knowledge of the newly revised game and understanding that a great deal of time was required to hone individual passing and receiving skills, Stagg devised a plan to get a jump start.

The University of Chicago had offered early-summer football seminars in previous years, but Stagg's 1906 football class was destined to be unique. Most returning undergraduate players were enrolled along with one former player and 1906 Chicago graduate, Jesse C. Harper. Harper and Stagg had built a great player–coach relationship. Harper had played both football and baseball for Stagg and had recently completed his fourth successful baseball season and was honored by being selected captain his junior year. Harper had accepted the head football position at Alma College in Alma, Michigan, and was taking the class to advance his knowledge and coaching ability on the new open-style passing offense. Harper had attended the

Stagg taught his receivers to catch the ball with their fingers and over their shoulder while running downfield, a major innovation at the time. (*The Chicago History Museum SDN-055814*)

summer football class before but knew Stagg was not about to teach the same old approach for winning football games.

Stagg began the summer football seminar by explaining to the group on how the 1905 football crisis was averted. He told them how coaches and college presidents worked together to form a new American Football Rules Committee responsible for governing intercollegiate football and eligibility nationwide. He also explained how the Western Conference presidents placed restrictions on Chicago's league teams. They reduced the length of the season to five contests, with none to be scheduled before October 20, and the practice could only officially begin on September 20, and not before. There was also no players training table allowed.[26] These restrictions developed by the league's presidents convinced the Wolverines to drop from the Western Conference from 1907 through 1916, thus eliminating the great Chicago–Michigan rivalry.[27]

Stagg warned his students how the game would change with the adoption of the new 1906 forward-passing rules. He provided copies of all his newly designed pass plays, sixty four in total, to his summer football students.[28] He also included material about his unique backfield shift and highly successful interference running plays.

Coach Stagg felt the newly adopted blocking rules required detailed attention. While he demonstrated his new offensive bridge-blocking technique, the students simulated and practiced the legal blocking skill. He explained that offensive players could no longer use their hands while blocking. A legal block was created with the blocker's body, shoulder, or the back of the arms. He emphasized that the revised blocking rule and newly adopted sportsmanship rules should make the game safer for players.

Each day over the course of the summer seminar, Stagg covered an additional football skill required for successfully implementing the open-style offense. He provided footballs for students to pair-off 15 yards apart for throwing and catching. Half of the class worked on throwing an overhead spiral pass while the receiver focused on catching with his fingers and hands extended and not cradling the ball with the arms or body. Like baseball players, the receiving technique included extending the arms as far away from the body as possible and looking the ball into "soft" hands with relaxed fingers. Stagg then instructed the receiver to tuck the ball into the pit of the shoulder and arm while turning upfield for gaining additional yardage.

In another drill, he had the receiver stand stationary with the body and head turned away from the passer. As the quarterback called "ball," the receiver looked back over his shoulder, caught the ball, tucked it away, and turned to run upfield. The next phase of catching and throwing practice included a player catching the ball while running a pass pattern. This helped the quarterback learn how to lead the receiver and deliver the ball with the proper trajectory.

Stagg explained that when both players were moving in the same plane, the quarterback should target the receiver's front shoulder. If the quarterback led the receiver running a pattern on the same plane, the ball would always be overthrown.

Finally, individual drills were stopped and a live scrimmage was practiced to simulate an offensive team running an open-style pass play. This gave the players the opportunity to better understand how a passing attack could complement the running game.

Stagg concluded the seminar by handing out a football to every one of the student athletes to use over the remainder of the summer months. The returning players developed an advantage by understanding the physical passing and receiving skills they needed to work on before reporting for fall practice in September. The young inexperienced coach, Jesse Harper, would now be capable of reporting to his new college assignment better prepared than almost all of his colleagues, many with years of football coaching experience.

In mid-September 1906, Stagg declared all preliminary football practice on Marshall Field stopped and the facility off-limits for his players; he even locked the gates. Stagg explained his whirlwind move by declaring Chicago had been accused of violating the Western Conference rules in commencing practice before school started. He had been vacationing in New York for three weeks and had no idea what was going on at Marshall Field. He did not want any suspicion cast on his players, and rather than take any chances for violations he ordered his team to find other areas for working out.

Walter Eckersall, captain and quarterback, immediately moved his teammates to the vacant lots adjacent to Hyde Park where the Maroons continued to prepare for the 1906 season.[29]

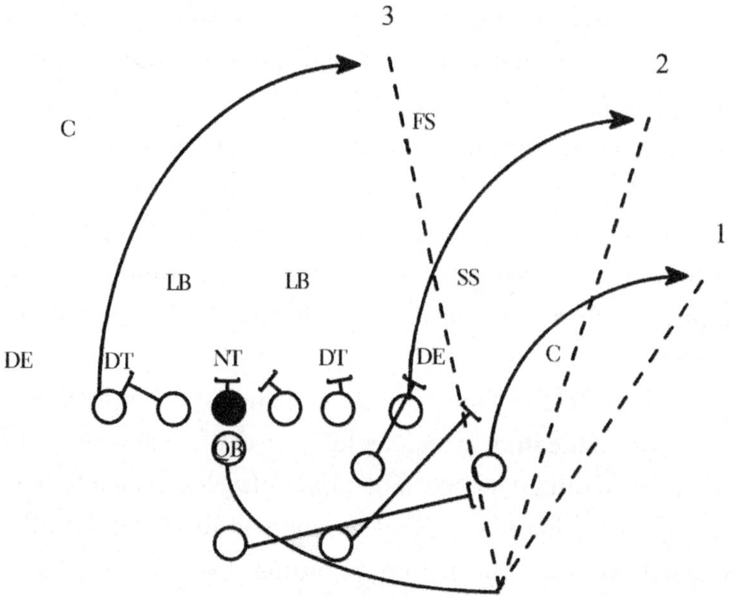

FIGURE 3.4 In Stagg's 1906 pass-play book, the first series called for the quarterback to sprintout with the option of passing to an open receiver or running the football.

Amos Alonzo Stagg's original pass-play book of 1906 is an important document worth examining in detail. That year, Stagg introduced a total of sixty-four pass plays, though most were duplicate patterns. In reality, Stagg designed roughly twenty interchangeable patterns for the receivers and multiple formations.[30]

Stagg cataloged his forward passes into series. His first series featured no backfield faking. The quarterback aligned behind the center, received the snap, and simply sprinted out to one side of the formation. He had the options of running or passing by flooding three receivers down the field in front of him. The backs and lead tackle were responsible for blocking the defensive tackle and end on the attacked front.[31] The pass could involve one or up to four receivers flooding one half of the field, including an end or wingback running complementary out routes. Stagg's coaching instructions were for the quarterback to throw a forward pass to the receiver providing the best opportunity for success.[32] Designed for Walter Eckersall, the All-American quarterback, a proficient overhand spiral passer as well as an excellent runner, it was considered Chicago's bread-and-butter play (Figure 3.4). Over a hundred years later, this option play is still found in playbooks.

The Chicago offensive assault was multifaceted. However, Stagg simplified his offense by running the same basic passing concept out of multiple formations. The quarterback was able to run the same sprint-out play by aligning 6 yards deep in the backfield and receiving a direct long snap (Figure 3.5).[33]

A variation of the quarterback sprint-out play had the halfback throwing the ball from a direct snap. The quarterback's alignment was offset from the center, and his assignment was to run pattern two (Figure 3.6).[34]

When Stagg's teams placed the ball into play adjacent to the sidelines, his second series of plays used an overshifted unbalanced line. The SY series overshifted to the right and QY overshifted to the left. Stagg developed three complementary plays for each series: a halfback off-tackle sweep, a sprint-out pass, and a quarterback sprint-out run. In an October 20 game against Purdue, Stagg utilized this series in their 39–0 win. A similar overshifted unbalanced formation was also used to create a guard-eligible pass.[35] A tackle shifted to the width of the field leaving only the left guard and center near the sidelines. The left guard's exposure made him a receiver, as the forward-pass rules called for only the two men on the end of the line eligible, in addition to all of the backfield players.

A strong overshifted formation to the width of the field involved moving an end and tackle over. The ball was centered

3

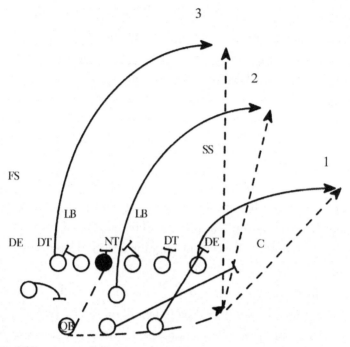

Figure 3.5 Stagg's quarterback sprint-out play placed the quarterback in "shotgun," 6 yards deep in the backfield, where he received a direct long-snap and had the option of running or throwing to an open receiver.

directly to the halfback. The backs led interference for the left halfback as he sprinted for the edge. The fullback blocked the defensive man covering the offensive end, and the right halfback was assigned to kick out the corner.

A third series involved play action with the quarterback faking the ball to a running back plunging into the line, running off-tackle, or around the end. The quarterback continued to fake until setting up to pass outside the offensive tackle's position.[36]

This play-action pass also included the quarterback boot play away from the faking back's direction. For play-action passes to be effective, a team had to successfully execute running the ball. Once the defense expected a running play, the short-flat or inter-

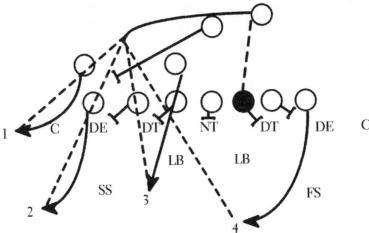

FIGURE 3.6 Stagg used the unbalanced direct snap formation when the ball was adjacent to the sidelines. Four or sometimes five offensive linemen aligned to the wide field side from the center, while one or two lineman aligned to the weak side of the center. The halfback had the option of running or throwing a pass. (*Photo: John Madill*)

mediate-flat passes were effective because the linebackers were not able to react fast enough (Figure 3.7).

The bootleg pass play was set up by establishing a solid off-tackle or sweep running play to the weak side of the formation. The quarterback faked to the running back, placed the ball on

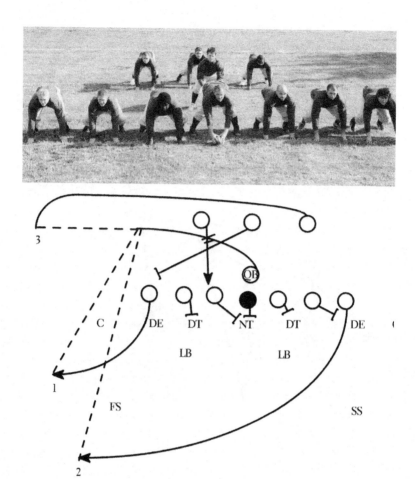

FIGURE 3.7 Another innovative foward pass formation was Stagg's play action, with the backs aligned in a T and the quarterback drawing in the linebackers with a fake, and sprinting to the outside where he could throw to an end or one of the backs coming out of the backfield. (*Photo: John Madill*)

his hip, and continued away from the run action. A short delay for timing was best as the number one receiver crossed from the opposite side of the formation.[37] The defensive team's focus was on the sweep, so the quarterback generally went unnoticed running a naked boot. The fake sweep to the weak side set up the

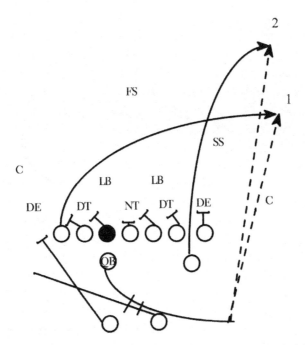

Figure 3.8 Stagg sketched a bootleg pass play—another formation which has become standard in playbooks—where the quarterback leads a misdirection action away from a faking back in order to hit an open receiver.

short 12- to 15-yard pass to the left end crossing behind the line-backers. If the corner dropped off, the quarterback had the option of running the football (Figure 3.8).

While the pulling guard or tackle was believed to have origi-nated with Harvard's freshman coach, W. Cameron Forbes in 1892, trapping or cross-blocking did not become widely used until fifteen to twenty years later. Stagg, in 1906, developed three short-side running plays where in two of them, the right tackle pulled out from the line and received the ball from the quarter-back, while a third featured the right tackle leading the interfer-ence on one short-side running play to the left (Figure 3.9).[38]

The fourth series involved the halfback throwing a running pass. The ball was centered to the quarterback who quick

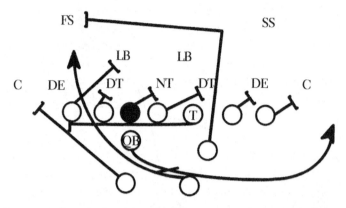

FIGURE 3.9 Stagg developed three short side plays with the tackle (T) pulling. In two of them the tackle pulled out and received the ball from the quarterback, while in the third, shown here, the tackle pulled and led the interference for a running play on the weak side.

pitched to the halfback. The play was designed to look like a quick running play around end. If the defensive corner reacted to stop the quick pitch, the ball was passed over his head to the wingback running a short-out pattern in the near flat area. However, if the corner dropped off in soft pass protection, the halfback could either run or throw a deeper pass to receivers two or three (Figure 3.10).[39]

A fifth passing series was the play-action pass, something Stagg referred to as a "double" or "triple" pass, even though only one forward pass would actually be thrown. Play-action passes involve a counter with halfbacks reversing the field. Stagg's misdirection crisscross play action meant the ball was exchanged from back to back. The defense had to play the end run, a reverse, and sometimes double-reverse action before realizing the play was a pass. Receiving the snap, the quarterback carried the ball to the wing reversing to the left. The wing continued to run with the ball until he cleared the offensive left tackle's area. The right end ran a crossing pattern 12 to 15 yards deep behind

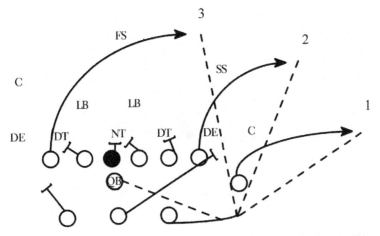

FIGURE 3.10 Stagg's fourth series of 1906 pass plays featured a halfback pass off the quick pitch from the quarterback. The back had three receivers to choose from, and if none were open, the back could run.

the linebackers. When the end opened up, the wing had a choice of passing the football to him or keeping it on a reverse. Stagg especially liked to use this play-action pass as he found it very effective against aggressive teams that pursued quickly to the run (Figure 3.11).[40]

The forward pass added a whole new dimension to the punting game. An end run off a fake kick was a trick play often used before the adoption of the pass. A punting team now possessed three scrimmage options. First, a team could place the ball into play with the punt and give up possession 30 to 40 yards downfield. Next, a team could fake a punt and sweep the end, with the ball carrier needing to gain the required distance for a first down or else the team lost ball possession at that point. The third option was to fake a punt and pass to an end faking kick coverage downfield—recalling the inadvertent forward pass in the 1895 Georgia–North Carolina game. The fake punt allowed for four potential receivers.[41] Since the quarterback generally doubled as

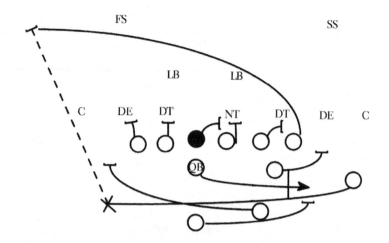

FIGURE 3.11 Referred to in his playbook as a "double" or "triple" pass, even though only one forward pass would actually be thrown, Stagg's fifth series of plays used a number of reverse and double-reverse play-action passes, involving a counter with halfbacks reversing the field and throwing to an end downfield.

the punter, he had the ability to punt, run, or pass the football effectively, giving the play a genuine triple threat (Figure 3.12).

The screen pass—one of the most important plays in the age of the forward pass—had not surfaced during the initial year of the new rule; however, there is a very interesting concept in one of Stagg's plays that was used from the punt formation series in 1906. The ball was long snapped to the punter, and while faking a punt he handed the ball off to a back sweeping to the right. The ball carrier stopped well behind the line of scrimmage and threw a short (screen) pass to the far left blocking back working from a position behind the rush end and defensive tackle (Figure 3.13).[42] According to Stagg, the first college coach to use the screen pass was Bob Folsom at Washington & Jefferson in 1912, and Stagg claimed he learned the screen-pass techniques from Folsom. Longtime Illinois head coach, coach of Oak Park High School, and friend of Stagg's, Robert Zuppke, recalled that

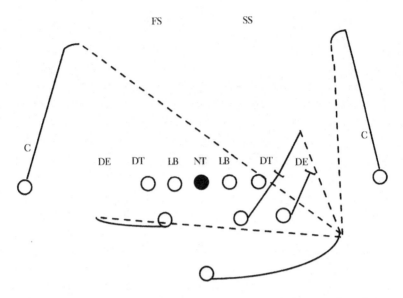

FS   SS

C

DE   DT   LB   NT   LB   DT   DE   C

FIGURE 3.12 Before the forward pass was legal, a fake punt relied on an end run. Stagg drew a series of pass plays off a fake punt formation that provided four options for the passer.

in 1908 or 1909 he (Zuppke) stumbled onto the screen pass while coaching at Muskegon High School in Michigan and "developed it at Oak Park High School in 1910." Zuppke added that, "We did not call the play a screen, but I asked my players to litter up the field so the disguised receiver could lurk behind the defense unnoticed."[43] Zuppke was not credited for having utilized the screen pass at the University of Illinois, however, until 1920.[44]

In a bit of outrageousness that was later made illegal, Stagg used a sleeper pass by quickly lining up ten men for an offensive play while one overlooked player retreated toward the sidelines and mingled with the players on the sideline. As the ball was put into play, the sleeper, unnoticed, sprinted onto the field running a deep route into the secondary uncovered.[45] Generally the sleeper play surprised the defense and resulted in a touchdown pass.

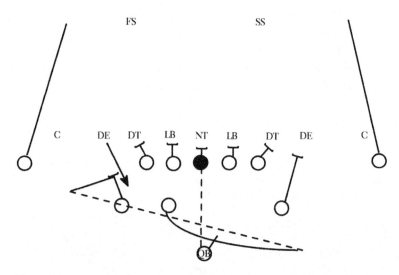

FIGURE 3.13 Stagg was one of the first to design a misdirection pass that resembles today's screen pass.

N early all of the forward-pass plays developed by Stagg were of the play-action variety intended to be set up for success by a strong running game. His passing game blended easily into the running offense. Stagg's system kept the defense off-balance: the defense could no longer play nine- or ten-men fronts because they would be unable to cover the pass. Before 1906, college defenses played with most players on the line and only one or two men deep as safeties. The defense attempted to smother the running game by overwhelming the offense with too many men up front to block. With Stagg's new offensive attack, opposing linebackers had to be concerned about covering the short passing game as well as shutting down the run. Strong secondary coverage called for two to three men playing the pass first and the run second. Every potential eligible receiver had to be accounted for by the defense in case a running play suddenly turned into a play-action pass.

The first defensive adjustment for covering the threat of the pass was the creation of man-to-man coverage. The defensive linebackers and halfbacks were assigned specific eligible receivers in man-to-man coverage. The toughest position to execute was playing linebacker with two opposing responsibilities, the run first and the pass second. Their assignment was difficult to execute when facing an offensive team capable of running or passing the football like the Chicago Maroons. Over the course of the next three years under a much-reduced schedule, the Maroons would tally a 10–2–3 record.

Most college coaches lagged behind in developing such a complex offensive system as Chicago's. Of those, however, in 1906, who were working on the forward pass, Stagg, Heisman, and Pop Warner were at the head of the class. But because of schedule changes, it would fall to another coach who had an equal passion for the forward pass to first demonstrate the devastating potential of the open-style play. That coach was Edward B. Cochems.

A helmeted player receiving a forward pass during a game between Chicago and the University of Illinois at Chicago's Marshall Field in 1908. (*University of Chicago Archives*)

4

A Perfect Spiral

WHAT WOULD THE 1906 SEASON BRING TO AN ORIGINAL NATIONAL treasure, a game developed by and through the interest and competitive nature of America's youth—a game that had evolved from a single rugbylike contest played thirty-seven years earlier to a sport that had grown so immensely popular that hundreds of colleges and high schools fielded football teams playing from five to twelve games a season? Stadiums were packed every weekend; rugged, closed-formation football had spread across America's vast countryside. What would be the reaction to the new game of football?

On the eve of the 1906 football season's opening day in September, the attitudes of players, coaches, and fans varied from excitement to resentment. A few coaches disdained the new rules and refused to adapt. Some bought into the changes and were energized about the future. Most coaches, however, were reluctant fence-sitters who needed to be shown the value of open plays. Preseason workouts did nothing to convince them that the new style of play was going to be easy to incorporate into the game. While preparing to play under the new rules, one word described the conditions confronting coaches and players at the start of the season: chaotic.[1] Unlike Stagg and a few others, in their early preseason practices most coaches found it frustrating to implement a complex passing game into their offense because new skills were difficult to teach and designing and practicing new pass plays in such a short period of time appeared impossible. College representatives and coaches said they had made the effort to incorporate passing into their game, but the results of their efforts would have to wait for the games to be played. The national press would not have to wait long.

On September 26, 1906, in one of the first games of the season, Coach Bemus Pierce and his Carlisle Indians played host to the Villanova Wildcats before the largest crowd ever to witness a game in Carlisle, Pennsylvania. Villanova received the opening kickoff and on the first play completed a forward pass for a 10-yard gain. The fans loved it. After a short gain on a line plunge, they lost ball possession on an errant pass hitting the ground untouched by either team.[2]

During the game there were many brilliant short inside bursts and long end runs with spectacular tackling, but the open play seemed constantly interrupted by bad passes and fumbles. The Indians' lone touchdown was scored by Hendricks Little Boy, with Charles Mount Pleasant kicking the extra point. Carlisle hung on for a 6–0 victory despite both teams trying long and risky passes for a quick touchdown.

Some people felt passing the ball was more of basketball's character and feared the game's toughness would be lost. Everyone agreed that well-executed passing was spectacular, but the penalty for an untouched incomplete pass was so great that it made the practice extremely risky.[3] On the other hand, gaining 10 yards consistently without sweeps, end runs, and forward passes seemed improbable even against weakened defensive alignments. Most spectators attending the Carlisle Indians and Villanova Wildcats contest appeared to enjoy the new style of open play more than the old sport.[4] But the sidelines were also filled with football experts harboring deep-seeded resentment, unwilling to accept the reality of change. The jury was still out and more games were needed to be played before a decision could be made on the game's fate.

Dartmouth's head coach Fred Folsom spoke out boldly by declaring the new football rules an imposition on the public and a farce and a fizzle. He felt Walter Camp, backed by the press, secured the 10-yard rule knowing full well that no team in the country could gain the distance in three downs without adding another attempt.

Concern was so great that on September 28, at New York's Murray-Hill Hotel over one hundred football coaches and administrators (most from eastern universities) convened to discuss the challenging new rules. They were seeking the football rules committee's interpretation of the changes to the game.[5] The rules committee members covered each rule in an attempt to clarify and clear up any confusion. However, to answer their real underlying concerns, there were no experts in attendance capable of offering the technical support required to explain how to successfully implement the multifaceted passing game into an offense.

The question most frequently asked was, can a team gain 10 yards in three downs? Invariably, the answer was no. Most coaches believed the requirement to gain 10 yards with two attempts, while possibly giving up possession on the third, weakened the offense. In practice scrimmages, coaches found it was virtually impossible to gain the necessary yardage by solely using the running game. The leading football experts agreed that unless defensive men were moved off the line to defend against the threat of a pass or an onside kick, competition between two equal teams would simply become an interchange of kicks, with luck and fumbles determining the game's outcome. If teams were able to perfect the passing and onside kicking game, these two offensive threats would require adjustments by the defense, and possibly make gaining the necessary yardage easier, but few teams appeared to be that far along.[6]

The day after the conference, September 29, was opening day for most teams across the country—and more opportunities to evaluate the new forward pass in action.

Controversy and vagueness has surrounded the verification of college football's first forward pass. Debate over who should be given credit for throwing the earliest one and in what college game the first official intercollegiate pass was thrown has been a mystery. A number of universities have been mentioned as the first, including the University of Notre Dame and Wesleyan University, a small institution in Connecticut, but none is correct.

Colleges generally scheduled their first football game a couple of weeks after the academic calendar year opened because the football program was required to be financially self-sufficient.

On September 22, thirteen colleges and one high school opened their season playing under the new forward-pass rules. The schools and the final scores are listed below.[7]

> Lehigh over Albright: 21–0
>
> Harvard over Williams College: 7–0
>
> Holy Cross College over Massachusetts: 6–4
>
> Penn State over Lebanon Valley College: 24–0
>
> Dartmouth College over Norwich: 5–0

Kansas over William Jewell: 18–0

Ohio University over Columbia East H.S.: 20–0

Other colleges started later. Wesleyan University's opening game was held on October 3. They were defeated by Yale, 21–0. In that game, a forward pass was thrown by Sammy Moore, the Wesleyan quarterback, and caught by receiver Irvin Van Tassell for an 18-yard gain. Notre Dame opened on October 6, with a 26–0 home victory over Indiana's Franklin College. A number of college teams opened as late as October 20, including the Western Conference members because of their season's limit of five games. Chicago crushed Purdue 39–0 in their opener with a well-executed open-style game featuring end runs, reverses, and forward passes.

So who actually threw football's first intercollegiate pass? Two midwestern colleges, St. Louis University and Carroll College, played their opening football game on Wednesday, September 5, 1906. Scheduling football games on Wednesdays was common during the early 1900s. Yale University competed in four home games within a two-week period from October 3 to October 13. The Bulldogs opened with Wesleyan on a Wednesday, Syracuse the following Saturday, Springfield College on the succeeding Wednesday, and Holy Cross that following Saturday.[8]

Edward B. Cochems, the St. Louis coach, was a University of Wisconsin graduate and a three-sport star, where he played football, track, and baseball. He had a brilliant football career while competing as a hard-running halfback on Wisconsin's outstanding 1899, 1900, and 1901 teams. During his four seasons, playing for head coach Phil King, Cochems helped his teams achieve thirty-five victories against four losses. In 1900, he scored four touchdowns in a 54–0 win over Notre Dame.

In 1901, Cochems tallied three touchdowns while playing against Chicago including a 100-yard kickoff return that still stands as a record. That same year, the University of Wisconsin went undefeated in nine games.[9]

After graduation in 1902, Cochems accepted the head football coach position at North Dakota leading the Aggies to winning seasons in 1902 and 1903. In 1904, he returned home to Madison to assist head coach Arthur Curtis for one season before accepting the head coaching position at Clemson.[10] In 1905, Cochems led the Tigers to three wins, two losses, and one tie.

In spring of 1906, Cochems accepted the head football coach and athletics director's position at St. Louis University, the same year the forward-passing game rules were introduced.

Cochems's mind was already stirred by this new concept of football. He tried to imagine the possibilities of developing an open-style passing offense while complementing his already successful powerful running game. He spent a great deal of time exploring answers to the question: How can the forward pass advance the game of football?[11]

Cochems's keen interest in the forward pass was highly influenced by open-game advocate, John Heisman. Heisman, eight years his senior, was now the head coach at Georgia Tech. At Tech, over a period of sixteen years Heisman would build a powerhouse program; between 1904 and 1919 his teams won 102 games, while losing only twenty-nine and tying seven.

Cochems and Heisman developed a friendly, respectful coaching relationship. On November 30, 1905, Heisman's Ramblin' Wreck from Georgia Tech prevailed in a hard fought 17–10 battle over Cochems's Clemson Tigers.[12] In 1906, Cochem accepted the head coaching position at St. Louis University. Heisman's passionate forward-pass convictions influenced Cochems so strongly that Cochems concentrated on developing a revolutionary offense for his new team capable of advancing the ball in the air as well as on the ground.

After Cochems read the 1906 official *Spaulding Football Guide* explaining the forward-passing rules, he masterminded a whole new game. He studied the proportions of the bloated football and discovered it was ideally designed for kicking and carrying in the armpit while running. Surprisingly, Cochems found the only way to hold and throw a spiral pass was by gripping the ball over the leather laces on its long axis. He had experimented with the old end-over-end throwing methods but found them ineffective.[13]

Eddie Cochems developed a highly successful forward passing attack in 1906 at St. Louis University. His Billikens defeated eleven opponents on the way to scoring 407 total points. (*St. Louis University Archives*)

Cochems understood, like Stagg, that for his St. Louis Billikens to become proficient in executing his open-game offense he needed more preparation time than the customary three weeks prior to the first game. He approached Father Patrick Burke, S.J., St. Louis University's athletics moderator, requesting permission to take his team to Wisconsin's beautiful Lake Beulah area for two months of advanced training.[14] The lake, about 25 miles south of Waukesha, was nestled among several quiet southeast Wisconsin communities. It was also the site of a Jesuit's community retreat where housing and meals were available. It was the perfect setting for studying and developing Cochems's forward-pass offense.

The Billikens team, comprised of nine former 1905 St. Louis veterans and winners of seven games, and seven transfers from various college football programs, unknowingly, were preparing

St. Louis University end and Wisconsin transfer student, Jack Schneider, a favorite target of Bradbury Robinson, caught the first legal college forward pass, a 20-yard strike. (*St. Louis University Archive*)

for a history-making season. Three of the transfers, former Wisconsin players Bradbury Robinson, Jack Schneider, and Frank Acker, had followed Cochems to St. Louis where they would become a part of his exciting new offense.[15] Cochems had coached Robinson in 1904 at Wisconsin and knew of his athletic ability. Robinson was a very capable football player and winner of a varsity letter with considerable playing time while at Wisconsin. He fit right into Cochems's ingenious technical-passing scheme.

Cochems understood that to produce a successful passing team his players needed to become proficient at throwing and catching a football. He instructed his players to place the throwing hand's index and middle fingers over the last two laces nearest the end of the ball's smallest axis while gripping the ball with the thumb and fingers spread, and to throw the ball from above the shoulder with a twist of the wrist on the ball's long axis.[16] His passing technique was advanced, but the receivers caught the ball with the old cradling method.

Robinson, a former high school baseball pitcher and a sturdy lad of six foot four with extra-large hands, practiced throwing a football to teammate Jack Schneider on the beautiful shores and grounds of Lake Beulah. One morning after a 15-minute warm-up session while passing at short distances, Robinson's ball rotation changed from a wobbly pass to a surprising spiral. Using

Cochems's instructions, he had found that by widening his grip and spreading his fingers over the last two or three of football's seven leather laces, slightly cocking his wrist, and releasing the ball off the index finger with an overhand baseball throwing motion, the ball spiraled instead of bobbing.[17]

Robinson's confidence and accuracy began to improve daily as he motioned at Schneider to move further and further away. With his receiver some 40 yards downfield, Robinson uncorked a long high spiral pass. Schneider watched the ball's perfect spherical flight then cradled it into his arms and chest for a successful

Bradbury Robinson, a St. Louis University halfback, the first to throw a legal college forward pass during the September 5, 1906 game against Carroll College. During that season, Robinson threw over fifteen forward passes a game, an output well ahead of its time. (*St. Louis University Archives*)

reception. The adrenaline flowed as they ran toward Cochems. Excitedly, Robinson yelled out, "Coach, I can throw the danged thing forty yards!"[18]

According to one reporter, "passing the ball forty yards for Robinson was easy because the halfback had already developed a throwing style when passing was illegal in 1904. He and Howard Savage were punters at Wisconsin and practiced kicking the ball to one another. One afternoon Savage, suffering from a painful foot injury, caught the punt and instead of kicking, threw the ball forty-plus yards back to Robinson. According to Bradbury, Savage was the first man he ever saw throw a football overhand. Robinson learned how to pass from Savage and spent a lot of time throwing a football just for fun."[19] After altering his technique, by changing his grip, Robinson could now throw a perfect spiral pass.

Cochems worked his team daily for over a month. Not only did they practice individual techniques, but also Cochems introduced his Billikens to a strong, deceptive running game and a well-balanced passing attack. His offensive formation always lined up with a guard or tackle moved over, thereby, producing a strong-side unbalanced line.

Cochems playing Robinson at left halfback called on him to run, kick, and throw, thus allowing Robinson to be the first triple-threat player in the history of football.

Cochems, assuming every football coach would use the forward pass, developed a defensive scheme to counter a passing offense. He employed his defensive ends and tackles in an upright two-point stance so they could rush the passer from a standing position, thereby, making them capable of batting down passes and blocking the passers' view of receivers. The secondary played a zone behind the six-man defensive line.[20]

After five weeks of practice, the St. Louis Billikens were ready to test their competitors' ability to contain their modern-day offense.

St. Louis's schedule was very competitive, including Kansas and Iowa, but they still had open dates to fill. Cochems had contact from nearby Carroll College's athletic manager Arthur Glyer exploring the possibility of playing a couple of practice games while the Billikens worked out at Lake Beulah.[21]

Carroll's former athletic representative, Fred Davis, had scheduled their opening home game on October 6 against Menomonee Falls High School. Carroll's coach Edgar Hutchins and captain Bill Williams wanted to open the season earlier. So on September 5, 1906, a home game was scheduled against the

St. Louis Billikens at Brown Field in Waukesha, Wisconsin.[22] Carroll College had ten veterans returning from their 1905 team, so expectations were high. Cochems, born and raised in Sturgeon's Bay, Wisconsin, was thrilled because he could now showcase his new St. Louis University football team to friends and family in his hometown.

The first part of the game was a scoreless tie with both teams not being able to move the ball effectively on the ground. Cochems had enough with his team's lackluster performance so he called a time-out and instructed his squad to break open the "air-attack."[23]

The first official pass play in football history was unsuccessful, as Bradbury Robinson's attempt fell short, untouched by the wide-open receiver or a defensive player, thus automatically turning ball possession over to Carroll College. However, on St. Louis University's next offensive possession, Robinson hit Schneider with a perfect strike on a 20-yard out pattern.[24] Schneider, catching the ball with his hands, realized there was no defensive player in his area and ran for a touchdown. The play surprised everyone in attendance, including the Carroll College defense. Here in Waukesha, Wisconsin, was the first legally completed pass in football history, and it was a touchdown.[25] In an interview nearly forty years later, a Carroll College player, Frank G. James, said, "The game will always stand out in my mind because it was the first time we ever saw a football passed." James added, "St. Louis was a far better trained team and their coach was kind enough to stop throwing passes for easy touchdowns."[26] The St. Louis Billikens ended up beating the Carroll College Pioneers by the score of 22–0.

Cochems had scheduled four games in Wisconsin during the month of September. On Saturday, St. Louis defeated Lawrence College 6–0. The next stop in Wisconsin was St. John's Military

Academy where his Billikens won 27–0 without using the forward pass. The fourth game of the preseason schedule was at Marquette University. The Billikens opened up their offense against the tough Hilltoppers winning 30–0.[27]

The new forward-pass rule restrictions kept most college football coaches from attempting the use of the risky play in 1906. But not St. Louis University's crafty Cochems who fully understood the impact the forward pass could have on the game.

On November 3, the Billikens defeated the University of Kansas 34–2 in a home contest. During the contest, Robinson completed the longest pass of the year, 48 yards, from the line of scrimmage. Cochems's philosophy was to score at least one touchdown on the ground forcing the defense to respect the running game. The opponents' inability to predict whether a play would be a run or pass was then exploited with his fast and tricky play-action passing attack. In the second half, Robinson completed seven of nine passes, one scoring a touchdown and the others setting up touchdown drives.[28] Kansas was no pushover, finishing the season with an outstanding record of seven wins and two losses.

In a home contest on November 29, St. Louis University overwhelmed Iowa 30–0. A working official for the Iowa game from West Point, referee Lt. H. B. Hackett, was amazed at the passing efficiency of Cochems's St. Louis team. The Billikens, playing a major university, offered proof that forward passing need not be used only in desperation, but rather as a companion to the run in a well-balanced offense. He had not seen any better in the East or West all season. Robinson had completed eight of ten attempts that afternoon.[29]

That eventful year of 1906, Cochems's powerful football team demonstrated the excitement and success of open-style football

The University of Kansas fell to St. Louis University 34-2 on November 3, 1906 at St. Louis Sportsman's Park. During the contest Robinson completed a 48-yard pass to Schneider Note the open formation that presages modern football offensive sets. (*St. Louis University Archives*)

by winning all eleven games with a formidable passing and punishing running game. St. Louis's passes included fast, short bullets of 7 to 12 yards as well as the 30- to 40-yard long-bombs for touchdowns. The Billikens amassed 407 total points, while defensively surrendering a mere 11.[30]

In 1949, St. Louis University discontinued their football program. Ironically, the university that provided the sport its most interesting and advanced play bid farewell to the game.[31]

One would think that exposure to the first well-executed pass play, such as the one thrown at Carroll College in Waukesha, Wisconsin, would have been replicated and become the wave of the future. Unfortunately, the East and West's media and football coaches had not heard of the successful open play of the small midwestern college football program. Even prominent newspapers in the Midwest such as the *Chicago Tribune* and *Milwaukee Sentinel* failed to report the first game or by-line the historic forward pass story. The St. Louis–Carroll College's breakout game was a well-kept secret.

R eviewing memoirs and historical accounts of the early days of the forward pass leaves readers with the impression that eastern university coaches were reluctant in utilizing the open-style play and lagged behind the not-so-conservative Midwest. Even Stagg, in his 1927 book, *Touchdown*, wrote, "The east eyed the pass dubiously, in general, and used it timidly when at all."[32] In January 1947, Grantland Rice, quoting Stagg's statements, said, "The middle west took to the pass long before the east ever discovered its value, despite the fact that Yale defeated Harvard 12-0, in 1907. After that, both Yale and Harvard forgot about the pass for several years."[33] The game's top-rated referee, West Point's Lt. H. B. Hackett, believed the eastern coaches spent more time preparing their defense for the new open-style play than on the offensive side. Therefore, the East played stronger defense but a slower type of offensive game.[34] Edwin Pollock, writing in *Franklin Field Illustrated*, said, "The coaches of Pennsylvania experimented with the pass, but were reluctant to employ it as an integral part of the attack until 1916."[35] Bob Zuppke, famed University of Illinois football coach, said, "The leaders of the open game as early as 1906 were mostly from the mid-west. The east as a rule was slow to follow. Michigan, Wisconsin, Chicago, Minnesota, Purdue, Notre Dame, and Illinois were the leaders. I saw more passing in high school than I did in college. However, the Carlisle Indians and Pennsylvania were also leaders in the new game."[36] Parke Davis, writing in the *Spaulding Football Guide*, said, "The eastern authorities couldn't see the forward pass as anything but as a foolish gamble."[37] Note that Pennsylvania was considered a leader and a reluctant user of the forward pass. But further investigation provides a clue.

The contemporary football books and written statements claiming the conservative East was not playing an open-style offense are contradicted by numerous 1906 newspaper game accounts. Covering eastern college opening football games played on September 22 through October 3, the sports sections have paragraph after paragraph of various teams attempting successful and unsuccessful forward passes. It is true that some early season games did not feature passes. Harvard opened the season under the revised rules by defeating Williams 7–0 in front of eight-thousand spectators while managing only three first downs for the entire game. The spectators expected new exciting plays, but none were used.[38]

In Hanover, New Hampshire, Dartmouth won their opener in a hard fought 5–0 score over Norwich. The general verdict on the new rules was unfavorable. Dartmouth was unsuccessful with the forward pass and quarterback kicks. They soon fell back to the old-fashioned style of line plunges. The new 10-yard rule prevented consecutive advances; only after hard work, did they score a touchdown.[39]

A tie game was played in Ithaca, New York, as Cornell and Colgate battled to a 0–0 score. Head coach Glen "Pop" Warner had Cornell working the forward pass extensively, as they gained 70 yards on three consecutive plays. Colgate used straight football tactics making large gains through the Cornell line. Neither team, however, was able to carry the ball over the goal line.

At West Point, New York, the Cadets defeated Tufts 12–0. Army was successful with their one and only forward pass for that afternoon.[40] Yale opened the season on October 3rd by defeating Wesleyan College at New Haven, Connecticut, 21–0. The Methodists threatened to score once, taking advantage of the new forward-pass rules, but they were thwarted in their attempt. Fullback Stuart Roome at 190 pounds tallied three touchdowns for Yale.[41]

During the second week of the season, Princeton and Washington & Jefferson played to a 6–0 score. The headlines stated, "Tigers Score Only Once-Forward Pass Tallies." On a wet, slippery field, Princeton was held to one score all afternoon. The Pennsylvanians were a heavy, fast aggregation and played good football. The game was especially interesting and helpful for one to understand how the new rules would work out under unfavorable conditions as Princeton used the forward pass several times. They scored on a short pass play and kicked the extra point, while holding Washington & Jefferson scoreless.[42]

In Harvard's second contest on September 26, the Crimson beat Bowdoin 10–0. The Harvard crowd waited patiently to witness the new forward pass, and when it occurred the entire gathering gave the Cambridge men a standing ovation. The pass was ordered as Harvard took over on the Bowdoin 35-yard line toward the end of the game. The ball was snapped directly to reserve quarterback Hall. After faking a short kick, he deliberately turned and threw the ball over the wing to left end Burnham. The pass was completed and the ball advanced a number of yards.[43]

The following week, on September 29, Harvard played its third game of the season. The improvement shown against Maine while demonstrating the open-style play surprised everyone. The home contest was one of open character and proved to be very interesting. Harvard attempted four passes in the first half and three quarterback onside kicks. Most of the plays were successful. The final score read Harvard 17 and Maine 0.[44]

Dartmouth's coach, Fred Folsom seemed to change his tune, as the Big Green defeated Holy Cross in their third game, 16–0. Playing with the new open game in a whirlwind fashion and taking advantage of Holy Cross mistakes brought victory to Dartmouth. The two squads were evenly matched, and the 10-yard rule prevented either team from making consecutive gains through straight football rushing, so the forward pass and onside kick were used successfully.[45]

On October 10, Bates University's only score of the game against Harvard came on a forward pass and a quarterback kick. The pass was labeled the prettiest play ever seen on Cambridge's Soldier's Field. The Crimson prevailed by a score of 27–6.[46]

In the second week of November, two big games were scheduled between the East and the West. Michigan traveled to the University of Pennsylvania and the Carlisle Indians of Carlisle, Pennsylvania, to Minnesota. It was the first time in 1906 that two intersectional teams squared off. Twenty-six thousand turned out in Philadelphia to witness the Quakers pound Michigan 17–0. Using a speedy and clever open-style offense, the red and blue Quakers outclassed the Michigan Wolverines. Gaining possession at midfield on a Michigan fumble, Penn completed a 20-yard forward pass to the 30-yard line followed by a 28-yard run to set up their first touchdown. Michigan passed twice during the game in desperation to avoid being shut out, but both fell incomplete.

In Minnesota, the Gophers lost to Carlisle Indians 17–0 in a hard-fought contest. The Indians pinned the only defeat of the season on the Gophers with a dazzling display of successful forward passes and quarterback kicks. The East had proven stronger in winning two huge contests over the West.[47]

Forward passes were flying frequently through the air and players scrambling to recover quarterback onside kicks as the 1906 football season winded down. Walter Camp said the Princeton–Yale game showed that both teams proved themselves versed in the new rule possibilities, open-style play, and made good use of forward passes and onside kicks.[48]

On December 1, a forward pass was also the turning point in the annual Army–Navy contest played in Philadelphia, a game that concluded the inaugural open-play season. In the second half, Navy was leading 4–0 thanks to a brilliant 45-yard field goal by big left tackle midshipman Northcroft. Scarcely had Annapolis's rooters' cheering ceased, when after an exchange of punts, Navy worked the ball into Army's territory. With a third down and four, Navy quarterback Norton dropped back in an apparent attempt to kick a field goal. Not anticipating a fake, Army played to block the kick. Ingram, Navy's fullback, lined up to protect the kicker, but as the ball was snapped he ran through the line like a shot. He caught Norton's beautiful bullet pass, sidestepped a would-be tackler, and dashed across Army's goal line for a touchdown. The jubilation of the Annapolis men started all over again and failed to cease until the game was over. The point after was good making the score Navy 10, Army 0.[49]

No one in the East despised the sport of football more than Harvard's president Charles Eliot. His distaste for the game was reported as early as 1893 in a *New York Times* article stating, "The evils of the intercollegiate sports as described in Harvard University's report for the academic year 1893-94 continued without real redress. The game of football grows worse and worse in regard to foul and violent play and in the number and gravity of the injuries of which the players suffer."[50]

After attending Harvard's 1906 game with the Carlisle Indians, president Eliot was very pleased with the overall open-style play, sportsmanship, and enforcement of the new rules. Just a year earlier, he had threatened to permanently ban Harvard's football program because of the game's brutal play. As Eliot left the stadium, he commented, "Today football improved immensely and did not possess the same elements of brutality and unsportsmanship as seen in previous years."[51]

For years, Walter Camp opposed the forward-pass concept and open-style of play. After witnessing the operation of the forward pass over the 1906 season, Camp had made a 180-degree turn. Camp reported in *Collier's* on November 24, 1906, that,

> The forward pass has had a deciding effect upon both the attacking and defensive team. It is safe to say no team or individual has mastered the art of passing as thoroughly as they will in another season, if the method is to be continued. The open-style play affords more opportunities for the offense. If a team has third down and five yards to go, they have three options provided with the new game. First, the old method of a long punt down the field, thereby surrendering the ball to the opponents, but a distance far from your own goal line; second, a short quarterback kick that shall strike the ground before reaching a defensive back, but giving the kickers side a chance for recovery and possession; third, the possibility of a forward pass which is more accurate than the on-side kick, but which carries with it more possible penalties. However, if the pass is successful for six to ten yards, even though the receiver is tackled, the necessary distance has been secured; the attack may be attempted once more with the running game. The forward pass and kick have been real intimidations for the defense, and are probably more effective than the plays themselves.[52]

Here, two of the biggest critics of football and the forward pass—Eliot who desired and ordered the game banned and Camp who lobbied against the introduction of the innovative passing and onside kicking game—had dramatic shifts in their attitudes toward the game of football.

The football subcommittee's primary reason for legislating open-style football play featuring the forward pass was to reduce the number of major injuries and deaths in the sport. Following the 1906 season, *The Chicago Tribune* published a two-year comparative study for football combatants. The title, "Casualties of the Football Season of 1906," recorded the total number of football deaths, including high school, college, and sandlot, as eleven compared to nineteen in 1905.[53] However, the number of game deaths in college remained the same, at three. College injuries were reduced from 88 in 1905 to 54 in 1906, while the total football injuries recorded decreased from 159 to 104.[54] This 35-percent injury reduction was extremely significant for one year. The greater portion of the injuries reported for 1906 were fractures of the hand, arm, rib, shoulder, nose, and leg.

The new rules clearly had a positive impact on the safety of the game. The adoption of a neutral zone on the line of scrimmage separating the offensive and defensive interior linemen by the length of the football, eliminated cheek-to-cheek positioning on the line that too often resulted in a crushing pile of bodies. The ban on using hands for offensive blocking cut down on the number of neck and facial injuries. Mass interference plays and the tackle-back formation were eliminated by ruling that only four men could be in the backfield and none of the five interior linemen could move into the backfield, unless they were taking a permanent position, and that position had to be at least 5 yards back behind the line of scrimmage. Another backfield player was then required to replace him on the line or was to move outside the end man on the line of scrimmage to assume a wingback position. Big interior linemen were prohibited from leading mass plunges into the line and delegated to lead less congested end sweeps and off-tackle plays. Some coaches circumvented this rule by playing their big men as ends and not tackles or guards. Ends were allowed to move into the backfield and carry the football on occasion.

Because of the publicity given the adoption of new rules and the effort to reduce violence in the game, the media downplayed injuries and deaths by not featuring them in headlines or focussing on them in game reports during the 1906 season. The fans and public figures were not exposed to weekly denunciations of the sport, and therefore people's attitudes were less affected.

Looking over the 1906 season, coaches across the country, with no prior experience and with no one to demonstrate successful individual football skills, did a remarkable job of devising and launching a rudimentary open-style offense. Midway through the season, teams began to loosen up their offense by throwing the ball and using the quarterback onside kick more frequently, In November, many teams were confidently throwing the ball between four and five times a game. Teams also used the onside kick extensively to maintain ball possession. Elementary football featuring a basic open-style offensive philosophy of ball possession was born—but if the modern balanced running and passing offense pioneered by Eddie Cochems and his St. Louis Billikens were to survive, it needed a national boost.

Jesse Harper in his University of Chicago uniform.
(*University of Chicago Archives*)

5

A Rookie Coach

In 1899, a young man named Jesse Clair Harper enrolled in South Chicago's Morgan Park Academy. His parents, James and Bertha Harper, decided he would be better prepared for university studies by attending a prep school.

Harper was born in Paw Paw, Illinois, but his family moved to Manson, Iowa, when Jesse was ten.[1] Living on a small farm, Jesse's dad always talked with him about possibly becoming a farmer someday just like he was, but Harper loved playing sports and desired to pursue an education with an opportunity to compete at the university level.

Harper could hit a baseball better than most of the other kids in his hometown and held onto a dream of someday playing in the Major Leagues. So at the age of sixteen, Harper left his family behind and moved to Chicago.

Morgan Park Academy played against some very competitive schools during Harper's three years of sports participation. He was the star quarterback on the football team and an outstanding center fielder in baseball. Harper was considered an excellent prep athlete with skills good enough to play at the next level. He had a terrific senior year while leading both teams to successful seasons.

Amos Alonzo Stagg contacted Harper early in his senior year encouraging him to look at the excellent opportunities offered by the University of Chicago; many people at the academy encouraged Jesse to consider applying there. They talked with him about the privilege of playing for Stagg, considered one of the finest football and baseball coaches in college athletics.

Harper was always interested in Chicago because he knew the Maroons scheduled some of the best teams in the country, including Michigan, Minnesota, Wisconsin, Indiana, Illinois, Iowa, and Purdue. Jesse set high standards for himself and wanted to compete against the best in the country. Coach Stagg made Jesse aware of the University of Chicago's challenging academic offerings because he knew Jesse was an excellent student. He also lined up a college visit for Jesse during a weekend after Morgan Park's football season concluded.

In the fall of 1902, Harper enrolled at the University of Chicago to study commerce and administration. He looked forward to Chicago's rigorous academic challenge. Walking across campus one day, Stagg ran across Harper and addressed him as "Jessie" instead of the correct "Jess," and the nickname stuck.[2]

Harper signed up for football and baseball his freshman year. He earned a varsity "C" in baseball but was unable to complete the football season because of bad ankles.

According to a newspaper article found in Stagg's scrapbook, while in college, one of Harper's sidelines was managing the refreshment stand at Marshall Field. The story is told that while he played football against Michigan in 1905, his partner in the enterprise was disposing of more than 3,600 hotdogs to appreciative customers at ten cents a dog. Needless to say, the business was profitable for these young entrepreneurs.[3] Harper also specialized in selling hams during school breaks for Chicago-based Swift & Company.

Harper had many positive experiences while playing football and baseball for Chicago. He had a great player–coach relationship with Stagg that had developed over four years of working together. Stagg challenged Harper to realize his full potential through a strong work ethic and positive motivation. Stagg especially emphasized the need for successful academics and said earning a degree from Chicago would help Harper in the future.

In March, 1906, coach Stagg received a letter from Alma College's president Dr. August F. Bruske. He was seeking a recommendation from Stagg to possibly fill their coaching vacancies and director of athletics position. Stagg immediately thought of Harper because of his leadership qualities, outstanding character, and competitive experience.

Chicago's sophomore quarterback, Walter Eckersall, an All-American candidate, was never replaced or injured so Harper did not have the opportunity to play quarterback under game conditions, but he studied the position and started at end and running back for a number of critical contests. His finest offensive performance was as a running back against Iowa on October 7, 1905, when he scored three rushing touchdowns in a 42–0 drumming.[4] Harper was virtually unstoppable while successfully converting numerous first-down attempts.

Harper was selected as junior baseball captain because he was highly respected as a quality team performer and leader. He was a center fielder during his freshman year but converted himself to the role of catcher where he started for three seasons. He was the Maroons top hitter for three consecutive years and as a junior led the team with a .311 batting average.[5] Blessed with excellent quickness and speed, Harper was an avid base-stealer.

Alma College was looking for a versatile young man with the talent for filling the multiple positions of athletic director and head coach for football, basketball, baseball, and track. The position paid a hundred dollars a month including Christmas and spring and summer vacations. Stagg told Harper, along with coaching, he would also be responsible for teaching history and gymnastics classes.[6]

Stagg said, "Being Presbyterian helped Jesse have an inside track on becoming Alma College's first head football coach because Alma was founded by the Michigan Presbyterians in 1886."

His recommendation for Jesse was the clincher. Stagg told Alma College's president that Jesse was a leader, responsible, and a clean living young man who would make an excellent coach and teacher for their program.[7]

Stagg always took pride in the hundreds of letters he received from colleges and universities requesting a Chicago graduate for their vacant coaching positions. He was respected across the nation as an outstanding man, leader, and highly successful and innovative football coach. He was a great mentor and related well to his players. He often reminded his team of the hard times in his early life as an Irish immigrant's son and being the fifth of eight children. He told many stories about events shaping his life.

Harper learned a lot about life from Stagg. There is no question Stagg helped influence Harper's philosophies of life and football. He considered Stagg to be his role model as a man and as a coach.

The excitement running through Harper's mind boarding the Michigan Central train in Chicago must have been overwhelming. He had graduated a couple of months earlier from the University of Chicago and was heading toward his first college head football coaching position. He was entering a new world full of challenges. His years of being a student and an athlete in training were coming to a close. Only 250 more miles of rail remained before Harper would assume the responsible roles of mentor, teacher, head coach, and leader.

As the train sped by seemingly endless rows of corn, wheat fields, and hundreds of acres of farmland, it passed over a bridge spanning the Pine River, and a small slumbering town appeared on the other side.

Flat roofs constructed above brick and wooden two-story buildings outlined Main Street, maybe four blocks long. Long, narrow, red storage buildings, a post office, and a bank appeared just a block from the tracks. Black smoke engulfed the passenger's windows as the train slowed approaching Alma's rail station. The train ride was over.

The college was only five blocks from the depot. Harper did not have to be concerned about searching for a place to rent because Alma College had offered him the opportunity to live in Pioneer Hall and act as the director of male students.

Professor James Mitchell was the first staff member to greet Harper. Mitchell's role was to represent the academic faculty and administration in overseeing athletics.

A few weeks later on Wednesday, September 12, 1906, coach Jesse C. Harper stood on the steps of the gymnasium eagerly awaiting the arrival of Alma College's football team. It was early autumn. The hot, dry summer had parched the brown grass on the football field's hard surface. The time had arrived for kicking off the 1906 football season.

Harper expected every team member to report for preseason training on time. Most players arrived by train, some locals by auto or carriage. Once on campus, they reported to coach Harper for obtaining their room assignments in Pioneer Hall. After arranging their housing, everyone headed to the college commissary to unload food they were responsible for bringing to camp. Coach Harper had sent a letter to each player explaining the program and listed the bushels of vegetables, fruit, or dozens of eggs to bring to football camp. Alma College players not only furnished food for preseason practices but were also obligated to pay for their college room, board, and tuition as there were no athletic scholarships at that time.

Academic classes were not scheduled to start until Tuesday, September 18. But Harper had the players report a few days ahead of time to get an early start on conditioning and to begin learning his new open-style football system.[8]

In the early 1900s, college football's opening game was normally scheduled in late September or early October, with the initial day of practice coinciding with the academic calendar's first day. Football coaches had no more than two to three weeks to prepare their team for the opening game. However, Harper's plan of two practices a day five days prior to opening day created a whole additional week of practice with no increased cost for the football program. Respect and enthusiasm were paramount on Alma College's campus, and the players bought into this young coach's innovative philosophy and approach.

Harper utilized Stagg's practice of requiring all football candidates to be physically tested for preseason conditioning levels. First, he weighed the players on the gymnasium scale, measured their height, and recorded the results in his leather-covered notepad. Next, he timed everyone in 40-yard sprints, an agility test, and two laps around the field. Harper had placed wooden stakes at the corners and positioned players at the far turn to watch while three players ran the course. Before retiring to the dorm, the team jogged a three-lap cooldown.

The next morning, Harper aroused the sleepy players by ringing a cowbell on Pioneer Hall's first- and second-floor corridors. The players responded by throwing cold water onto their faces to wake up and after toweling off, jogged 2 miles as a team around the Alma College campus.

A complete breakfast followed with Harper expounding on the value of proper nutrition. Using Stagg's format, Harper explained the importance of eating plenty of meat, eggs, vegetables, and fruits to fuel the body for the rigors of practice and achieving successful academic studies. He personally checked with professors, on a weekly basis, for reports on players who were failing or had inconsistent class attendance.

Harper scheduled a 9:30 a.m. practice everyday as well as a late afternoon session. He scripted the entire practice in his leather-covered notepad just like coach Stagg had done with his team.

Harper was instructed well by Stagg who believed the team needed to work on basic fundamentals every single day in practice. Prepractice started with Harper talking to the team about the importance of their blocking and developing interference for the ball carrier. He demonstrated a three-point offensive stance and emphasized the need for the linemen and backs to report early every day to work on stance, takeoff, bridge blocking—where a player would lean down, clasp his hands close to his chest, and extend his elbows out—and pulling for interference.

The brief instructive period was followed by the entire team running 40-yard punt coverage to improve their conditioning levels. In 1906, there were very few substitutes used in a game, so players had to be ready to play the entire 60 minutes without a break.

Coach Stagg always called his team together for a pep talk before starting the warm-up period. Like Stagg, Harper had players huddle around while he talked about the importance of giving 100 percent in practice. He emphasized a no-tolerance rule for drinking or smoking. Like his mentor, Harper stressed that a clean life made it easier to become a fit player.

The team completed 15 to 20 minutes of exhausting calisthenics and moved into the next period. Individual football-technique training was scheduled for the next 40 minutes. Harper demonstrated the proper techniques of throwing and receiving and then handed out footballs. The backs divided into groups of two for practicing passing and receiving. The quarterbacks also worked on handoffs for running plays while the backs learned to receive the handoff, carry the ball, and follow interference by making the proper downfield cuts.

Harper split his time for coaching the backs and the linemen into 20-minute sessions. To the linemen, he stressed a rapid release and taught them their position requirements: line splits, stance, getting off the ball snap, and blocking execution.

Coach Harper's open-style offensive playbook featured the T-formation, shifting from the T into a direct snap, a strong tackle-back and a short-punt formation. The total offensive plays numbered around forty, including simple plunges through the line as well as bucks, where the quarterback would hand the ball off to a back following a lead blocker into the line, and cross-bucks, where the quarterback would fake the ball to the fullback diving into the line and hand the ball off to the halfback who would run around to the weak side of the defense. Harper also added a few more end-sweep plays because spectators liked to see potential long runs, not just running up the middle.

Harper's playbook contained misdirection reverse plays by starting the ball in one direction and handing off to a back or an end coming from the opposite side of the formation. It also contained double-reverse and triple-reverse plays. Out of the exciting sixty-four play-action passes Stagg developed, Harper planned on teaching only a total of six to eight passes. He felt the quarterback sprint out with the pass-run option was excellent. He also favored the play-action three-man routes and swinging a back out of the backfield for a short pass. Harper realized there was an enormous amount of material to teach in a short period of time, so he eliminated much of Stagg's offense. The players had never experienced such creativity and were excited about learning the new formations, the passing game, and trick running plays. Harper was planning on using a simple but multifaceted offense.

The final phase of team practice was punting and kickoff coverage. The backs, ends, and linemen sprinted downfield as soon as the ball was punted. They also practiced scooping and recovering the ball for possession. During this period, coach Harper worked individually with the quarterbacks to instruct and correct their passing technique.

The young men vying for the starting quarterback's position had no previous experience passing the football overhand. The concept was difficult to learn, and they struggled with the new techniques.

Harper soon realized that successfully executing the overarm football passing skill, for an athlete never performing it before, was going to be a major challenge. The players had a tendency to push the ball from the hand and shoulder rather than releasing the ball from the fingers and hand. Their action resembled someone putting a shot in track.

Stagg and Harper had worked hard learning the proper throwing and catching techniques. Even after a few weeks of Harper's summer football class, receivers continued to catch the ball with stiff wrists and cradled arms despite practicing the proper receiving technique for many days. Breaking old habits was difficult. The receivers also attempted to trap the pass with their body causing the ball to bounce off their chests or arms and fall incomplete.

Harper began to better understand that developing an effective passing game required a great deal of time, patience, and training. Stagg was leery about the risk created by the pass and had warned Harper how difficult it would be to implement it into an offensive scheme within a short period, let alone the first season.

Harper now understood Stagg's concern. Stagg said passing the ball was eventually going to dramatically change the game from the original football creator's intent, but the process would be a slow one. After a week of practice, of the entire series of pass plays Stagg provided, Harper now expected his Alma College team to use only two.

On October 6, 1906, coach Harper's Alma gridders were scheduled to open the season against Ferris Institute (now Ferris State University) in Big Rapids, Michigan. A squall blew horizontal sheets of rain during the entire train trip; the unforgiving downpour created 3 inches of mud on the playing field.[9] The adverse playing conditions, combined with a new 10-yard first-down rule, challenged the physical capability of both teams. Attempted passes were erratic, either dropped or thrown off target. The receiver and quarterback never seemed to coordinate with one another. Neither college established a consistent, quality offense as they experienced difficulty maintaining possession and converting first downs, resulting in more punts than when Harper had played the game in his college years.[10] Harper's men,

The 1906 Alma College football team was coached by the rookie, Jesse Harper, who stands in a bowler in the back right. (*Alma College Archives*)

however, played an excellent game on defense, but the team and coach were disappointed with the final outcome, a scoreless tie.[11]

Harper was frustrated, but he was confident his team's ability and success would progress week by week as his individual players' basic football fundamentals improved.

Alma's gridders buckled up their leather helmets during the next week and prepared for the tough Michigan Agricultural College (now Michigan State University) team.[12] The Michigan Aggies were the 1905 Michigan Intercollegiate Athletic Association (MIAA) champions and fast becoming an archrival. They opened their season on September 29 by defeating Olivet College 23–0, crushed Albion College the following week 37–0, and entered the Alma contest sporting a perfect record.[13]

Alma College's Davis Field was not in the best of condition on October 13. The rain had halted just two days prior leaving the playing field muddy and covered with puddles. However, according to the December 1906 *Almanian*, the locals were not put off by the adverse field conditions and watched in good numbers while their gridders unveiled the forward pass and catchy shift plays. The game ended with Alma College and the favored Michigan Aggies in a scoreless game.[14]

Despite claiming a moral victory and playing hard, coach Harper attributed the team's inability to score during the first two games on deficient offensive execution.

During the following weeks of practice, Harper went back to basics, spending time coaching individual football techniques that included blocking, tackling, passing, and receiving.

When Alma took on Ferris for a second time, Harper's team prevailed 4–0. On October 27, Alma traveled to southern Michigan to take on the Hillsdale College Baptists and an old teammate of Harper's, J. W. Boone. Boone had played on Chicago's 1905 championship squad and was also in his first year of coaching. The game showed the strength of the Alma team better than the others because the men were of equal weight and weather conditions were ideal for the game.

After a Hillsdale miscue, fullback Harry "Hal" Helmer scored an Alma touchdown. Roy Marshall's kick failed, and the score read Alma 5, Hillsdale 0. The lead did not last long, because later in the first half an Alma fumble in the end zone gave Hillsdale a touchdown. Their kick also failed leaving the score tied at 5.[15] The touchdown scored by Hillsdale was the first allowed by Alma's defense.[16]

In the second half, Alma used a delayed forward pass out of the backfield with Helmer catching the ball for a gain of 75 yards. Alma worked to within 2 yards of the goal, but Hillsdale's defense stiffened and held them scoreless.[17]

After a Hillsdale punt, Alma drove the ball from midfield for a touchdown with short passes, end sweeps, and line bucks.

Marshall successfully kicked the extra point raising the final score to Alma 11, Hillsdale 5.

Alma's next foe was Olivet College, a team favored to win the MIAA championship in 1906. The whole state was shocked when the Michigan Aggies held Olivet scoreless in winning the season opener. The showdown at Alma College would advance the winner to the top spot in the MIAA conference. The Alma gridders had not scored on Olivet since 1902 when they won 10–0.[18]

A punting duel resulted in a scoreless first half. Many football experts had warned the rules committee that extending the distance for a first down would result in a kicking contest and that a fluke or long run would probably win the game. Alma met its first defeat of the season on a third-quarter field goal, 4–0, having failed on two attempts of their own.

But Harper was not about to allow his team to dwell on the loss.[19] Like Stagg, who performed magic season after season by always being positive, Harper urged his team to move past defeat by learning from their mistakes. He convinced his players to grow, improve, and focus on Kalamazoo College, their next opponent.

When they met Kalamazoo at Alma's Davis Field on November 10, torrential rain delayed the start, then forced a cancellation of the game. Both head coaches agreed to call the contest a draw, declaring it a scoreless tie.[20]

Knowing his players were disappointed, Harper called the Michigan Aggies coach. He knew Albion College had forfeited its game to the Aggies the previous Saturday. Because Alma and Michigan both had been unable to play that week, they agreed to compete that Monday afternoon in East Lansing. The Aggies prevailed, defeating Alma College 12–0, but in the players' estimation their game performance was the best of the season.[21]

The Alma team was eager to take on its next opponent, Albion College, but a few days before the game was to be played Albion's management informed Harper they could not play and would forfeit. So in the record books Alma received a 6–0 victory.[22] The cancellation meant Alma ended its season with the frustration of not playing the final contest on the schedule and having lost its last on-field game.

I n 1907, the college's student newspaper cited the progress and enthusiasm that Harper brought to the entire college during the 1906-07 academic year. The student writer stated, "Jesse C. Harper, a graduate of the University of Chicago, is the best coach among the colleges of Michigan."

Harper learned many lessons in his first year of coaching. A touch of success, despite the failures, moved Harper ahead of the coaching curve as he began to understand the value and importance of individual football skills. Jesse now realized more time was required to develop players' skills and concluded the off-season was the best time for players to improve their football techniques.

At the advice of the young coach, Alma's president Bruske committed the college to offer an off-season student physical training program. Bruske recognized the importance of holistic human development involving the mind, body, and spirit. He approved a course titled "Physical Training for Men and Women"; Harper was identified as the instructor. The course description said, "In recognition of the importance of regular and systematic physical exercise during the formative period of student life, the authorities of the college have decided to put this work on a credit basis. At least two hours of physical culture credit was required of students before graduation."[23]

Harper made sure his football, track, and baseball players were enrolled in the physical training course which focused on conditioning and individual-sports skills technique. This class provided his football players an opportunity to develop and successfully execute passing and receiving skills.

Harper's whole life now centered on the academic, social, and athletic life at Alma College. He lived and ate with the male students and was ultimately responsible for their conduct at Pioneer Hall. Teaching academic classes during the day and coaching teams year round, Harper had no down time. He always needed to be focused and at his best.

Harper was young with high energy levels, but he was consumed by the demands of his job. Being close to his family had always been a priority for Harper, and he had been able to travel home during vacations or on long weekends where he could relax when enrolled at Morgan Park Academy and the University of Chicago.[24] But at Alma this was nearly impossible. So he eagerly looked forward to returning home to Iowa when classes ended in June until he had to return in early September.

Alma valued Harper's leadership and prominent roles played on campus. They appreciated his teaching and coaching ability as well as his influence on the entire community. He was an ideal role model and mentor. Not wanting to lose this remarkable young man's talents, Alma awarded Harper with a new merit contract calling for an annual salary of $1,800, an incredible $600 raise.[25]

In his initial year of coaching, Harper had sparked a new level of community optimism creating positive and upbeat campus talk. He gained respect from the faculty by demanding excellence in all phases of the students' lives.

Harper believed academics came first, before anything else. He never held practice for more than 2 hours because it would infringe on players' study time, and he called off all practices during exam week to allow athletes time to study. He produced a very stringent eligibility requirement for all athletes by expecting them to be at least 77 percent academically successful in every class.[26]

Many of Harper's athletes worked diligently in the physical training course and during the summer, returning with a new sense of enthusiasm and resolve to succeed for the 1907 football season.

Having spent quality downtime with his family, Harper felt revitalized and well rested. He returned to Alma's campus during the first week of September with a new zest and determination.

Harper realized that his first year at Alma College was not only challenging but also had set the standard for years to come. Taking the Alma College football program to the next level was now the task ahead of him.

Harper's valuable leadership training, playing experience, and mentoring by Amos Alonzo Stagg would now come into sharper focus. He had learned many crucial lessons as an athlete, especially as the baseball captain his junior year, where the captain's position called for more than just acting as a communications liaison between coach and players. The captain assumed the role of a coach on and off the field. The head coach trained the captain in every phase of the game and depended on his judgment for making critical decisions.

Harper's role in football as the backup quarterback had provided the necessary training and understanding of what was essential to produce a successful football team. He spent countless hours with Stagg and Eckersall learning to successfully apply individual and team football techniques. He learned to throw the overhand pass, starting behind the ear and above the shoulder; it was a natural progression from baseball to football. He also assimilated Stagg's philosophy and application of team offensive and defensive strategy. But more important, as a backup quarterback, Harper learned the value of evaluation through observation, listening, and asking questions. He patiently viewed the game through perceptive eyes, attentive ears, and an inquisitive mind. He played the game as a running back but thought as a quarterback.

An assessment of Harper's first year as a college football coach revealed a team deficient in basic techniques. This contributed to a lackluster offensive performance. The offensive line, with few good athletes, lacked the ability to successfully bridge block and create interference. Backfield fundamentals, including quarterback exchanges, fielding kicks, ball carrying, and especially passing and catching the football, were subpar. The result was an offensive breakdown with an output of a mere 15 points in five games. Harper realized averaging 3 points a game would not win many football games.[27] Although the weather was a factor in the team's poor performance in a number of games, it was no excuse. He was determined to improve the offense in 1907.

Excitement was high with twenty-seven young men reporting to camp on September 17, 1907.[28] Alma College never saw the likes of so many talented football players in one year. Coach Harper would have three full weeks to develop a competitive football team with the first game at Kalamazoo College scheduled on October 5.[29]

"He's Still Smiling," were the headlines in the local paper describing coach Harper on his team's readiness for the 1907 football season. "Winning athletics alone do not make a college, but a first class faculty and winning athletics do. As a direct result of last year's victories, more young men entered the freshmen class than any previous time in the history of the college."

The second day of the season found coach Harper driving one team up and down the field while team captain "Hal" Helmer was putting another, equally as good, through their paces. Throughout the summer, Alma College rooters looked forward to an exciting new football season.[30]

Harper did not bring instant excellence to the college, but in a year's time his ingenuity, outstanding leadership qualities, dedication, and abilities to motivate and teach rallied an entire community. In one short year, coach Jesse Harper won the hearts of students, faculty, alumni, administrators, and the local community. This "small northern burg," as some newspapers referred to Alma, swelled with pride over the prospects of fielding winning sports teams.[31] There was no denying the strength of Harper's 1906 team was its rock-hard, smash-nose defense with rib-jarring tackles in every game. Defensive players were quick to the point of attack, stripping runners of interference, and making clean tackles.

The defensive team in 1906 gave up an average of just 3 points a game. This was considered successful football. Now the question was whether Harper's 1907 team could move to the next level by becoming a dominating force on defense and offense.

In 1907, Harper added a surprising new twist to the offense. The backfield, aligned in a balanced-line T-formation, shifted on the quarterback's cadence, flowing as though a dance choreographer had designed the routine. Harper had taught the shift concept during the first season, but inconsistent centering and lack of precision ball handling prevented his team from using motion under game conditions.

During the shift, the center snapped the ball directly to the left halfback going in motion to the right. The backfield formed a wall of interference by leading the runner through a seam

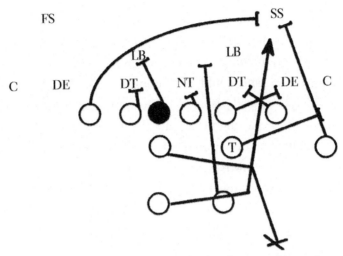

Figure 5.1 At Alma College in 1906, Harper developed a successful complementary play-action pass from his favorite off-tackle running play (above). The backfield action was mirrored for both plays making it difficult for the linebackers and defensive half-backs to differentiate between the running or passing game. If they committed to the run, a pass would exploit their position, so they played cautiously back on their heels and were generally late providing the necessary defensive run support to counter the off-tackle running play.

behind the right end and tackle. Rules allowed continued move-ment with the shift and did not call for the players to stop, but only to pause. Therefore, the defense was generally caught short at the point of attack by the momentum of the leveraged offen-sive players. The shift created an offensive advantage when run-ning off tackle (Figure 5.1), sweeping around end, and reversing the field with misdirection.

Another boost for the offense was a decision by the 1907 foot-ball rules committee to reduce the severe penalty on an untouched incomplete pass. Instead of loss of possession on an untouched pass, they adopted a 15-yard penalty from the previ-ous spot. Although the penalty was severe, this decision eliminat-ed much of the risk involved with passing the ball.

In the season opener against Kalamazoo, Alma's defense limited their opponent to a total of two first downs the entire game. The game was uncompetitive because Kalamazoo had practiced only one week and could not perform up to Alma's expectation.[32] Harper's squad prepared a robust running game with a full complement of passing plays. Most of the afternoon, Alma ran plunges with few opportunities for passes or trick plays. Alma scored six touchdowns—including a spectacular 70-yard pass and run from quarterback Dan Duncanson to fullback Irwin E. Bradfield—with Marshall successfully adding the points after goal making the score 36–0.

Michigan's weather in mid-October was normally crisp and clear. But on Saturday, October 12, for Alma's second game of the season against Hillsdale College, a cold raw wind from the north made playing conditions almost unbearable. To make things worse, intermittent thunderstorms soaked the energetic Alma College boosters. Despite the rugged conditions, the loyal fans hung in to root for their team. The game was marred with ragged play with the forward pass being unsuccessful for either team. The bright elements of the Alma attack were the excellent punting of Helmer, a 75-yard run by Hugh Ferguson, and Roy Marshall's successful field goal and extra point. The touchdown was scored by Helmer on a short plunge. All the scoring in the 10–0 Alma victory was in the first half.[33]

The 1907 football rules forbade sideline coaching and only allowed the players to make decisions on the field. The rules clearly stated only five men could walk up and down on each side of the field. The players, water carriers, coaches, and all admitted within the bench area were required to remain seated throughout the game or suffer a penalty of 10 yards for a violation.

Therefore, Harper, like all other coaches during that era, had to make sure his quarterback was well schooled in understanding and applying the offense during diverse game conditions. He met with his signal callers everyday for at least 30 minutes to an hour to improve their knowledge of that week's opponent's weaknesses and strengths and how that opponent was to be attacked under varying game conditions.

Several players with Alma's third opponent, Ferris Institute (now Ferris State University), grew up in Alma, creating an interesting game flavor. The Ferris Institute loyal were looking for revenge over past defeats. Alma's Irwin Bradfield was not going to allow this to happen as he scored a touchdown in the first 2 minutes of play, and Marshall's point-after attempt was good making the score 6–0. Helmer added another score on a short plunge, but Marshall's kick bounced off a goal post upright, making the score 11–0. Then an Alma fumble near the goal line set up a Ferris touchdown for an 11–5 score at halftime.[34]

Helmer scored again as Alma dominated the second half. Marshall's extra point was again successful. Alma's offense used brilliant line bucking and skillful forward passes in recording its third straight victory with a convincing 17–5 decision.[35] Everyone agreed Alma improved immensely from the previous week's win over Hillsdale.

Harper had arranged a perfect schedule for the weekend of October 26, prior to their showdown with MIAA favorite Olivet College on November 2. The void from competition provided a longer weekend, so Harper gave the team Saturday and Sunday to rest and heal up. On Monday, the team reported back for a light practice. Alma College ended up with ten days of practice instead of five to prepare for Olivet. Alma entered the Olivet contest undefeated while yielding only 5 points. The offense had amassed 63 total points while averaging 21 points a game.[36]

On November 2, the whole town gathered at the train station and paid tribute while sending off Alma's gridders. The band played the college fight song followed by a chorus of students chanting "Go Alma, Beat Olivet" over and over again.

Despite the high spirits of the players, the weather conditions were unconquerable. An early morning rain rendered Olivet's Reed Field slippery and muddy with pools of water covering many parts of the gridiron. To make things worse, the wind-driven rain was raw and cold.[37] But the bleachers were packed with fans wearing hats, gloves, and overcoats. The players' moleskin uniforms soon became soaked and covered with mud and grass. The successful survivors of this game would certainly be those best adapted for playing under these conditions. No tricks, no passes, no sweeps; only straight-forward smash-mouth football with plunges into the line.

Alma completely dominated play on both sides of the ball during a scoreless first half but suffered during the halftime break.[38] There was only one dressing room at Reed Field, and Olivet's players used it to rest and wash off the mud, and don clean and dry uniforms. The Alma team, drenched by rain and covered with mud, were forced to sit down on the open field in a raw, damp wind, then went into the second half weighted down by their mud-covered suits to meet the refreshed Olivet team. The home team managed to hold Alma scoreless in the second half and won 14–0, ending the visitors' three-game winning streak.[39]

On November 9, the Alma gridders traveled 15 miles north to take on Central State Normal College (now Central Michigan University). Anxious to redeem their Olivet defeat, the gridders were primed to play.

Alma received the kickoff and scored a touchdown in the first 3 minutes of play. By the end of the first half, the visitors were ahead, 17–0. The second half was a repeat performance, and the game ended with Alma on top, 35–0.[40] The *Weekly Almanian* recorded that the team played outstanding possession football, blending a mix of the forward pass with a brutal running attack that simply outclassed Central offensively and defensively.[41] The win on the road raised Alma's record to four wins and one loss, with Albion College the next opponent.

Midway through the following week, Michigan Agricultural College unexpectedly announced it was withdrawing from MIAA. Albion College's cancellation of its scheduled game at East Lansing apparently precipitated Michigan's withdrawal.[42] Albion gave no reason for the cancellation; though there may have been a feeling that Michigan was becoming too strong for the other colleges in the league. However, since the first MIAA Championship season in 1894, Michigan Agricultural had won only two titles while Albion had captured four.[43]

Harper was concerned about Albion's forfeit and the Michigan Aggies's withdrawal because Alma was scheduled to play Albion on the upcoming Saturday, followed by the Michigan Aggies. But a phone call from Albion assured Harper that the game was still on.

The game at Albion, on November 16, was scheduled to start at 3:30 p.m. but was delayed nearly an hour with darkness already settling in. A Helmer touchdown gave Alma a 5–0 lead, but the extra point was missed. The second half lasted fewer than 10 minutes before the game was halted because of darkness, and victory was awarded to Alma. *The Weekly Almanian* reported Albion was at no time within striking distance, spending the entire afternoon punting to Alma.[44]

During the train ride home from Albion, Harper learned that the Michigan Aggies had defeated Olivet, 55–4.[45] This was a concern to Harper because Alma would now face, in its final game, the team that had routed Olivet and the only foe to defeat Alma College's men.

When the Michigan Agricultural team came to Alma's Davis Field on November 23, Harper knew coach Chester Brewer's Aggies were on a mission to prove they had outgrown the MIAA's other teams. The Aggies's only blemish had come at the hands of Fielding Yost's University of Michigan squad by the score of 46–0.[46] Alma had not scored on Michigan Agriculture for the previous three years, losing 40–0 in 1904, 18–0 in 1905, and 12–0 in 1906.[47]

Harper designed a game plan by opening with two forward passes, but both failed. After receiving a punt, the Aggies attempted a forward pass that Alma's Dan Duncanson intercepted near the goal. With the ball on the 5-yard line, Helmer punted out of danger on first down. The Aggies received the ball in good field position and smashed forward for 5 yards. They gave back 5 on an end run as Marshall broke through, dropping the ball carrier for a loss. The Michigan kicker missed a long drop-kick in front of the goal.[48]

The second half found both teams exchanging the ball between the 20-yard lines with neither team able to score. The Aggies missed on three field goal attempts, and Alma failed on one.[49] The game ended in a 0–0 tie.

The 1907 football season concluded with Alma playing a brilliant game against the tough Michigan Aggies. This moral victory helped take the sting out of the Olivet defeat.

Alma's administration recognized the gridders' exceptional 5-1-1 season with a reception and celebration in Wright Hall.[50] The evening was filled with speeches, songs, laughter, and plain old-fashioned college spirit.

Following in Amos Alonzo Stagg's footsteps, Harper had become a great leader, teacher, coach, and, above all, an outstanding young man of values and talent. But something was missing.

When the school year ended, Alma's alumni and students were unaware that, although the administration hoped to negotiate a new contract with Harper, the coach was seriously considering becoming a business partner in his father's farming and brokerage company. He had many great experiences at Alma College, but the thousand miles between him and his family made it difficult to maintain a quality relationship with them.

Harper informed the Alma College administration that he had decided to leave. As coach, Harper had developed his 1907 Alma offense into a well-disciplined scoring machine, averaging almost 15 points per game. The defense had shut out five opponents while surrendering only 19 points during the entire season.[51] Jesse Clair Harper demonstrated he had the potential to be a great coach, but life does not always follow an expected pattern. Here at the start of a successful career, he was walking away.

The 1912 Wabash College football team. (*Wabash College Archives*)

6

South to Wabash

JESSE HARPER ALWAYS LOVED THE COMPETITION OF ATHLETICS, whether playing or coaching. There was something special that excited him about the spontaneity of the game. Sports were not just physical activities, they were great mental and emotional challenges for his mind and spirit.

Harper thrived on involvement. But his experience at Alma College had taken a heavy toll on him. He had literally spent two years immersed in athletics. He had successfully met every challenge head on and thoroughly enjoyed his responsibilities. But he needed time away to reflect and to make a decision about his future. He had made his mind up, during his summer break, that Alma would not be his permanent residence. So he headed home to partner in the farming and brokerage business with his father.

He worked closely with his dad in the family business from July 1907 through March 1909. Having been away for so many years, Harper enjoyed the family relationships he had missed so much. For a short period, during the summer of 1908, Harper became a canvasser peddling atlases in Kansas for a Chicago publishing house. His success in disposing of the books was not as marked as the romance that followed his meeting a certain nineteen-year-old Miss Melville Campbell from Wichita, Kansas.[1]

Enduring the college baseball and football seasons of 1908 was long and difficult. This was Harper's first full year of life without being involved in sports either as an athlete or coach. Although he was a highly successful businessman, Harper missed the players, the challenges, making crucial and spontaneous decisions, and the excitement of the college scene. The fire had returned.

In January 1909, coach Stagg received a very well-penned and sincere letter from Harper. In the letter, he explained that he wanted to get back into coaching college football and asked Stagg for a recommendation to universities seeking to fill their football coaching vacancy.[2]

Stagg always admired and respected Harper. He followed his short coaching career with great interest. He was proud of what Jesse had accomplished at the University of Chicago and continually bragged about his excellent coaching record achieved at Alma College.[3] Stagg wrote, "J.C. Harper is a first class fellow and a man of excellent habits. He has played football, but for two years while with us; however, he played on the Morgan Park Academy team for three years before he entered the university. During his first two years with us, he was handicapped by having rheumatism and did not try out for the football team. He had been making a study of football with the idea of coaching. He had experience as quarterback and halfback, the larger part of his game playing being at halfback."[4]

In two short years, Stagg's respect for Harper had grown from recognizing him as a fine fellow and accomplished athlete, to the level of a fine man and addressing him in writing as Mr. Harper. In Stagg's eyes, Jesse Harper had arrived as a professional coach.

Stagg recommended Harper again in February 1909 when stating, "Harper had unusual success as a coach in football at Alma College, which is one of the smallest of the Michigan Colleges. He prepared himself well in my football class during the past two summers, and is well qualified to coach the new open game."[5] He added, "My own personal knowledge of the man is that he would make an excellent director of athletics. About a week ago I had an occasion to recommend him to Wabash College, which is a strong small athletic college in Indiana."[6]

On Thursday, May 6, 1909, the headlines in the Wabash College student newspaper, *The Bachelor*, read "Harper, Chicago, '06 to Coach Men, former Maroon star and Director of Athletics at Alma College will be here this coming gridiron season."[7]

According to Stagg, "Mr. Harper is one of the most promising coaches he has knowledge of in the west." Concerning the new coach's past record, the following letters from coach Stagg of Chicago, and coach Chester Brewer of the Michigan Aggie's are significant.[8]

Stagg summarized Harper's sports and playing time at the university and then added, "He made great success as a Director of Athletics at Alma College. His coaching records in football and baseball were outstanding although the college had a very small number of students. He is a fine man, personally clean and upright and will be thoroughly respected and liked wherever he goes. I have every confidence in him as a man and in his ability as a coach. Wabash College will be fortunate to secure him."[9]

Chester Brewer, Michigan Aggies head coach, gave Jesse Harper a glowing recommendation. His letter to Harry Eller, athletic manager for Wabash College and published in *The Bachelor* stated, "I know Mr. Harper very well and consider him one of the best football coaches in the west. He is a fine, clean fellow, a tireless worker, and one who is popular with all the students. His work at Alma was very successful and they let him go only after trying in every way to raise money enough to keep him. I am sure you can make no mistake in Mr. Harper."[10]

On May 6, 1909, Jesse C. Harper was now officially and publicly named the new head football coach of Wabash College. Prior to accepting the Wabash coaching position, Jesse and Melville Campbell dated and developed a close relationship. With Jesse leaving for Wabash, there would be time to test the relationship as he would be able to return to Wichita only during breaks and over the summer. But as luck would have it, Jesse's mother and father moved to Wichita that June, and their home was only two blocks from the Campbell household.

Harper was scheduled to begin his new position on September 1, 1909, because college and university contracts were concurrent with the school's academic year. Once a person was under contract, he was obligated legally to fulfill all remaining days agreed on. Even though Harper would not officially start for three months, he began working behind the scenes to get everything in place that needed to be organized for a successful football season.

Wabash College's student body comprised an all-male enrollment. In the fall of 1909, there were 310 registered students, up forty from the previous year. The freshmen class made up the largest share with 140 new members. The college predicted an enrollment in excess of four hundred by the year's end.[11]

The large enrollment of new male students was good news for Harper. In comparison, Alma College had a male population of seventy five from which he built a solid football program. The bad news was that Harper inherited a Wabash College football program with only two starting veteran linemen from the previous year. Two substitutes with limited playing time, a center, and a back-up quarterback returned. Most of the returning players had been substitutes from the 1908 team with little or no playing time.[12]

The freshmen squad was the best to report in many years. A large number were recognized as high school stars. According to the student newspaper, *The Bachelor*, "One of the best pieces of luck which the college has had in several years was the securing of Mr. Jesse Harper for football coach of this year's eleven. Mr. Harper and his fine record were well known to all students. He is very optimistic over the prospects, but will make no definite statement for publication."[13]

Harper continued to believe in a well-organized 2-hour daily practice.[14] The Wabash campus academic and sports calendar published football practice times scheduled from 4 to 6 p.m. every week day and 2 to 6 p.m. on Saturday, with a day off on Sunday.[15]

Coach Harper had only three weeks to develop a competitive Wabash team from a large number of inexperienced players. He had brought an exciting open-game offensive package to Wabash, including multiple formations, shifting, play-action passing, end sweeps, plunges, bucks, and much misdirection.[16]

The newly named football coach explored opportunities for scheduling stronger opponents to bring Wabash College national and regional recognition. When completed, coach Jesse C. Harper's maroon Little Giants 1909 football schedule was loaded up with quality heavy-hitting opponents. Not only were the games challenging, but also Harper's crew had to pack their travel bags for almost an entire season.

On October 9, following the season's opening game at home with Illinois State, the Little Giants were scheduled to play the DePauw Old Gold at Greencastle, Indiana. Next, on October 16, they would travel to East Lansing to battle the tough Michigan Aggies. The strong passing team of St. Louis University would be the next foe on the road on October 23. Without unpacking their bags, Wabash would have to board the train for Lafayette, Indiana, to play Big Nine foe Purdue on November 6.

After an open date, coach Harper's team would head to South Bend on November 20 to take on the tough blue-and-gold Notre Dame Catholics. Wabash's last game was scheduled with Butler at Indianapolis, Indiana, on November 25.[17] Harper's team was scheduled to play Hanover College for homecoming on October 30, sandwiched in between all the road trips.

The opening football game resulted in a victory for the young Wabash Scarlet team. The score at halftime read, Wabash 16, Illinois State 0.[18] On the following Monday, *The Bachelor* headlines proudly proclaimed, "Wabash Defeats Illinois Eleven 27 to 0."[19]

Harper was praised by students and fans attending the first game. They were excited about dominating Illinois State and by shutting them out with such young players. The community's expectation was growing stronger with the future looking bright for Wabash College football. Roger Wilson, a 1908 substitute center, was named senior captain of the football squad. He was recognized for his leadership, dependability, and honesty.[20]

A new week found a challenging opponent and a paper painting a gloomy picture for Wabash College's football success against DePauw to be held on Saturday, October 9.[21]

Harper worked the squad on improving individual blocking and tackling techniques. He also continued to add more plays to the offense. Because inexperienced players were performing in critical roles, he made a decision to introduce the entire offensive package in stages to the Wabash team. He wanted each play to be executed flawlessly under game conditions and was meticulous with the details in his coaching. It was important, Harper taught, that each player understand each play and what the team could achieve on the field.

Harper organized a second daily mental practice by meeting the entire team or sometimes specific players for evening blackboard sessions. He felt these blackboard sessions were just as an important training tool as the physical practice on the field held earlier in the afternoon because it reinforced the learning curve. Harper believed players must understand their role and how their level of football knowledge contributed to the strength or weakness of overall team performance.

Over one thousand loyal fans jammed DePauw's McKeen Field in Greencastle, Indiana, expecting a knock-down, drag-out, competitive game. The kickoff was scheduled for 3:30 p.m. DePauw's quarterback caught the opening kick on the run and started upfield where Wabash's captain Roger Wilson was bearing down at top speed. One thousand hearts ceased beating for a few seconds as the collision could be heard in downtown Greencastle. Both men dropped to the ground and lay motionless. Wilson was so severely injured he was forced to leave the field. William M. Cochran, a sub, took Wilson's place at center. DePauw's starting quarterback also was taken out and replaced.[22]

The second half was evenly played between the two fierce rivals. First, one team would have an advantage, then the other.[23]

An interesting contrast of opinions on how the game was viewed occurred in the reporting newspaper, *The Bachelor*. "The

Scarlet held the Methodists to a 0-0 score, Saturday, in one of the fiercest gridiron games ever fought between the Scarlet and the Old Gold. Wabash's practically green team held the veteran DePauw eleven to a scoreless tie. The play was surprising to the Greencastle people who had expected to register a victory after having lost the last five times the teams had met. Wabash was well satisfied, but DePauw crushed."[24]

Coach Harper's defensive team had improved in tackling and pursuit of the ball by taking out the interference for the ball carrier. There were not many long gains for the DePauw offense, as the defensive team created numerous punting downs in shutting out the Old Gold. However, Harper knew his Little Giants needed to attain an even higher level of hitting for their next opponent, the tough Michigan Aggies from East Lansing. The Aggies had held the University of Detroit and Alma College scoreless in their first two contests. Offensively, the Aggies had amassed a total of 61 points.[25]

The game was over quickly. The Aggies took little time in scoring 28 unanswered points and held Wabash scoreless in recording their third straight victory in the young 1909 season.[26] Coach Brewer praised Harper and his young team for putting up a valiant fight.

The Bachelor reported that, "The Wabash squad held stiff scrimmage practices each day preparing for St. Louis. The first team had a chance to practice new plays which would be used the remainder of the schedule. In addition to straight football some plays strong on strategy were being perfected, which should fool St. Louis and Purdue."[27] It also stated that twenty men would travel Friday evening for St. Louis, Missouri, in preparation for Saturday's game. Fans were encouraged to purchase train fares and accompany the team. A rate of $2.50 was listed for the round trip or four dollars more would engage a berth.[28]

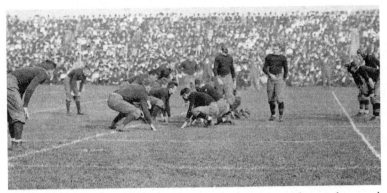

An excellent photograph of the October 17, 1908, Yale–Army game showing the neutral zone, offensive and defensive formations, and appearance of typical college football players of the period. Note the well-tended field and the simple uniforms. Yale, on the left, ended up winning the hard fought game, 6-0. (*Library of Congress*)

"St. Louis University turned the trick again Saturday and the Scarlet pigskin artists returned home Sunday morning dragging a zero behind them. However, the 14-0 score does not tell a story of absolute defeat. Wabash, with a bunch of crippled men was distinctly in the game. The Billikens' first score came after four minutes of play, being the result of a cleverly executed drop kick. In the second half, St. Louis scored a touchdown on a pass and then scored a field goal from a straight kick."[29]

Wabash's offense had now been shut out for three consecutive weeks in recording two losses and one tie. This was now the turning point of the season. The team had four weeks of game experience with over twenty players gaining playing time. For the homecoming game against Hanover, Harper overhauled the starting lineup for the fifth straight week, debuting a surprising backfield of P. J. Hawkins at left halfback, freshman Kent "Skeet" Lambert at quarterback, A. S. "Stony" Yount at right halfback, and R. L. "Smiley" Markle at fullback. Wabash ran over and around Hanover all afternoon. The blocking of the front seven was outstanding, and the revised Wabash lineup responded by scoring 33 points in the first half and 15 in the second, making the final score 48–0.[30]

Wabash's successful offensive play had arrived. After a multitude of injuries, rotating inexperienced players, learning a new offensive system, and competing against quality opponents, Harper's patience and perseverance had finally paid dividends with a satisfying and decisive win. *The Bachelor* stated, "The defensive players tackled with good form. The offense used very few trick plays, straight football tactics brought excellent results and there was no need to utilize the new plays designed for use against Purdue."[31]

The game results of Wabash's next three opponents found Purdue losing to Illinois 24–6, Notre Dame winning over Pittsburgh 6–0, and Butler losing to DePauw 12–6. Harper knew in his heart that traveling to Lafayette and beating Purdue on their home turf at Stuart Field would be an uphill battle. However, he finally had a positive outcome on which to build and help vault the team to the next level of play. Wabash had the same upper-class starting lineup returning for the first time all season. Injured players were actually healthy and capable of playing.

P urdue University was an original 1896 charter member of the Western Conference and bound to comply with its bylaws. In reaction to the public outcry of football's evils in 1905, the conference presidents restricted member schools to only five scheduled football games in 1906 and 1907. They also amended the constitution to make freshmen ineligible for intercollegiate sports, so athletes could only compete beginning their sophomore year. Consequently, while scheduling football and basketball competition outside of the conference, the Western

Conference schools could only contract those schools agreeing to comply with Rule Six covering the limitation of participation.[32] How this affected Wabash was that no freshmen could suit up and play in the Purdue game.

This was a blow to the development of Harper's football program. He had been nurturing many outstanding freshmen who were playing critical starting and backup roles. Wabash was stripped not only of player depth but also most devastating of all was the loss of freshman "Skeet" Lambert, the Little Giants' starting quarterback. He had played a major role in the win over Hanover after the upper-class quarterback, Hawkins, had injured a shoulder earlier in the season. But the news was not all unfortunate. It turns out Harper had convinced Lambert's older brother, Ward "Piggy" Lambert, a junior forward in the basketball program, into working out with the football team during preparation for Hanover College. Piggy played a limited time at quarterback scoring two touchdowns in the scrimmage. Piggy enjoyed his experience and returned to practice all week to help the team get ready for the Purdue contest. Even though Hawkins could play the position, instead of returning him to quarterback, Harper kept him as his halfback. Harper was convinced that Piggy Lambert would be physically capable of executing the offense. The Purdue game would be a huge test for the unproven two-week rookie quarterback and a major gamble by Harper.

Harper scouted Purdue against Illinois after the Hanover game, and he had been working hard all week in preparing the Wabash eleven with a number of new ideas. The starting team scrimmaged against the freshmen every evening and was showing promise in their offensive execution. Witnesses reported the team was preparing trick plays with misdirection reverses, forward passes, and straight bucks and sweeps.[33]

By Friday, every Wabash supporter was ready for the game of the season. The papers predicted that two thirds of the Wabash students would join the team in Lafayette. The whole college and Crawfordsville's community were excited about the Purdue contest. The Scarlet team was scheduled to depart on the Monon Special train Saturday afternoon at 1:13 p.m., with kick-off at 3:30 p.m. sharp.[34]

Purdue won the toss and opted to receive. Wabash kicked off to the Boilermakers; but when unable to convert a first down they were forced to punt on third down. Wabash's Hawkins field-ed the ball cleanly and outmaneuvered the Purdue pursuit for a 40-yard return. The defense soon settled in as both teams exchanged punts. Purdue's quarterback threw a 20-yard pass downfield to Wabash's 15-yard line where Wabash defensive back Sam Starbuck stepped in front of the receiver and inter-cepted the football. Everyone in the stadium rose to their feet as Starbuck avoided would-be tacklers and scooted down the side-line for an 85-yard touchdown run.[35] The point-after attempt was good. The Wabash fans went wild with the scoreboard reading Wabash 6, Purdue 0.

Soon after the kickoff, Wabash again regained control of the ball on its own 45-yard line after Purdue was unable to sustain possession. A 5-yard fullback plunge placed the ball at midfield. Starbuck lined up at right end. Piggy Lambert took the snap from center and pitched the ball to Hawkins, sweeping right. Out of nowhere, Starbuck took the handoff from Hawkins run-ning a misdirection reverse around left end. Purdue's defensive end attempted a tackle only to be straight armed to the ground. Starbuck knocked down the defensive back cutting across to his right, running over the would-be tackler. Only the safety stood between Starbuck and the goal. Attempting a touchdown-saving tackle, the safety was pushed into the ground as Starbuck galloped across the goal line. The roar from the Wabash supporters was deafening.[36] The Wabash kicker missed the point-after attempt making the score stand at Wabash 11, Purdue 0.

Wabash elected to kickoff to Purdue following the touchdown. After completing a series of successful first downs, Purdue worked the ball close to Wabash territory only to be stopped short of a first down. On second down, Purdue tried a quarterback quick kick into an open area downfield attempting to surprise the defense. Not to be outdone, Wabash's Ray "Sis" Hopkins beat the Purdue players to the ball, scooped up the pigskin, and rambled 60 yards for a touchdown, making the score Wabash 16, Purdue 0.[37] With time expiring in the first half, the Purdue cheering section sensed a defeat bearing down.

Early in the second half, Wabash took possession in its own territory only to fumble the ball away. Purdue recovered, and on the next play the quarterback ran a well-executed 25-yard touchdown jaunt, but they missed the attempt and the score read, Wabash 16, Purdue 5. *The Bachelor* reported the Boilermakers' weight and fresh players began to tell on the lighter locals, and aided one of their back's brilliant work, Purdue pushed over another score. Miles's kick was good, making the score Wabash 16, Purdue 11.[38] The fans expressed concern, but coach Harper took an important timeout and confidently talked with his Scarlet eleven to settle them down, instructing them not to panic, and he successfully refocused the team.

The Little Giants returned to the field for the kickoff with renewed vigor and determination. A long Wabash punt placed the ball on Purdue's 4-yard line where Nickey and basketball player Piggy Lambert hit Purdue's Chapin with such a driving force that they rolled him back across the goal for a Wabash safety.[39] The score now read, Wabash 18, Purdue 11. The momentum shifted to Wabash's favor with this devastating dual tackle.

Who would have guessed that an athlete not expected to play Wabash football in 1909 would provide such an outstanding performance and be transformed from a spectator to a football hero in just two short weeks.

Purdue scored its last touchdown on a disputed punt return making the final score 18–17 in favor of Wabash. With the sound of the whistle signaling the end of the game, the Wabash rooters rushed onto the field and celebrated with their victorious, but exhausted heroes. Both cheering sections demonstrated genuine spirit and were complimentary and respectful of their worthy opponents. Unfortunately, Piggy injured his leg in the final moments of the game and was seen leaving the field supported by a pair of crutches.[40]

Coach Harper was elated with this satisfying, but most difficult victory. After the game, he praised every member of the Scarlet squad, but in his heart he felt a special admiration for the young man daring to come out of the stands and willing to do whatever it took for a Wabash victory.

But football victories are short lived. Monday's scouting report on undefeated Notre Dame's defense read, "Tough," as they had allowed but a meager 14 total points in their first six games. Notre Dame held Michigan to a single field goal in their 11–3 win and only allowed two touchdowns while massacring Rose-Poly Tech 60–11. They had shut the door on Olivet, Michigan State, Pittsburgh, and Miami of Ohio. When Notre Dame had the ball, they amassed points in a hurry, averaging 33 points per game.[41]

On Tuesday, Piggy Lambert was still on crutches and ruled medically out for the remainder of the season. His services would be sorely missed as he had performed brilliantly against Purdue.[42]

Harper knew the Notre Dame contest would be an uphill battle. Mentally he began to reconstruct the starting offense for the sixth time in their past seven weeks of competition. The student newspaper declared, "The next job for the Little Giants will be to hold down Notre Dame. This is the most tremendous task required of the Scarlet all year, but it is far from impossible if the men played as they did against Purdue." The paper went on to say, "The Catholics have one of the strongest teams in the West. Their victory over Michigan could not be equaled by any other Indiana institution."[43] This was an understatement, as Notre Dame inflicted the Wolverines' only loss of the season. Michigan meanwhile mowed down such worthy opponents as Ohio State 33–6, Syracuse 43–0, Pennsylvania 12–6, Minnesota 15–6, and tough Marquette in a squeaker 6–5.[44]

The Bachelor said, "Coach Harper, in his characteristic style, is saying nothing, but is preparing the team diligently for the Notre Dame game, as hard work is the key."[45]

The week flew by as Harper prepared to travel on Saturday morning with twenty Wabash young men committed to giving their all for the Scarlet. A large crowd was expected to follow the team for the 3:00 p.m. kickoff, especially after such a great showing against Purdue the previous week. Notre Dame ended up dominating the injury-plagued Wabash Little Giants. After an early 45-yard field goal by Notre Dame's quarterback Don Hamilton, the Blue and Gold scored four unanswered touchdowns and extra points to lead 27–0 at the end of the first half. The second half was more competitive as Wabash drove many times into Notre Dame territory and within scoring distance, only to be held short of the goal line. Notre Dame scored two easy touchdowns with one coming off a 40-yard returned fumble, for a final score of 38–0.[46] The following week, the season ended with a thoroughly weary and crippled Wabash losing to Butler, 12–0.

The 1909 Wabash football season was one that Harper would never forget. Despite numerous injuries to key players; having to juggle the starting lineup every week; working with a pool of inexperienced players; having freshmen play prominent roles; traveling to play on the road six times; playing a schedule that included major competition with Michigan State, Purdue, and Notre Dame, he thoroughly enjoyed the challenges, frustrating as they were.

The Bachelor was very complimentary as it stated, "This fall has proven the worth and ability of Coach Jesse Harper. From somewhat scanty and mainly new material he has built up a team which credits his name and added credibility to the reputation of the 'Little Giants.' The 1909 football season was now history. The victory over Purdue was the crowning point, while the loss to Butler was the low ebb."[47]

The announcement that coach Jesse Harper had signed an extended contract ensuring his services at Wabash College was welcomed by the Wabash community. He had formally agreed with the administration to take over as athletic director for the remainder of the current 1909–10 academic year until June 1911. The article added that Harper would leave after Thanksgiving and return home to Wichita, Kansas, for a month's vacation. He was scheduled to resume his duties the first day of winter term by taking charge of all the college athletics with the exception of basketball.[48]

Harper grew as a professional football coach during the challenging and trying times of his first football season at Wabash College. He demonstrated great leadership and effective communication. He displayed exceptional emotional control and patience in leading the team through adverse conditions. He was innovative and adapted his open offense to the level and capability of the available personnel. His team demonstrated great motivation and positive focus throughout the grueling season despite many setbacks. He elevated his players' football knowledge and techniques on and off the field through various learning tools, such as evening blackboard sessions. The team believed week after week they had the ability or could find a way to win despite their shortcomings. He established high academic, social, and physical player standards. Above all, he instilled a level of respect in every man, which brought out the best in him, his team, and for Wabash College.

Jesse Harper had now coached football for three seasons without experiencing the traumatic result of a major injury or death that many of his peers around the country had to live through. Eleven college players had died during the 1909 season. This number was twice that of 1908, with six deaths, and two in 1907. The overall number of 1909 football fatalities jumped to an alarming twenty-six.[49]

During the first week of November, Harvard's University Athletic Association met to discuss plans for creating safer play after the tragic death of West Point cadet Eugene Byrne in a massing play in the October 30 Harvard–Army football game.[50] They sought to lead the movement in lessening the number and severity of football's injuries in the present game played with primitive head protection while involving brutal blocking and tackling tactics.[51]

Army cancelled its remaining schedule, including the annual Army–Navy clash that highlighted and concluded the end of every football season. Navy also suffered the loss of a midshipman during the 1909 season when quarterback and all-around athlete Earl Wilson sustained a broken neck in the Villanova game on October 16. He would die six months later.[52]

Archer Christian, a first-year student at the University of Virginia in 1909, was a standout halfback. According to historian John Watterson, Virginia was crushing Georgetown on November 6. Christian had kicked a field goal and scored the team's third touchdown to put Virginia up 21–0. When Virginia regained possession, they put the ball back into Christian's hands while running a line buck. Being mass tackled, he went straight to the bottom of the Georgetown pile. While getting up, he stumbled to the sideline before collapsing into a coma and dying within hours of a brain hemorrhage.[53]

These well-publicized cases made the front page of *The New York Times* and other major newspapers and immediately struck a match to the public opinion tinderbox of college football. Once again, some university presidents called for the abolition of football.

On December 28, 1909, more than one hundred professors and football coaches met in New York City to discuss elimination of the dangerous aspects still haunting intercollegiate football. After much deliberation, five recommendations were adopted for the rules committee's consideration.

The first change was to prohibit players from carrying, pushing, or pulling a ball carrier; second, when making a fair catch, no opposing player should approach within 3 yards of the catcher until he had possession; third, seven men were required to be on the offensive line; fourth, the present forward-passing rules should be dropped substituting only those passes completed behind the line of scrimmage; and last, to make compulsory the removal from the game of any player requested by the trainer, doctor, or captain.[54]

Three years had elapsed, and few coaches had developed the confidence or the expertise to implement forward passing into their offensive scheme. Many coaches felt the forward-passing

Football practice at Columbia University in 1908. Rough and dangerous play remained common across the country and after several highly publicized fatalities in 1909, a ban on college football was once again considered. (*Library of Congress*)

rules were restrictive and a great risk to use. Something needed to be done immediately.

The official 1910 football rules guide reflected the strong response from the football rules committee. They astutely eliminated many of the forward-pass restrictions. Instead of requiring a pass to cross over the line of scrimmage 5 yards out from center, the passer was now obliged to be at least 5 yards deep for any pass thrown crossing the line of scrimmage. This adoption legalized forward passes thrown into the middle of the field. To eliminate potential injuries, protection was given to the pass receivers while catching the pass. The rule read, "If the side in possession of the ball makes a forward pass, no players of the side not in possession, shall in any manner interfere with the opponents who have crossed the line of scrimmage until the ball was caught, except in an actual attempt to catch the ball themselves."[55]

The penalty for the defense was a loss of 10 yards from the spot of the previous play and the offense awarded a first down.

The restrictive rule that a pass must touch a player before striking the ground was eliminated. However, a limit of 20 yards downfield was placed on the length of the pass. This odd rule was enacted to prevent indiscriminate heaves downfield. If an incomplete pass was thrown on third down, the ball went to the opponents at the spot of the preceding play.[56]

After spending the Christmas and New Year's holidays with his family and Melville Campbell, Harper returned to Wabash College in early January well rested and ready to hit the ground running. He made an all-campus call stating, "Anyone expecting to play football in 1910 must either go out for basketball or play a spring sport." He added, "These activities would be good off-season conditioning programs."[57]

Harper was interviewed in March concerning the new football rule changes and expressed pleasure with the new revisions. He believed coaches would use the forward pass more frequently because of less risk for losing possession. He also felt the pace of the game would be faster resulting in requiring an improved player conditioning.[58]

With twenty-four returning players, Harper was upbeat for the 1910 fall season. Only three Wabash starters graduated, so experience and depth were prevalent for the 1910 squad.

Harper had recruited an outstanding freshmen class augmenting team strength. One freshman, Ralph Wilson, a promising athlete from Crawfordsville High School, possessed good speed and strength and earned a starting running back role. Wilson had been president of the Clionian Debating Society of Crawfordsville High School and was commencement speaker as president of his graduating class. He was elected vice president of Wabash's class of 1914. He was respected by all who met or knew him, easily making friends wherever he went.[59]

In the season's opener, the Little Giants made quick work of Georgetown University 57–0. In their second contest, Wabash defeated Purdue 3–0. The Old Gold and Black had now lost for the second straight year to Harper's eleven.

On Saturday, October 15, last year's loss to Butler was avenged with a 48–0 shutout. St. Louis University's Billikens, 14–0 winners over the Little Giants in 1909, were next on the schedule. Expectation was high for Wabash as the team headed to St. Louis, Missouri, for the October 22 contest.

Wabash College freshman Ralph Wilson died of a cerebral hemorrhage after making a knee-high tackle in the game against St. Louis University. (*Wabash College Archives*)

Leading by a score of 10–0 in the third period, Wabash College's football team appeared headed for their fourth consecutive win. Not a single point had been scored on the Little Giants' defense.

Wilson was playing defensive halfback when a St. Louis back carrying the ball around end turned the corner while outrunning his interference. Wilson was the last Wabash player between the ball and the goal line. While closing in on the runner tackling him low and hard, the St. Louis player's knee struck Wilson's head, dropping both players to the ground. Wilson struggled to get to his feet even while being assisted by Wabash's team captain. St. Louis quickly lined up for a play, and Wilson, still staggering, said, "Time out, time out."

Play was delayed while Wilson was escorted to the sideline by two Wabash players. Collapsing unconscious, Wilson was removed from the field area and taken to the gymnasium for observation by a physician. He was then moved to the team's headquarters, the American Hotel. Upon regaining consciousness, his first response was to ask coach Harper, "Did Wabash win?" Wilson then reassured everyone he would be all right as soon as he got some sleep.[60]

At approximately 11 p.m. Saturday night Wilson was taken to the St. Louis Baptist Hospital and then moved to the Josephine Hospital for an operation designed to treat a severe closed-head injury. Dr. F. J. Lutz performed the surgery and discovered a fractured skull and three blood clots. Ralph Wilson never regained consciousness and died at 5:45 p.m. the following afternoon. Dr. Lutz commented, "It was a mystery to me that death had not been instantaneous."[61]

Two funerals were held for Ralph Wilson on the following Wednesday. A morning service was held at 11 a.m. at the family home, and a 3:00 p.m. ceremony was held at the First Methodist Church in Crawfordsville where over five-hundred family, faculty, students, and friends paid tribute and reverence. Wabash's president Dr. Mackintosh delivered an emotional eulogy. "The brilliant and beloved young man has so suddenly passed from the visible world to the world invisible. He was a manly man, whose heroism and excellent qualities have secured for him a lasting place in the memories of Wabash men."

Coach Harper memorialized Ralph Wilson by stating, "Not only was he a wonderful athlete and a great young man, but Ralph possessed a brilliant and well-trained mind, promising to become one of the finest students ever to attend Wabash College."

Ralph's casket was attended by ten members of the Wabash College football team, and he was laid to rest in Crawfordsville's Oak Hill cemetery. Inscribed on his tombstone were the words, "Did we win?"[62]

That same week Harper recommended that the 1910 football season be suspended with all remaining games cancelled. President Mackintosh and administrators agreed and announced publicly that the season was over because Wilson's tragic death.

An article in the November 2nd *Bachelor* titled, "Question of Football's Future Now Open," stated, "The cancellation of the remaining games was taken as a matter of course, but the pertinent question now among the students and others interested in Wabash athletics remains whether or not the game will continue to thrive after this year?"[63]

A tribute paid to Ralph Wilson by a student's article in the November 10th issue of the Wabash College magazine said, "It is not often that one with us for such a short time is able to influence our lives so great by gaining our interest and admiration. Nor is it often that bonds of friendship and good fellowships are more painfully met. We are sorry that such a terrible accident should come to mar the promising outlook the athletic season held for us, but we are more deeply grieved that we can do nothing further out of respect to Ralph Wilson than prevent a recurrence of the fate which befell him. We hold power over the future only. What might have been done is past consideration."[64]

After much debate over football's impact and future on Wabash's campus, it was decided that for the good of the student body and college spirit, the game would resume in 1911. In March, football was reinstated by the Wabash administration.

The Wabash magazine featured an article on football stating, "The 1911 football team is an uncertain quantity because of the fact that two players are on the verge of giving up the game, two others will graduate and two have left college. The genius of Harper will probably fix things up all right and we may expect a complete season." A full football schedule was announced with commitments to play Marquette, Earlham, Purdue, Rose Poly, DePauw, Michigan Agricultural, Notre Dame, and St. Louis.[65]

Coach Harper and football team members underwent a tremendous amount of emotional stress while enduring the death of a teammate. Each person experienced considerable soul searching while questioning if he were capable of playing or coaching the game again. Some members lost intensity for the game while others kept the thought of being seriously injured in the back of their minds. Playing with these restrictions eroded self-confidence and the ability to compete with reckless abandon. Everyone had to overcome these intense conditions to start over with no mental blocks in their minds.

In reflecting on the season *The Wabash* magazine said,

> Football this year started with a question mark. Many doubted that Wabash would have a team, let alone a good one. Rooters hesitated at first from urging the players on, remembering the accident last fall. Yet, we have stepped to the front and with true Wabash spirit have taken a distinct lead. This does not mean the man who was lost last year was forgotten. It means the spirit of life is showing itself to good advantage right here in our little college. A fallen comrade holds a special place in our memories and we must still keep up in the race.[66]

And so, football prospered in Wabash again.

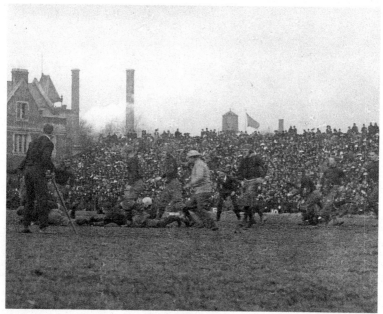

The 1912 Army–Navy Game. (*National Archives*)

7

A Change of Plans

DESPITE THE ATTEMPT TO PUT RALPH WILSON'S DEATH BEHIND them, the 1911 Wabash College football season started with a huge question mark. There was a team, but two major queries remained: How would the returning players react on the field after experiencing such a devastating tragedy? And, how would it affect coach Harper?

Jesse Harper had struggled every day with thoughts of the tragic accident. In quiet times, they conquered his soul. They tore at his being as he attempted to move on with life and responsibilities at Wabash College. Jesse shared his grief with Melville. She had the capacity to listen, console, and provide the love and support Jesse needed, and she helped him realize that he was unable to turn back time and change the past. He quickly understood his leadership was desperately needed. He knew the young men at Wabash College were hurting, just like he was, and cried for consolation after suffering the loss of a true friend and teammate.

In time of great adversity, Harper somehow found the inner strength and faith to help others cope and find their way back.

He became the beacon of leadership that the young men needed. He decided the way to deal with Ralph Lee Wilson's loss was
to become immersed with the young men in activities on a daily
basis and help them to move on with their lives.

Harper attempted to help heal the young men as they rallied
around one another. He listened, counseled, and provided direction. Harper's role on campus changed dramatically from being
a young respected coach to becoming a friend and mentor. He
was the one everyone admired and looked up to. That summer,
Jesse and Melville became engaged.

As athletic director, Harper called for developing an institutional intramural sports program. He believed if sports activities
were good emotional and physical tools for the varsity athletes,
they would even be better for the whole Wabash community. So
in addition to coaching football, basketball, baseball, and track,
he oversaw the intramural sports program. Hundreds of young
men became involved.

Before the 1911 season, Harper had decided to open his
offensive game plan with an even greater emphasis on the
passing game and welcomed the new 1910 passing rules. His
quarterback was throwing the ball between eight and ten times a
game, but the key factor was when to use the forward pass. The
quarterback called for a pass play based on the defensive formation or a defensive weakness of either alignment or personnel.
When the defense crowded the line of scrimmage expecting a
running play, Harper's team would elect to run a play-action pass
or a choice pass. Wabash had a higher number of passing plays in
their playbook than most schools at the time, which is not surprising considering the majority of football coaches across the country still had a conservative attitude about using the forward pass.

Harper was one of the first coaches to develop the concept of a receiver's forward-passing tree. The tree consisted of a series of individual pass patterns. The player was required to learn multiple pass routes while starting from a stationary position. The routes were not named but numbered. The quarterback called a number designating the receiver's pattern to be run into a specific defensive-zone area. This combination of knowledge coordinated the quarterback and receiver, thereby enhancing the probability for success. Harper taught the receiver to catch the ball with soft hands and with the fingers spread in contrast to the cradle catch. He also taught receivers how to catch the ball over the shoulder similar to a baseball player running down a fly ball.

These advanced forward-passing practices provided the offense with greater flexibility. Harper's offensive philosophy had moved ahead of nearly all of the nation's football coaches. His highly successful football program was becoming a unique model.

The passing and receiving techniques that Harper used are still employed in modern passing attacks today.

Skeet Lambert, a mobile and excellent passing quarterback, was now a third-year starter in Harper's program. Harper's football instruction helped Skeet develop into a well-schooled signal caller capable of performing under pressure in a big game.

Harper had three general types of forward-pass plays designed for his quarterback. The first was the spot pass designed for an individual receiver to run a route, ending up in a specific location where Skeet threw the ball. Second, an individual receiver ran a well-defined pass route to get open in a defensive zone's soft spot. Third, a choice pass was designed to allow Skeet to select one of three or four receivers running routes down or across the width of the field. He was very adept at recognizing the open man and completing forward passes 15 to 20 yards long.

When attempting a forward pass, quarterback Lambert was instructed on how to react when pass-protection blocking broke down. If he was being closely pursued behind the line of scrimmage, he was to throw the ball into the ground. Harper was a perceptive student of the game and did not miss a trick when reviewing the football rules manual. He was the first to recognize a flaw in the 1911 forward-pass rules that permitted a player being closely pursued to intentionally ground the ball with no penalty other than giving up a down.[1] Today this action is penalized with loss of a down plus 10 yards from the previous spot. Using this loophole, Skeet was never sacked for a loss during the 1911 and 1912 seasons.

On October 8, 1911, thirty young men reported to football camp. Many new faces stared at coach Harper as they gathered around him on the practice field. Leading the returnees from the 1910 season were seven top starters, including Lambert. This team made a remarkable comeback after having suffered such a distressing tragedy just a year earlier. They bravely fought their way to three victories, including a third consecutive win over Western Conference foe, the University of Purdue, tied one game, and lost to Marquette, Michigan Agricultural, and Notre Dame (who was crowned Indiana state champions in 1911).[2]

The Notre Dame game was one of the most thrilling gridiron struggles of the season. After a series of ball exchanges with neither team able to maintain possession, Wabash recovered a Notre Dame fumble at midfield. After two failed attempts, Skeet Lambert punted the ball back. Notre Dame's big fullback, Ray Eichenlaub, ran two line plunges, but Wabash's defense stiffened and stopped him for no gain. Eichenlaub punted to Wabash's halfback Elgin who was tackled in his tracks by ends Knute Rockne and Charles Crowley. On first down, Wabash's quarterback Skeet Lambert ran a successful bootleg for a 10-yard gain around left end. The Little Giants followed with an end sweep for a second consecutive first down. After two running attempts placing the ball in front of the goalposts on the 30-yard line, Lambert sent a drop kick squarely through the uprights for a score.[3] The first quarter ended with Wabash 3, Notre Dame 0.

In the second quarter, both teams punted several times despite Wabash's continued success with the forward pass and end sweeps. Each series ended with Notre Dame's defense stiffening and preventing Wabash from scoring. The first half ended with Wabash holding onto a slim 3-point lead.

In the third period, a remarkable catch of a forward pass from Skeet Lambert to Wabash's left end Howard set off a wave of excitement in the Crawfordsville's home stands as he outran the Notre Dame defensive secondary for an apparent 60-yard touchdown. After much discussion and the referee measuring the distance of the pass, it was ruled a 21-yard catch, and therefore the touchdown was disallowed. The rule—the ball having passed over the 20-yard limit—was considered an incomplete pass with no penalty.[4]

Early in the fourth quarter, with the Little Giants hanging onto their slim lead, Notre Dame's Eichenlaub drove a long wind-aided punt across Wabash's goal. The ball was placed on the 25-yard line with a first and 10, and then the roof caved in. Skeet Lambert put the ball into play with a 5-yard gain but was seriously injured by a crushing hit, fumbled, and was forced to leave the game. Notre Dame gained possession on Wabash's 35-yard line.

The Blue and Gold resorted to their bruising ground game with a series of line smashes from Eichenlaub, Al Berger, and Joe Pliska. Unable to contain the barrage, the Little Giants buckled. Berger scored, carrying the ball over from the 2-yard line. Gus Dorais kicked the extra point giving the Catholics a 6–3 lead late in the fourth period.[5] Notre Dame held off Wabash's desperate attempt to score as the game ended.[6]

The Little Giants, utilizing an open-style offense and a stifling, swarming defense, fought bravely throughout the contest. Wabash's Lambert passed nineteen times while completing over half of his attempts. The Notre Dame defense was excellent containing Lambert's running threat throughout the game. The Blue and Gold's defensive team was frustrated from chasing the elusive quarterback. The defense pursued Skeet sometimes 15 to 25 yards behind the line of scrimmage and looked as though they would throw him for a substantial loss, but just as the defender closed in for an apparent quarterback sack, Lambert fooled him by purposely grounding the ball for an incomplete pass. The ball was then returned to the previous spot with only a loss of down.[7]

Notre Dame's quarterback was quick to learn from Lambert's uncanny tactics, using them in his final game against Marquette and during his remaining two seasons.

In a tribute, the Wabash magazine said, "The year 1911-1912 has been a successful one in Wabash athletics. And to our 'Peerless Leader' Coach Harper, belongs a large share of the credit." In summary, it also said, "The noted Wabash spirit is again perching among the campus trees. Win or lose, the teams are cheered. The student body is back of every team and every man, realizing this fact every player puts his whole strength into his play. And, 'Coach Harper' is largely responsible for this. Thanks, Harper."[8]

In 1912, the football rules committee approved four downs to earn a first down instead of three. This rule created an advantage for the stronger, heavier players like those of Notre Dame who could batter their opponent's defense with three rushes instead of two. By averaging 3 yards plus on each attempt, they could earn a first down by overpowering the defense. The Committee also adopted legislation to allow a forward pass to be thrown to any part of the field, no matter how long, including over the goal line that would count as a touchdown. Scoring was changed too, with a touchdown becoming 6 points, a field goal dropped from 4 to 3 points, while the point-after-touchdown remained 1 point.

The forward pass now had been part of the game for five years, but only a limited number of colleges, either eastern or western, had adopted an open-style offensive strategy. Most coaches did not dare to take the risks involved in the complex passing game and therefore did not spend time practicing or developing the skills necessary for a passing game. There were, however, a few innovative college coaches that found success with the forward pass. Their programs, unfortunately, have largely remained unheralded.

In 1908, Hugo Bezdek, a 1906 Chicago graduate and a Stagg protégé, was named head coach for the Arkansas Razorbacks. His team was badly beaten by coach Eddie Cochems and his St. Louis University Billikens, by a score of 24–0. The Razorbacks recovered and completed the 1908 season with a 5–4 record.

To strengthen the offense, Bezdek called for help from his former coach, Stagg, and teammate, all-American passing quarterback Walter Eckersall. Stagg and Eckersall traveled to Fayetteville to teach Bezdek's players the techniques of forward passing.

For the next three years, Arkansas, utilizing the forward pass, went undefeated in 1909 and lost but three total games in 1910 and 1911.[9]

At Denison University in Grandville, Ohio, coach Walter "Livy" Livingston's Big Red gridders had discovered the exciting forward pass while playing Wooster College's Fighting Scots of Ohio in the third game of the 1912 season.[10] Wooster College's coach, H. B. Lloyd, was one of a few possessing the newly printed football rules manual and subsequently developed a highly successful, forward-passing attack based on the relaxed forward-passing regulations. In an interview years later, attorney George Roudebush said, "The Fighting Scots threw the ball all over the park and we couldn't figure out why or how."[11] A lesson in forward passing was well learned as the Denison players and coach organized an impressive strategic plan from their newly acquired information.

George Roudebush, the backup quarterback, had enrolled in Denison "off the farm where he had practiced throwing stones and corncobs at hogs and chickens." Coach Livingston found Roudebush could also throw a football just as well as a corncob. Livy elevated Roudebush to a starting halfback role to take advantage of his excellent throwing ability. Denison's two senior ends were sure handed and very capable of catching the football.[12]

David Reese, an outstanding basketball player, played center on the football team, but coach Livingston concluded that if Reese could catch a basketball, securing a football would be no problem.

Livingston devised many new pass plays but also included some involving a line shift where Reese was eligible by being uncovered as the end man on the line of scrimmage. Livingston thus created a brilliant passing combination during the last half of the 1912 season. Denison went on to score over 200 points while winning their last five games compared to a meager 19-point output in their first three games. Denison crushed the Otterbein Cardinals 60–3, then the Wittenberg Tigers 68–0. Impressive wins were also recorded against three larger universities as the Big Reds defeated the University of Cincinnati 31–13,

The 1912 Denison University football team featured one of the finest passing games in the county that season. (*Denison University Archives*)

Miami of Ohio 13–0, and West Virginia University 17–6.[13] Former backup Roudebush starred at halfback as the passing attack worked wonders for the Big Reds.

Newspaper reports heralded Roudebush and Denison University's success as they completed five to six bewildering forward passes a game that were 30 or more yards long. "The young Denison sophomore led the revolution in modern football by elevating the forward pass into a dominating offensive weapon."[14]

During the 1913–14 seasons, on the arm of Roudebush, Denison University developed into a football power. In a 1913 game against Ohio Wesleyan, he completed nineteen forward passes out of forty-two attempts. In the fourth quarter alone, he connected on thirteen passes for 150 yards. In 1914, Roudebush led Denison to an Ohio Conference football championship. In 1915, Roudebush entered law school at the University of Cincinnati. He was then drafted by the Canton Bulldogs, a professional football team, and played in their backfield with the famed Jim Thorpe.[15]

For three consecutive years, West Virginia Wesleyan, a small Methodist college, defeated cross-state rival West Virginia University by utilizing the forward pass with the scores of 19–14 in 1912, 21–0 in 1913, and 14–9 in 1914. They were undefeated in 1912 sporting a 7–0 record, joining major programs such as Harvard, Penn State, and Wisconsin that also won all their games in 1912.

Jesse and Melville Campbell were married in Wichita on February 5, 1912. They moved to Crawfordsville, Indiana, not far from the Wabash College campus. That year also brought even greater success to the Little Giants as they won five and lost two, outscoring their opponents 263–65. Wabash's stingy defense shut out every team they defeated. The Scarlet's only losses came at the hands of undefeated 7-0-0 Notre Dame and 7-1 Michigan State.

The 1912 *Notre Dame Scholastic* said, "In the greatest game that has been played on Notre Dame's Cartier Field in many a year, the varsity clinched its claim on the Hoosier state football championship last Saturday by decisively conquering Wabash 41-6. The down-state eleven put up the most obstinate defense possible, but the lighter Little Giants players could not withstand the terrific hammering from four rushing attempts of the Blue and Gold offensive line and backs."[16]

Walter Eckersall, the great University of Chicago quarterback and now sports writer for the *Chicago Tribune*, wrote, "Skeet Lambert, one of the best quarterbacks in the West, was the only Wabash player effective against the powerful Notre Dame squad. The Catholics' decisive victory entitles them to be rated as one of the strongest elevens in the West. They are equally strong on offense and defense. Although they do not use forward passes with any degree of success, their crushing and varied attack would confront any team in the nation."[17]

Despite this overwhelming victory, the Notre Dame team had developed great respect for Wabash College, and especially for coach Harper. The players did not know him personally but were aware of his coaching ability. His Wabash football, basketball, and baseball teams had challenged the powerful Catholics over four consecutive years and garnered wins in basketball and baseball while competing to the wire in all sports contests.

Jesse Harper about the time he was hired away from Wabash by Notre Dame. (*University of Notre Dame Archives*)

Notre Dame realized the Little Giants were totally prepared, competed to win, and never quit. Coach Harper's teams executed with a high degree of efficiency. It was even more remarkable that Harper coached every Wabash varsity team, whereas Notre Dame contracted a different head coach for each varsity sport.

In the state of Indiana's ranking of football powers, Wabash trailed champion Notre Dame as the number two power for all colleges and universities in the state, putting them ahead of Western Conference members Indiana University and Purdue University and all remaining small colleges.

A common concern among Notre Dame's fans and administration was their football schedule lacking quality competitive national teams. John (Jack) L. Marks, a former outstanding Dartmouth player and graduate, had coached Notre Dame to undefeated seasons in 1911 (6-0-2) and in 1912 (7-0-0). Most of their 1912 opponents matched Notre Dame's enrollment, but not their football skills. The strongest team played in 1912 was Pittsburgh (3–6), with Notre Dame winning by the score of 3–0. The Blue and Gold demolished St. Viator 116–7, Adrian College 74–7, Morris Harvey 39–0, Wabash 41–6, St. Louis 47–7, and Marquette, 69–0 to run the table in earning an unbeaten season.[18] Looking for a greater challenge, Marks suddenly resigned from Notre Dame at the conclusion of the 1912 campaign. This event initiated Notre Dame's officials to seriously evaluate their athletics program and its philosophy.

Notre Dame's administrators were concerned with the financial weight of their athletics program. The cost burden of individual sports coaches, road trips, and general athletics expenses far outweighed the insufficient income generated from home contests. By not being self-sufficient, athletics were losing money and costing the university precious dollars.

Another major administrative concern was the inability of their coaches and athletics manager to schedule the relatively close and competitive Western Conference universities such as Indiana, Purdue, Illinois, Chicago, Michigan, and Wisconsin. The Western Conference members avoided scheduling Notre Dame because they believed the university did not measure up to their conference's academic and athletic eligibility standards.

Notre Dame allowed freshmen and transfers to become immediately eligible on matriculation, whereas Western Conference rules prohibited students from competing until they established residency for one year. There were also rumors about a religious prejudice, with the public universities not wanting to compete against the Catholics. The Notre Dame administration believed immediate and dramatic changes in the athletics department had to be undertaken.

A friend of Harper's, an attorney and Notre Dame graduate living in Crawfordsville, Indiana, was amazed with Harper's athletic philosophy and coaching ability and Wabash's successful sports programs. He and Harper had many discussions about athletics and how athletics should be financially self-sufficient. Hearing of Notre Dame's open football position and believing in the Wabash coach, he traveled to South Bend to meet with Father John W. Cavanaugh, Notre Dame's president, to recommend Harper. Interested, the president summoned Harper for an interview.[19]

In early December, Harper boarded the Wabash railroad and headed to Notre Dame to meet with the president and vice president Father M. J. Walsh. After a few hours of discussing athletics philosophy and procedures, Father Cavanaugh hired Harper on the spot. Harper really liked Father Walsh's personality and sincere approach. They seemed to have a lot in common with their educational and athletics philosophies. They recognized the potential for a close and lasting friendship. Father Walsh was especially pleased that Harper had agreed to become Notre Dame's athletics director and head coach for football, basketball, baseball, and track. He genuinely looked forward to working with him because of his honesty, experience, and proven leadership. Harper called his wife Melville, explaining Notre Dame's offer, because he knew the university's responsibilities would create even greater demands on their lives, especially on family time. Harper's first contract at Wabash called for $1,500 a year while he was responsible for coaching four sports, teaching, and performing the athletics director's duties.[20] Excited about the possibilities of settling in South Bend, Indiana, they had agreed to make the move, but the final decision would ultimately be Jesse's. Before heading back, Harper signed an initial contract for an annual salary of $2,500. Harper was contracted to become Notre Dame's first full-time athletics director, as well as head football, basketball, baseball, and track coach. Within one day, all of Notre Dame's four head coaching positions were eliminated and replaced by Jesse C. Harper.[21] Harper became Notre Dame's thirteenth head football coach in the university's twenty-five years of football history.

Departing Notre Dame's beautiful sprawling campus, Jesse Harper's heart swelled with pride on being selected their new athletics mentor. But his thoughts were centered on concerns for his wife Melville and their week-old newborn daughter Katherine, back in Crawfordsville.[22]

Boarding the train and settling in for the 4-hour ride back to Crawfordsville, Harper's mind mulled over his day-long conversations. The administrators had thoroughly scrutinized Notre Dame's athletic problems while inquiring how Harper would engage and solve them. He addressed their concerns with conviction and honesty.

Harper knew he possessed the ability to solve Notre Dame's problems, but the issue undoubtedly clouding his mind was where he would find the time to manage all these responsibilities and a new family. Time, unfortunately, was his primary limiting factor. The second factor affecting achievement was in Harper's favor, his ability to work efficiently. He had the intellectual capability and the necessary experience to take control and meet Notre Dame's challenges head-on.

The timing of Harper's hiring was in his favor. Wabash's football season was over, and he had already held tryouts for the Wabash varsity basketball team.[23] Fortunately, December was an academically shortened month. Christmas break was scheduled at the conclusion of exam week on the 20th, so he would have over two weeks with no pressing Wabash College demands.

Headlines in the December 14, 1912 *Bachelor* said it all: "Harper Accepts Offer as Notre Dame Coach. Jesse Harper signed a contract with the authorities at Notre Dame University and beginning next September, will have charge of their athletics program." Harper was to remain at Wabash College during the 1912–13 academic year continuing to coach basketball, baseball, and track, even though he would be competing against the very institution and teams he would be coaching the following year.[24]

The announcement that Harper was leaving Wabash was not entirely unexpected because his outstanding record as the coach of four sports had attracted a great deal of attention from various athletic boards. An article titled "A Debt of Gratitude" stated, "Harper's new position at Notre Dame marks the passing of a man to whom Wabash College owes much. He has set and maintained high standards for the teams and himself. His superbly coached athletes were very capable of competing with the larger universities as well as the smaller ones. Harper's work as a coach and athletic director has been exceptional and it will be difficult to find a man to adequately fill his position."[25]

Harper's dilemma was the burden of successfully executing the responsibilities for two full-time positions. One was to continue performing his coaching and athletic directorship obligations at Wabash by providing leadership and direction for the young men involved in athletics. Second was to establish a new course of action for the athletics program at the University of Notre Dame while living 180 miles from the campus.

Knute Rockne leads the Notre Dame team out onto the field for the first game of the 1913 season. (*University of Notre Dame Archives*)

8

Blue and Gold

On December 16, 1912, William Cotter, Notre Dame's athletics manager, sent Harper a congratulatory letter saying,

> Notre Dame has been fighting against misinterpretation for the past four or five years and were denied opportunities to play our logical opponents. Now with your hiring a brighter day lies ahead. I wish you the greatest success in your efforts because scheduling for this school is indeed a tough proposition. However, I feel confident when it is published with your name, it will speak for itself and be the finest Notre Dame Football schedule ever produced.
>
> I have forwarded all previous football correspondences and negotiations and encourage you to consider playing Ohio Northern in the first game on October 4. They will make a fair practice game, although I believe a guarantee is negotiable at this point.[1]

The initial challenge for the Notre Dame football team was to arrange a competitive schedule incorporating a number of prestigious opponents. Harper's goal was to attract large numbers of enthusiastic college football fans to Notre Dame's Cartier Stadium by competing against well-respected football programs.

On December 17, 1912, Harper penned a letter to William Cotter asking, "How many people will your present bleachers accommodate? I want to see how large of a crowd we can generate."[2]

The week after his hiring, Harper sent numerous letters to well-regarded eastern, midwestern, and far western college football programs asking their representatives to consider competing against Notre Dame's Blue and Gold in South Bend, Indiana. Letters were sent as far as Nebraska, Texas, South and North Dakota, Kentucky, West Point, Yale, Penn State, Pittsburgh, Syracuse, Carlisle, Michigan, and Michigan State. He also sent correspondences to the eight boycotting Western Conference's institutions hoping to receive a positive response from them; they had refused to schedule Notre Dame during four consecutive years from 1909–12.

Notre Dame had defeated Indiana 11–0 in their last competition played in 1908. The Blue and Gold had played against Michigan, a former conference member, in 1909, winning 11–3. Other than scheduling smaller midwestern colleges, Pittsburgh was Notre Dame's only formidable national opponent in 1911 and 1912. Notre Dame's 1912 team steamrolled their seven opponents by a total score of 389–27 while racing to an undefeated season.

Harper was astute in understanding most college teams preferred to play at home. His ability to attract major opponents to play at Notre Dame was problematic at best. By December 18, he had mailed close to seventy-five letters, completely depleting his supply of Notre Dame's stationery; he wrote Cotter asking for more letterhead paper as soon as possible.[3]

Promoting Notre Dame was easy for Harper as long as other universities cooperated by showing an interest in scheduling the Blue and Gold. Harper had made a commitment to Notre Dame's administrators ensuring he would develop a financially self-sufficient football program while building their 1913 football schedule.

Harper knew there were various options in solving the challenging issue. The obvious was to generate increased paying customers by exhibiting a more appealing game, though he knew this would be difficult to achieve during the first year. He believed by playing a top-quality, competitive national schedule, instead of lesser known regional colleges, fans would flock to the stadium. In other words, his goal was to produce more gate receipts for home games.

Harper found a few universities interested, but they were demanding such large travel guarantees it was impossible to meet their requests. Notre Dame's football budget had been in the red for years because their gate receipts were unable to cover expenses. Over a ten-year period the revenues from fifty home games were minimal. They had also played twenty-eight road games without a guarantee to cover travel expenses.[4] Harper was about to put an end to this practice of supporting other colleges' football programs. His long-term goal was to restore Notre Dame's reputation and competitiveness by scheduling the highly respected and close-by Western Conference universities.

A number of athletic managers had shown an interest in scheduling Notre Dame but requested to play at home. Without hesitation, Harper decided his alternative was to take them up on their offer by negotiating guarantees in excess of his team's travel expenses. He needed to generate income for the football program, and this option appeared to be his most viable.

Harper described himself best on accepting the Notre Dame position by stating, "It was my sound business skill that caught the attention of Notre Dame, where the economics of football proved to be a drain on university funds."[5] He went on to state, "We just had to make football pay for itself; they didn't take in much money for home games in the early days, so I scheduled four on the road in 1913 and five in 1914."[6]

To pay the expenses, Harper secured lucrative guarantees from the home team opponents. Nebraska, as an example, agreed to a $6,000 guarantee for Notre Dame's football team to play six games at Lincoln, commencing in 1915.[7] Harper tried to negotiate at least a $1,000 guarantee or 50 percent of the net gate, which ever was greater, for every road trip.

Texas was the first major college to respond positively to Harper's letter seeking football games. Pulling off a major coup, on January 29, 1913, Harper secured a one-year contract. This included a $2,500 guarantee or 50 percent of net gate receipts from the University of Texas to play in Austin on Thanksgiving Day, November 27, 1913. Harper had initially requested a $3,000 guarantee in his letter posted on January 1, 1913, but Texas countered the offer, stating, in 1912, Oklahoma had received a postgame check for $3,400 which represented half of the net gate. Texas preferred to contract a lesser sum to insure their coverage of the guarantee, not realizing at the time how attractive the Thanksgiving game would be to their fans.[8]

Harper had an exceptional plan for killing two birds with one stone. He agreed to an $800 travel guarantee to play the Christian Brothers in St. Louis, Missouri, on Saturday, November 22. His scheme was to board the Missouri Pacific Railroad's train heading for Texas following the contest instead of returning home, thereby eliminating a 500-mile round-trip back to Crawfordsville.[9] His team would only have 885 miles of travel remaining to Austin, Texas, instead of 1,150. His idea was to cover the two games' travel expenses with the Texas guarantee, with Notre Dame's football program's budget pocketing the excess. The plan was brilliant as the players would only miss two academic days of classes because of Thanksgiving break.

On January 21, 1913, Penn State University's athletics gradu-ate manager, R. H. Smith, sent a Western Union telegram offer-ing Harper a one-year playing date. Later that winter, Smith agreed to Harper's $1,000 guarantee request, and a contract was signed to play at State College, Pennsylvania, on Saturday, November 8, 1913.[10] Penn State's coach, Bill Hollenback, had led his Nittany Lions through two consecutive unbeaten seasons in 1911–12. His 1912 team had an impressive 37–0 win over Ohio State and appeared as a very formidable national opponent for the Blue and Gold.[11]

Rumors preceding the 1912 Army–Yale game set in motion a circumstance that unintentionally benefited Harper. Earnest Graves, the Black Knights' interim coach, along with their athlet-ic representative, Lt. Daniel Sultan were discussing the annual game with first-year Yale coach Arthur Howe. Commencing in 1893, Yale University competed with Army for the past twenty consecutive years. These two football programs were great rivals with Yale emerging the superior thirteen times while tying four and Army winning three.[12] Graves and Howe concurred that the game demanded too much from both teams. However, neither team had formally agreed to cancel the yearly competition.[13]

In the winter of 1912, while developing their 1913 season's football schedule, Yale excluded Army's playing date by contract-ing Lehigh as their opposition. Harold Jones had been hired as Yale's new football mentor and found his schedule was completed. West Point had also hired their first-year coach, Lt. Charles Daly, Harvard's former All-American quarterback. Inadvertently, no one had informed Army of the unprecedented move, as traditionally West Point always held an open date for Yale. Cadet football manager, Second Class Hal Loomis, calling Yale to confirm the November 1st game, was appalled, to say the least, when he learned of the cancellation.[14]

When the Cadets heard there would be no trip to New Haven to do battle with the Old Eli, the grey West Point corps were extremely disappointed. Nothing could reverse this unfortunate predicament. It was now Daley's responsibility to finalize Army's schedule. As soon as he discovered that all of the eastern teams were booked, he instructed Loomis to find a suitable football team to fill the open date.[15]

On December 18, 1912, Harper had sent a letter to West Point notifying them of Notre Dame's open dates and sincere intent to schedule a game.[16] Hal Loomis received the letter, but having never heard of the Blue and Gold proceeded to study this small midwestern university's background. After consulting the 1912 *Spaulding Football Guide,* he found Notre Dame was located in Indiana, not in Illinois as he had previously thought. Checking out Notre Dame's 1912 football scores, he discovered an undefeated team with an unbelievable ability to score points while massacring their smaller college opponents. Loomis, convinced that Notre Dame would at least be a worthy opponent, wrote back to Harper expressing an interest in scheduling them for a home contest.[17]

Responding to Cadet Loomis's positive letter requesting Notre Dame to travel to West Point on November 1, Harper sought additional information. Specifically, he wanted to know how much money Army could guarantee to cover their travel expenses.[18] This was a first for Loomis because colleges always paid their own expenses when playing at West Point.

Army desperately needed to fill their open date, so a sum of $600 was allotted for Cadet Loomis to offer Harper. After several correspondences back and forth, Harper replied that Notre Dame had no funds to subsidize the trip that would cost them over $1,000 for travel expenses, including feeding and housing the team. Loomis went back to the drawing board, meeting with his superiors, until they finally approved a $1,000 guarantee that Harper was demanding.[19]

The football game contract between Army and Notre Dame secured by Jesse Harper in early 1913. (*University of Notre Dame Archives*)

Harper's persistence and business savvy paid off. They agreed to a long-standing verbal commitment with West Point to play one another. Army also agreed to play one game during Notre Dame's spring baseball tour through the East.[20] A formal contract between the two colleges was finalized and signed April 8, 1913. Unknown to either team, the stage was set for the football game of the century.

The second half of the 1913 football schedule was filled up with four road trips, so Harper knew he had to locate three teams willing to compete at Notre Dame. Realizing three contracted teams were major national powers, Harper did not want to overburden his Notre Dame team's competitiveness by scheduling too many major opponents during one season.

During the 1911–12 season, Army, Penn State, and Texas had a two-year combined record of thirty-nine wins, seven losses, and two ties.[21] Harper knew it would be difficult to schedule larger schools at home, so he concentrated on communicating with highly successful but smaller college football programs.

Notre Dame had opened their 1911 season by defeating Ohio Northern 32–6.[22] The Huskies had scored the season's lone touchdown against the Blue and Gold's defense while Notre Dame shut out six other opponents. Ironically, Harper's former Wabash Little Giants were the only other team to score all season on Notre Dame's defense when losing their close contest 6–3. Harper offered Ohio Northern a $250 guarantee to play in South Bend on October 4, 1913. With Ohio Northern agreeing to his proposition in late December, Harper was now well on his way to completing Notre Dame's toughest football schedule ever assembled.[23]

Harper contacted his former superior and friend, Alma College's athletics supervisor professor James Mitchell, inquiring if they were looking to fill a 1913 football date.[24] Alma College's 1912 season was outstanding, losing only to the nonleague Michigan State Aggies 14–3, while capturing the Michigan Intercollegiate Athletic Association's championship. The Presbyterians' offense averaged 39 points a game while winning six, including an impressive 6–0 win over the University of Michigan's freshman team. In their nonleague competition, Alma defeated the University of Detroit 28–20 and destroyed Central State 106–0.[25]

Harper believed his previous two-year coaching stint at Alma College would add an interesting flavor to the contest. He felt Alma would be a competitive opponent, but not overpowering. Mitchell notified his coach, William Bleamaster, concerning Notre Dame's inquiry to play in 1913. He was thrilled at the opportunity to compete against this well-known regional midwestern power. Bleamaster was eager to schedule Notre Dame because he believed it would add immediate credibility to

Alma's football program and possibly help to attract promising young high school graduates.

Professor James Mitchell replied that October 18, 1913, would be a satisfactory playing date. He also requested a guarantee of $250.[26] Harper agreed to his request returning the contract with his letter stating, "The guarantee is a little larger than I had hoped to pay because the game will lose money. However, I still have loyalty to Alma and believe this game with Notre Dame will mean a great deal to her. A good showing against Notre Dame will boost your football stock a great deal."[27]

Notre Dame's schedule remained unfinished. Harper still needed one additional opponent to fasten down a seven-game season. He felt the budget was insufficient to support eight games, and Notre Dame had traditionally played only seven. A surprising but welcomed response was received from South Dakota, a team Harper had contacted earlier. Harper was unfamiliar with the university and their football program. Studying their background, he found them to be a very formidable opponent, but more important, they were interested in traveling to South Bend.

In 1912, the South Dakota team had proven itself as one of the best teams from the West, battling to a 5–1 record. Their lone defeat was a tight 7–6 loss to the University of Michigan Wolverines. They had beaten Western Conference member Minnesota 10–0 in their impressive opening contest.[28] Minnesota played a respectable season with a 4–3 record including two close losses to Wisconsin and Chicago. South Dakota's 1913 team returned many veterans from a lineup averaging 40 points a game while defensively surrendering only 14 points the entire season.[29]

One dilemma remained. South Dakota's lone open playing date was October 18th, not the 25th. Harper had already scheduled the 18th with Alma. So he wrote to James Mitchell asking if they would be willing to change their playing date to the 25th. Mitchell replied positively, opening up the game date for South Dakota's team.

On March 19, 1913, Harper sent a letter to Alma College's James Mitchell thanking him for changing their contracted football date. Harper said, "It enabled me to fill our home schedule with South Dakota on October 18th and play an away contest on November 1st with the West Point Military Academy."[30]

Harper immediately sent South Dakota a contract for October 18th to include a $1,000 guarantee.[31] South Dakota returned the signed agreement. Notre Dame's 1913 football schedule was complete.

The challenges were now clearly defined and firmly in place. Harper had written to Notre Dame's assistant manager of athletics, John F. O'Connell, notifying him of the pending football schedule. Thinking everything was finalized, O'Connell publicly released the 1913 Notre Dame football schedule in late March. It was published in many newspapers including *The Bachelor*, Wabash College's student newspaper. The article revealed an unusually strong Notre Dame schedule, including games on October 4 with Ohio Northern; October 11, the traditional game with the Notre Dame freshmen; October 18 with South Dakota University; October 25 with Alma College; November 1 at West Point Military Academy; November 8 at Penn State University; November 22 at Christian Brothers, St. Louis; and November 27 at The University of Texas in Austin.[32]

Notre Dame's administrators were pleased with Harper's promise of developing a challenging football schedule. Within three short months, Harper had not only produced an enormous amount of paperwork but also achieved two of his five goals for

Notre Dame's athletics program. He knew his next obligation was to contact Notre Dame's returning football players to develop a schedule for meeting with them before college dismissed in late spring.

Despite coach John Marks's impressive undefeated 13–0–2 record for the 1911 and 1912 football seasons,[33] Notre Dame's football program struggled. The 1911 home contests only netted between $80 and $140 per game. Because their three road trips were unsubsidized by their opponents' guarantees, the overall football program lost over $2,000. This was a mere pittance when compared with the financially disastrous 1912 football budget that skyrocketed to over $12,000 in the red.[34]

When hearing of Harper's hiring, many campus people, including students, strongly questioned the year-end release of their four coaches, the athletics manager, and his graduate assistant. Few really believed, let alone were convinced, that one man could adequately fill the shoes of so many respected and well-liked men.

Jesse Harper had won round one. However, he realized it was now time and extremely important that he meet the returning football veterans. He felt the young men needed to understand his athletics philosophy and expectations. The Notre Dame players knew Harper as Wabash College's coach and the Blue and Gold's respected enemy.

Harper understood there was a challenging road ahead, but he had faced tougher obstacles. He decided his first move would be to contact Notre Dame's new 1913 football captain so as to develop a strong coach–player relationship in helping to ease the transition of changing head coaches. Harper wrote to Father Walsh questioning who the newly elected football captain was and how he could get in touch with him. Father Walsh responded in a letter dated March 25, 1913, that the captain was Knute Rockne, located at Corby Hall, Notre Dame, Indiana.

Spring break commenced on Thursday, March 20, continuing through March 26. Easter Sunday was early in 1913, falling on March 23. The Blue and Gold baseball team was practicing and playing games and Harper knew football veterans Henry Berger and Edward Duggan were key players on the squad. He also realized that three outstanding players, namely Knute Rockne, Ray Eichenlaub, and Alfred Bergman were off competing with the track team.[35] It would be impossible for Harper to meet the team until after every athlete returned to campus.

Harper contacted Rockne by letter and scheduled a football meeting after all spring sports scheduled had finished. Harper arrived at Notre Dame's campus on June 8 and stayed until Saturday June 14. He spent the week meeting players, students, faculty, and staff and observing conditions of the athletics facilities.[36] Learning that Harper had scheduled Army, Penn State, and Texas, Rockne and quarterback Gus Dorais were excited about the challenge. At the first football meeting with the entire squad Harper introduced his philosophy of athletics and expectations to the team members.

Winning over the confidence of the players would require Harper's patience and time. He had been coaching long enough now to know positive relationships were not built overnight. Some players would still have an allegiance to their former coach, John Marks. Some were probably skeptical of Harper's ability, let alone any one man, to lead the team successfully with so many demands and responsibilities. Some looked at the positive opportunity of proving themselves to a new coach and starting over with a clean slate. Some could care less and just wanted to play football. Most, however, had a great deal of respect for

Harper because they had competed against his highly motivated and competitive Wabash teams. Harper was well aware he had to work closely with each team member to gain his confidence and trust.

The key individuals Harper needed to garner support from were his two senior leaders. Credibility and acceptance from the team members would be much easier to attain with their assistance. The first leader was his elected football captain, Knute Rockne. Harper had an inside track with his team's captain because, though Rockne had grown up on the south side of Chicago, he was unquestionably a Chicago Maroons football fan.

Rockne hung around their football field watching and learning while the team drilled in practice. Like any other kid, Rockne made sure he was not a nuisance as he enjoyed the interaction with the older college football players. Sometimes he caught a pass or kicked the football to a player or just hung around the facility. For Chicago's home games, Rockne and his friends saved money by entering the field through the undermanned motor-car gate instead of the turnstiles.

Chicago's 1905 and 1906 All-American quarterback, Walter Eckersall, was young Rockne's idol while Eckersall was still in high school directing Hyde Park High's championship football teams.[37] Rockne admired Eckersall's ability to carry the ball with quick feet and elusive speed. He was spellbound by Eckersall's brilliant ability to lead the offensive team with precision and confidence. He watched in awe as Hyde Park destroyed an eastern Brooklyn Poly Prep team by the score of 105–0. As time ran out, Rockne and every other young boy left the field chanting Eckersall's name. He headed home with a deeply imbedded vision of someday becoming a star quarterback, just like Eckersall, while leading his team to glory.[38] Rockne's dream was not to unfold in high school. He did not make Northwest Division's highly successful varsity football team until he was a senior.

Rockne continued to follow Eckersall's Chicago Maroons football career and Stagg's outstanding teams. Working as a mail dispatcher after graduation, Rockne attended Chicago's games for three more seasons until matriculating to Notre Dame in the fall of 1910.[39]

Frank "Shorty" Longman was a recent college graduate when he assumed Notre Dame's head football position in 1909. Longman had played for Yost's outstanding unbeaten Michigan teams from 1903–05. He tossed first-year Rockne off his 1910 football team after just three days of practice for not performing well at fullback. Upset and disappointed, Rockne was on a mission to prove Longman wrong. He went out for Notre Dame's track team to display his athletic talents to his football coach. Rockne, possessing great speed, was capable of running the 440-yard dash in under 52 seconds. He had also cleared 12 feet 8 inches pole vaulting despite his undersized physique.[40] He quickly made his point by earning a varsity track monogram.

Needless to say, Rockne earned a starting end position for his new coach John Marks on Notre Dame's 1911 undefeated football squad. Marks, also a recent college graduate, had been a former All-American halfback on Dartmouth's 1907, 1908, and 1909 successful football teams.[41] Years later, Rockne was quoted in describing his former coach, "Marks made us over from a green, aggressive squad into a slashing, driving outfit. Marks even gave attention to the forward pass."[42]

By the end of the 1911 season, Rockne's name was being tossed around as a possible All-American candidate—a complete turnaround after being cut only two years earlier.

At the age of twenty-nine, Harper was Notre Dame's first head football mentor with proven college football coaching experience, and someone Rockne could look up to. Rockne, an older student, had entered Notre Dame in 1910 at the age of twenty two. Their age differential also helped Rockne and Harper ease the transition as respect became paramount in their coach–player relationship. Harper's Chicago Maroons athletic background and his close relationships with Stagg and Eckersall no doubt also played a major role in influencing Rockne and helping to facilitate their coach–player bond.

Gus Dorais, well-known to Harper, had led Notre Dame to victory over Harper's Wabash Little Giants in 1911 and 1912. He had earned the starting quarterback position for three consecutive years. Before Longman arrived on the scene and during Dorais's first season, Notre Dame passed the football underhand or end-over-end like most other university football programs. When Longman became Notre Dame's coach, first-year player Dorais began throwing the ball overhand. Longman approached him and said, "You'll never be able to handle a wet ball like that. It will slip out of your hand." To make a point Longman placed a football in a pail of water for an hour and had Dorais attempt a pass with the water-soaked ball. When demonstrating he could throw the ball successfully overhand, Longman elevated Dorais to Notre Dame's starting quarterback.[43] Gus Dorais had possessed the passing, kicking, and running abilities equal of any All-American.

Harper had the greatest respect for Dorais's athletic skills, but even more for his proven leadership qualities. Dorais was a tough competitor and a perfect match for Harper's open-style offense. Dorais also knew of Harper's innovative approach to the game and was excited about learning from this forward-thinking coach.

Harper's reputation was well known to these talented young men. Both team leaders knew Harper was well schooled in passing and receiving techniques and looked forward to working closely with him to advance their football skills. Harper was equally as thrilled with the opportunity to teach these talented athletes.

Rockne and Dorais took to Harper's candid approach as he revealed the critical leadership roles he had planned for them. He emphasized it was their team and their sole responsibility to reinforce player expectations. He also made it clear and imperative they follow through with each player to help him prepare 100 percent physically, mentally, and emotionally for a challenging season.

Notre Dame's campus was buzzing after Harper met for the first time in June 1913 with his football squad. It became apparent to everyone that Harper was a winner. He communicated candidly with the players so there were no unanswered questions remaining. Every player knew what was expected, and it was up to each one to develop a commitment to excellence. Harper assured the young men they were the team's foundation and all starters would be selected from the group within the room. He made a promise of not recruiting or accepting any tramp athletes or transfers joining their team.

Harper was emphatic about upholding academic standards. All players were required to attend their daily scheduled academic classes with no excuses or exceptions. A doctor's or nurse's excuse slip was required to explain any absence. He checked on the players' weekly attendance with all of their professors. He demanded academic excellence and would not accept any classroom effort below a 77 percent average. If a player fell below this standard, he would become ineligible until his grades improved.

First-year students were ineligible for varsity athletics competition. First-year athletes would not be able to compete and take over a starting or back-up role of an upperclassman. A campus-wide intramural football program would be established so all new students would have an opportunity to participate. Any first-year athlete interested in playing varsity football during his sophomore year had to improve his football skills by playing campus ball.

Harper believed by being positively committed to raising Notre Dame's academic scholarship and eligibility standards, not accepting transfers, and by holding freshmen out of competition he could improve their standing with the Western Conference members. In raising Notre Dame's athletics program standards to those established by the Western Conference universities, Harper assumed they would begin to schedule his teams in all sports. His long-term goal was to improve and restore Notre Dame's good favor with the Western Conference schools.

Harper had presented himself, his proposal for success, and his objectives for achieving his following six major goals for Notre Dame's athletics program. He had committed himself to arranging a major competitive football schedule; developing a financially self-sustaining football program; raising Notre Dame's student-athletes academic standards; creating eligibility standards for freshmen, upper-class players and transfers; reestablishing respect for Notre Dame's working and playing relationships with the boycotting Western Conference members; and achieving national recognition for a highly successful Notre Dame football program.

Notre Dame seniors Knute Rockne (left) and quarterback Gus
Dorais in 1913. (*University of Notre Dame Archives*)

9

Creating a Modern Team

BEFORE LEAVING FOR NOTRE DAME, HARPER STILL COACHED baseball and track at Wabash College in the spring. During their June Baccalaureate ceremony, the Wabash College graduating class surprised Harper by making him a 1913 Honorary Alumnus.[1] The citation described him as a man who was victorious on and off the Wabash College athletic fields. Over a four-year period, Harper led the Little Giants football team to a 15-9-2 record, including three consecutive wins over Purdue.

Following graduation, Harper, his wife Melville, and their daughter Katherine packed all their belongings and headed for Kansas to visit both of their families for the summer.

While spending time with his family, Harper found it difficult to keep his mind off the enormous obligation and responsibilities awaiting him in two short months. Having met with his Notre Dame football players in early June, he was finding it difficult to communicate with them over the summer months as they were scattered across the country and on their own. Harper could only hope they had the burning desire to physically prepare for the challenge he put before them at the spring team meeting.

At the end of the spring meeting, Harper repeated Stagg's policy of distributing footballs for everyone to wear out during their summer conditioning workouts. He had covered a detailed off-season workout plan with the receivers, halfbacks, ends, and quarterbacks. Each player's position responsibilities were detailed. The exercise regimen concentrated on the players catching and throwing the football while working on speed and conditioning. The linemen also received a heavy-duty exercise schedule.

Rockne had told Harper that he and Dorais were employed during the summer at a seaside hotel at Cedar Point, Ohio, on Lake Erie. They took a couple of Harper's footballs with them so they could work out together.[2]

No one could have predicted what Notre Dame's two leading student-athletes, Knute Rockne and Gus Dorais, encountered when meeting their new coach Jesse C. Harper for the first time and what it would mean to the game of football. Harper was the Notre Dame seniors' third coach in four years. Their two former coaches had talked about using the forward pass but seldom was the pass utilized much more than a mere threat to disguise the run.

Rockne and Dorais knew Harper was unique. They experienced his capability as an innovative coach while competing against his deceptive open-style offense for three seasons. Not only were Harper's forward-pass plays exceptionally well conceived, but his passing and receiving techniques were also distinct because his receivers caught the ball on the run or over their shoulder with their hands.

Notre Dame's former football coaches had taught Knute Rockne to cradle catch the ball, similar to the receiving style of

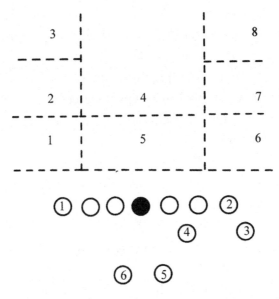

FIGURE 9.1 Harper's defensive field chart that he developed for quarterbacks to help them to visualize the designated zone for directing a forward pass.

the eastern teams. His favorite pattern was the button-hook pass. Rockne would run downfield and suddenly stop and turn, facing Dorais expecting the ball to be thrown directly to him. Harper was concerned about Rockne's stiff wrists while catching the ball with his arms and body. He told Rockne great receivers were highly mobile and caught the ball with soft hands and wrists.[3]

Harper spent a great deal of time explaining the summer workout program to Rockne and Dorais. He wanted his quarterback to be able to develop a better touch and greater accuracy while throwing to a moving target. Harper presented Dorais with a defensive field chart for writing down the pass play or receiver's route in identifying where his passes were to be thrown. During practice, Dorais called the defensive zone to attack, while Rockne ran Notre Dame's new individual pass routes designed to get him open in that area (Figure 9.1).[4] He emphasized to

Rockne the art of catching the ball with the wrists relaxed and fingers spread.[5] He covered all of the individual pass routes he expected them to practice. Rockne and Dorais would have an excellent opportunity awaiting them when they returned in the fall. When they returned to campus, Harper wanted them to believe they were the finest dual passing and receiving combination in the country.

Rockne and Dorais headed off to Cedar Point for a summer of clerking, janitoring, and waiting on tables. For this, they would get a room, meals, and about twelve to fifteen dollars a week in wages, excluding tips.[6] Packed away in with their sparse luggage were two footballs. Between working hours and enjoying the sand on the beach, they would diligently practice the forward pass.

A fortuitous change in equipment made their task a little easier. Since 1896, college teams were expected to play the game with a fat rugbylike ball. Only quarterbacks possessing unusually large hands and long fingers, like St. Louis's Bradbury Robinson and Denison's George Roudebush, were capable of gripping and successfully throwing the bloated ball. In 1912, the ball was reduced in size to approximately 28 inches circumference around the ends and 22.5 to 23 inches around the middle with a weight of 14 to 15 ounces, making it even easier for players like Gus Dorais to successfully throw the ball.[7] But despite the smaller football, many eastern universities still were not about to alter their tradition of running the football, and most continued to use the forward pass sparingly.

After completing their daily throwing and catching warm-up drills, Rockne and Dorais spent hours perfecting Harper's offensive pass plays and techniques. The longer Dorais and Rockne practiced together, the more they understood how to complement one another. After a few weeks, Dorais began to recognize the pass route Rockne was using while attacking a specific defensive passing zone.

Running in all directions, Rockne practiced catching the ball from different angles. To make their summer sessions as game-like as possible, Dorais would call out a series of numbers prior to his cadence to set Rockne in motion. For example, he called, "Ready, 27, 35, 42, Set, Hike, Hike, Hike." Rockne sprinted off the line on the simulated snap and attacked the zone called by Dorais.[8]

People who came to watch their practices at the beach shook their heads over the intensity of Dorais and Rockne. Dorais learned to throw the ball short, medium, and long distances. He also developed a better touch by altering the trajectory and speed of the ball. He learned how to lead Rockne on long passes or to throw to his shoulder on sharp cuts. Each week Dorais's passes became more accurate and stronger. The two seniors were no longer satisfied with the button hook or trying to outrun the defense. They worked diligently to perfect their timing on every pass route.

There have been many stories about Rockne's and Dorais's exploits at Cedar Point, most of which are wrong. The popular 1940 movie, *Knute Rockne All American*, portrayed Rockne as the inventor of the forward pass and the two seniors as architects of the forward-pass plays. According to Harper, "There've been many stories about their summer practicing the forward pass at Cedar Point and they are all bunk. The truth was that Rockne had always caught the ball in his stomach. I told him he had to learn to catch it with his hands and that I wanted him to learn my offensive pass routes with mobility."[9] He then went on to say, "When they say that the two of them used to practice on the beach for hours at a time is not correct. Dorais and Rockne did a lot of running in the sand because it was good for their leg muscles. They also did toss the ball around a bit on the beach, but the duo worked out mostly on a turf field nearby their hotel. They had to, in order to perfect what they had been instructed to accomplish and to get their timing down pat."[10]

The film also showed Rockne and Dorais devising the summer workout plan, and they were so thrilled with themselves they decided to take on Army in the fall. Rockne biographer, Michael R. Steele, agreed with Harper's comments about the passing duo's 1913 summer experiences, stating, "The fact is that the team knew about the scheduled Army game in the spring and Rockne and Dorais actually went to Cedar Point with a plan already hatched; they did not go there, hear the good news, and immediately start running post patterns they had drawn in the sand. The entire matter was really quite important to the Irish. Harper worked hard to arrange the game and then inspire his men. Rockne and Dorais took the charge with solemn hopes. But a film cannot readily capture the gradual build-up to the climax."[11]

Harper had coached Dorais on quarterbacking techniques and expected him to master them. Notre Dame's offense demanded the field general to understand the use of four basic types of passes: individual, choice, run-pass option, and delayed.[12] Out of the four passes Harper developed for his offensive arsenal, the choice pass was probably his favorite because all receivers were eligible and permitted to catch the ball.

The individual pass was the simplest to execute because the quarterback passed the ball to a primary receiver in a definite location. The weakness of the individual pass was the nonprimary receivers' role as decoys. If not coached properly, they often ran their patterns inconsistently because they knew they were not live targets.

The run-pass option play was designed for the passer to have a choice of either passing or running the football. These types of passes were either sprint-out or bootleg actions with the passer attacking the corner on the run. Depending on the player responsible for maintaining defensive leverage, the amount of pressure applied from the outer edge determined whether the ball was thrown or tucked under the arm and carried up the field.

Harper's offense employed the direct snap and centered on the stationary pass as well as the running-pass technique.[13] He felt the stationary pass allowed the passer more time to look over the defense making it easier to recognize the open receiver.

Harper's personal preference was the play-action pass because it involved more run deception, thereby complementing Harper's open-style running and passing offense. Often with the play-action pass, defensive players overreact to the feigned run causing them to lose their leverage and creating an open passing zone.

In 1913, the huddle was not an important component because following each successive play the offense realigned on the line of scrimmage as quickly as possible. Aware of his team's readiness, the quarterback called an audible from the line signifying the specific play to be performed. On a forward-pass play, the quarterback called the primary receiver's number first and then the defensive passing zone's number (Figure 9.2).[14]

All pass plays had distinct patterns so that the quarterback could follow the receiver and know where to throw the ball except for the "choice" pattern, where the quarterback did not have advanced knowledge of how the receiver would run his pattern while attacking the defensive zone, but only where the receiver was going to end up so he could deliver the football successfully. Effective communication and successful execution of the passing offense by the quarterback and receiver was only achieved by running the same route over and over.

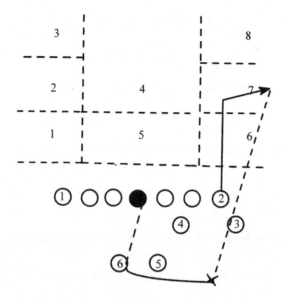

FIGURE 9.2 Harper's forward pass audible system with pass play "27" called. Here receiver number 2 is designated to run a pattern into zone 7.

Rockne learned that if there was an art in throwing, there was also an art in receiving. After weeks of practice, Rockne realized it wasn't finished work to have the ball bounce against his arms and chest when catching it in breadbasket or medicine ball fashion. There were too many chances for fumbles with the old cradle catch. He also learned to run his patterns with varying and controlled speed allowing him to adjust to the ball by either increasing his speed or throttling down. Patterning himself after a baseball player, Rockne gained the confidence to catch the ball with his hands while his arms were extended from his body. He kept repeating the phrase, "mobility, mobility and change of pace. That's what we need. They're not going to know where we're going or when we get there."[15] There was no more running out for a pass, turning, and waiting for it to arrive. He had learned to catch the ball in full stride.

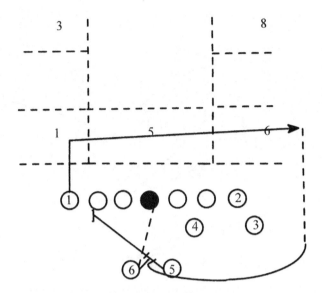

FIGURE 9.3 Harper's play-action pass with the quarterback faking the running play "65" while receiver number 1 heads to get open for a pass reception in zone 6.

Focusing his eyes on the front of the football helped Rockne develop better concentration and dexterity while catching with one hand. Gaining greater confidence, Rockne caught the ball with his left hand equally as well as his right. But when reporting for fall practice, Harper insisted on Rockne catching with both hands. Rockne later stated he was quite possibly the first receiver ever to attempt catching the ball with only one hand.[16]

Devoting time perfecting their respective roles, Rockne and Dorais developed perfect timing for each specific pass route. Anticipating exactly where Rockne would cut, Dorais would lead and hit him over the shoulder or put it right into his chest on a curl back. Instead of being only a threat with the running game, with the forward pass incorporated into a system of offensive plays along with leads, cross-bucks, off-tackles, and end runs, their team could offer a truly double threat to a defense.

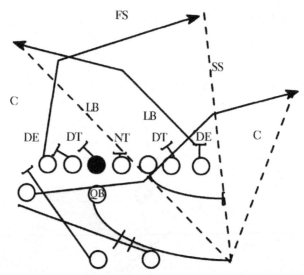

FIGURE 9.4 Harper's choice pass showing multiple receivers with none designated as the primary target.

Harper especially liked the play-action passes designed to complement the running game (Figure 9.3).[17] Rehearsing daily, Dorais and Rockne perfected every play-action pass drawn up in their new offensive manual. Dorais practiced faking the ball to an invisible back while developing his techniques of throwing the ball either on the run or from a stationary position.

Harper's passing offense contained a great deal of flexibility because it had the potential to exploit a weak player as well as a specific defensive area. On every pass play, Dorais had the option of calling one or multiple receivers. Designating a primary receiver identified where the ball was to be thrown, and all other eligible receivers were considered decoys requiring them to run routes away from the designated hot zone (Figure 9.4).[18]

Choice pass plays were designed to attack the defense with crossing routes or by flooding one side of the field with short, medium, and long receivers. Generally, all receivers attempted

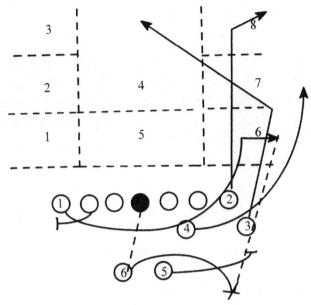

FIGURE 9.5 Harper's delayed pass with multiple decoy receivers and one designated primary receiver running a short under or delayed route.

to run their choice patterns to perfection because none were decoys. The quarterback's responsibility was to throw the ball to the most receptive receiver in the field.

A few eastern teams had installed the delay pass because it was one of the safest plays to execute (Figure 9.5).[19] Delay passes required the primary receiver to pause for at least a 2-second count before running a short underpattern. All other receivers were required to clear the field for the delay route by running through the deep passing zones. This forward pass was sometimes thrown like a basketball pass with two hands because the receiver was positioned only a few yards from the quarterback. Harper's delayed pass, like his mentors, was short, but the receiver was in motion and not stationary.

Harper's forward-pass offense, like Stagg's, was very well conceived and demonstrated much ingenuity and football virtuosity.

Some one hundred years later, we find a number of Harper's pass-play designs are still used in football today.

Rockne and Dorais went so far as to have some young men at Cedar Point put up a defense against their forward-pass plays in a mock scrimmage.[20] Creating a live experience helped Dorais anticipate what his opponents' reactions would be to the multiple pass routes. Practicing with live defensive backs, the two learned a great deal about their explosive offense.

Having been informed by Harper that the forward pass was frowned on in the East because it was too complex and unreliable to execute, Dorais and Rockne could not wait to demonstrate their newly acquired passing and receiving skills, particularly because they were scheduled to play two of the East's strongest teams, Penn State and Army. Years later, looking back on the football experience at Cedar Point, Rockne believed that their summer workouts on the beach had been the turning point of their lives.

Notre Dame's Cartier Field flourished with cautious optimism as the football squad arrived for their first preseason practice. Coming off an undefeated season with seven returning starters and two outstanding leaders, the Blue and Gold exuded confidence and excitement.

Although classes were to resume on Monday, September 15, 1913, Harper's strategy called for greeting his two senior team leaders, Rockne and Dorais, and their thirty-plus teammates one week earlier.[21]

The new coach's first week's practice plan was designed to focus on individual fundamentals and introducing the big pictures of team offense and defense. Harper did not overlook conditioning as his morning and afternoon practices consisted of minisegments of intense kick coverage and returns. The players welcomed the idea of their new coach challenging them to strive to achieve their full potential.

With no classes during the first week, Harper had time to conduct three daily physical and mental practice sessions. Morning's practice focused on individual blocking and tackling skills, kick coverage, and total team defense. In midafternoon, Harper introduced individual passing and running game techniques, kick returns, and total team offensive strategy. In the evening, he went over on the blackboard the passing offense they had practiced on the field during the day. Harper concentrated on making sure his players' understood their individual and team responsibilities. Harper expected his players to become emotionally, physically, and mentally immersed into his style of football.

During the first and second week of classes, Harper maintained a rigid 2-hour practice schedule demonstrating that academics came first. Cartier Field had not seen the likes of such strenuous football workouts. The first couple of weeks of practice for the 1913 season revealed major team challenges. Devoting a great deal of time to the kicking game, Harper had fullback Ray Eichenlaub working as a place kicker, in the event Dorais was unable to handle the kicking during a game. Harper wanted to have a reliable backup ready. The weakness in the offensive line was compounded when two 1912 starters, right tackle Paul Harvat and right guard Walter Yund, failed to return, creating an enormous rebuilding challenge for the new coach.[22] Nagging injuries also took a toll. Starting halfback Charles (Sam) Finnegan was out with a strained ligament in his side, and a tall potential end, Rupert (Rupe) Mills, had suffered an ankle sprain.[23] Both of these players were ruled not ready physically for the opening home game against the Ohio Northern Huskies on October 4. Starting center Al Feeney reported late to preseason camp and as a consequence was being held out of the Blue and Gold's first contest.

Alternating days of individual instruction and all-out scrimmage tested what the players had learned about Harper's offense and defense. The effects of Harper's training schedule were evident when the varsity and freshmen squad, the latter under the tutelage of ex-Notre Dame team captain Howard "Cap" Edwards, often battled for nearly 2 hours a scrimmage. The freshman team provided the varsity with competition in practice scrimmages so that they could learn Harper's system and improve their football skills.

Heading-up the offensive line for the opening game were three 1912 starters: left end Knute Rockne, left tackle Keith (Deak) Jones, and right guard Freeman (Fitz) Fitzgerald. Four new faces were selected from the 1912 backup players: left guard Hollis (Hoot) King, right tackle Ralph (Zipper) Lathrop, right end Allen (Mal) Elward, and center John Voelkers. The good news was a solid experienced backfield returned with three-year starter Dorais, the All-Western 220-pound bruising fullback Ray Eichenlaub, and a quick and speedy right halfback Joe Pliska.[24] Alvin Berger was scheduled to start for injured Sam Finnegan at left halfback.

No one expected the onslaught from Notre Dame's land and air attack in overwhelming the undermanned Ohio Northern Huskies 87–0.[25] The visitor's defeat was not quite as devastating as the previous years St. Viator's 116–7 crushing loss. But the three-thousand fans jam packed into Cartier Stadium witnessed the Blue and Gold's open-style offensive display in awe. Forward passes were mixed brilliantly with sweeping end runs and line smashes. The only thing stopping the newly found Notre Dame offense was the clock. Fullback Ray Eichenlaub plunged over for four touchdowns in the first half.

A moment of dead silence occurred late in the second period when Rockne was tackled hard and failed to get up after catching a pass. Dislocating and severely tearing a floating rib from the cartilage, he grimaced in great pain as he left the game. He was replaced at left end by Paul (Curley) Nowers. Harper substituted freely in the second half as the reserves scored 20 points while playing in the final two quarters.[26]

Dorais was brilliant in leading Notre Dame's eleven to its first victory of the season. Joe Pliska scored three touchdowns, two by rushing and one by snagging a beautiful 35-yard strike from Dorais.

To avoid a week off, Harper initially scheduled a varsity weekend game with the freshmen team at Cartier Field on October 11. With three starting players out with injuries, Harper decided to cancel the contest and schedule a freshmen game with Culver Academy instead. The light physical week was welcomed by the varsity, allowing them to concentrate on perfecting total team offensive and defensive play plus conditioning with the kicking game instead of the hard-hitting basic fundamentals.

Meanwhile during the week, the University's Board of Control over Athletics voted to accept Harper's proposal compelling freshmen ineligible to compete on varsity teams. This ruling allowed freshmen athletics teams to have schedules as well as making freshmen eligible to play on their intramural hall team. Adopting this university policy aligned Notre Dame's athletics program with the Western Conference regulations. Harper had won round two and achieved another major goal of improving Notre Dame's academic standards and norms for student-athletes.

On October 18, a pack of Coyotes from South Dakota invaded Cartier Stadium, providing the Blue and Gold an opportunity to show their heart. Fumbling on their own 25-yard line on the first play from scrimmage, Notre Dame's players had their backs to the wall. Unfortunately, Deak Jones, the Blue and Gold's left tackle, was injured on the play. Notre Dame lost not only the ball but also one of their premier defensive players. Playing without injured Rockne and now losing Jones was a huge blow to the Blue and Gold.

Taking advantage of the emotional letdown, Ferguson, the big Coyote fullback, drove the ball from 5 yards out for the first half's lone touchdown, giving the Coyotes a 7-point lead.[27] Trailing by 7 points, the Blue and Gold made critical halftime adjustments to the Coyote's swarming defense. For the first 30 minutes, the visitors had been playing their secondary close to the line of scrimmage, creating a ten-men front but leaving their intermediate and deep areas vulnerable to the forward pass.

Opening up their offense during the third quarter, acting captain Dorais had never been better. His multiple forward passes were cool, swift, and accurate. In targeting his receivers fifteen times, he never made a bad throw. The Notre Dame backs and ends eluded cover, catching the ball from all angles. The confused Coyote's secondary moved back to cover the pass and weakened their front, resulting in successful end sweeps and plunges.[28] Eichenlaub, with the help of superb blocking, ran over and around the defensive front scoring on a 7-yard run in the third period to tie the game. Dorais kicked a 20-yard field goal later in the period to elevate the Blue and Gold ahead for the first time. The goal was set up by successful forward passes.

In the final quarter, Notre Dame scored another 10 points. An 18-yard field goal by Dorais was followed by a 40-yard touchdown pass from Dorais to substitute Curley Nowers.[29]

The story of the come-from-behind-victory over South Dakota packed the stadium the following week with high expectations. Squaring off at Cartier Field were the Catholics and the

Halfback Joe Pliska running through a hole opened up by his blockers during the second half of the game against the University of South Dakota. (*University of Notre Dame Archives*)

Alma College Presbyterians. Not to let down the energetic crowd demanding another supreme display of offensive scoring power, Notre Dame swept to a 62–0 victory.[30] The crowd was also pleased to see the return of Rockne, Jones, and Finnegan. Notre Dame was now at full strength. Harper, remembering where he got his start, substituted twenty-one players freely throughout the contest as the Blue and Gold overwhelmed the undersized visitors from Michigan.

The forward pass worked well in the second half of the South Dakota game; but for most of the afternoon against Alma College, Notre Dame kept the ball on the ground and did not resort to the pass.

Following the contest, Harper met with Alma's professor James Mitchell and presented him with a travel check for $250.

Notre Dame now had three victories and no defeats, although South Dakota gave them a scare. Harper knew the first three home games were against teams his Notre Dame squad could beat. However, he kept reminding the team during these first three contests to stay focused and not to overlook anyone or to look ahead to Army.

Prior to the 1913 season, the Cadets from West Point were considered as one of the class teams of the East and possibly in the nation. They were big, strong, fast, and powerful with their running game. On defense, they hit like bricks. They were one of a handful of eastern teams that used the forward pass. Quarterback Pritchard and their All-American receiver L. A. Merillat were rated as one of the top passing combinations in the country.

Over their past twenty-five football seasons, Notre Dame had seldom scheduled a team strong as Army. Over their past five football seasons, starting in 1907, Army had swept over twenty-six opponents while dropping only nine and tying three for a .743 winning percentage.[31] Three of their nine losses were to perennial powerhouse Yale and four losses to their number one rival, Navy.

Army opened their season with a 34–0 victory against Stevens College. Unlike Notre Dame, the Cadets did not have an open date on their schedule, and following the Stevens contest, Rutgers, Colgate, and Tufts had all fallen in order to the Cadets. Army was undefeated and had only allowed a single touchdown to Colgate in their first four games.[32]

Army had sent their scout and assistant coach, Capt. Tom Hammond, to evaluate Notre Dame's playing abilities against Alma College, the game where Notre Dame happened not to showcase their forward-pass offense. The Alma defense offered little resistance to the advanced Blue and Gold's athletes. Their smaller players were overwhelmed by Notre Dame's running game as the Catholics ripped off yard after yard. It was unnecessary to use the forward pass for maintaining possession. Hammond reported that Notre Dame had a brilliant ball-handling quarterback and a ferocious slashing fullback, but they should pose no problem for Army's defense.

Quarterback Gus Dorais scrambling to throw a forward pass against South Dakota in 1913. (*University of Notre Dame Archives*)

10

The Rebirth of Intercollegiate Football

FACING HIS TEAM'S IMPENDING DEFEAT AT HALFTIME TO A tenacious South Dakota team, Harper had to make crucial adjustments. South Dakota's defense had overwhelmed the Blue and Gold's offense the entire first half as time and time again Notre Dame's ball carriers were smothered behind the line of scrimmage. Stacking their two rolled-up halfbacks behind their defensive tackles, South Dakota's ten defensive men were positioned right at the line of scrimmage.[1] Panic set in as the Blue and Gold continued to run into a seemingly brick wall (Figure 10.1).

Harper and his players were aware of the two basic football defenses. One was composed of a seven-man front with one middle linebacker and a three-deep diamond-shaped secondary. This defensive alignment used either a man or zone pass coverage.[2] A second base defense used a similar seven-man front but contained two outside linebackers and a two-deep box secondary playing either man or zone pass coverage.[3] Pioneer coaches, like Heisman, Cochems, and Stagg, understood while creating the open-style passing and running offensive attack, they needed to reciprocate and develop an equally progressive tactical defensive alignment that could defend against their newly devised passing game. Although not featuring a passing game, South Dakota had clearly taken an innovative defensive step toward countering the open game.

The Coyote's unorthodox overshifted defensive front baffled Dorais and his blockers on almost every play providing Harper's football team a serious character test. South Dakota's individual players were bigger in size, but Notre Dame's players were faster. In his halftime talk, Harper instructed Dorais to utilize a fake-run action into the line with Eichenlaub to draw the defense out of position. South Dakota's overreaction to the run fake would create holes in the Coyote's secondary, giving an opportunity to his receivers. With man-to-man coverage, Notre Dame's receivers were instructed to run crossing patterns to not only force the tight secondary deep but also to confuse and outrun the Coyote defensive backs.

In the second half, Dorais picked South Dakota's defense apart with his speedier backs running short under and flat routes as well as throwing to the wide-open deeper crossing receivers. In an attempt to cover the pass, South Dakota adjusted their secondary by playing deeper, thus leaving their defensive front vulnerable to the run. Mixing a strong blend of play-action passes with an occasional running play in the second half, Notre Dame scored 20 unanswered points.[4]

The South Dakota game was a blessing in disguise. It was a badly needed wake-up call that exposed Notre Dame's offense's vulnerability.

Despite Dorais's previous three-year experience as a starting college quarterback, it did not prepare him for directing an open-style passing and running attack. Dorais had outstanding athlet-

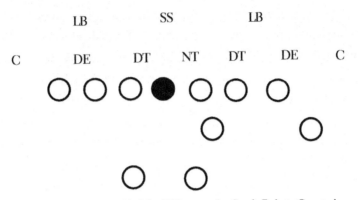

Figure 10.1 During the first half of the 1913 game, the South Dakota Coyotes's over-shifted defensive front while playing man-to-man coverage completely confused Notre Dame's offense.

ic passing ability and leadership tools making him potentially a great quarterback, but he still needed more training and experience to successfully direct Harper's open-style offense and understand opposing defensive sets.

The timing couldn't have been better as Harper had two full weeks to prepare Dorais and back-ups Hardy Bush and Joe Gargan before Notre Dame faced tough and heralded Army.[5] Holding strategy sessions over lunch and every evening, Harper drilled and tested his quarterbacks on their offensive preparation for West Point.

Directing Notre Dame's multifaceted offense required a great deal of practice and concentration. Not only did Dorais have to learn to recognize the opponent's various defensive fronts' strengths and weaknesses, but he also had to specifically understand what to call on the line of scrimmage when counterattacking. Harper tutored Dorais to make quick decisions by helping him analyze the defense and creating a mental picture of the best way to attack the opponent. Dorais learned valuable lessons about the complex offense's "big" picture. His newly acquired knowledge ensured him of improvement in future games.

Preparing for the Army game made for a short week. Harper put his gridders through a light workout on Monday while rehearsing their total team offense against Army's anticipated defensive fronts. Expecting the unexpected, Harper's gut told him to coach and prepare his team for unusual unorthodox defenses including overshifted, seven-man fronts, like South Dakota's innovative six- and five-man fronts, as well as the standard seven-man defenses. Conditioning was completed on Monday by running all phases of the kicking game's coverage.

L t. Charles Daly was a first-year Army head coach, replacing Ernest Graves; but, despite being a novice, he was one of the first college gridiron mentors to apply a systematic approach to scouting opponents.[6] Daly entered Harvard at the age of sixteen where he became a legendary quarterback. While an undergraduate at Harvard, President Roosevelt asked him to help strengthen the West Point football team. Daly coached them during the summers of his last two years at Harvard. Graduating in 1901, he went on to West Point where he played football until 1902. The next two years, he was a West Point assistant coach. In 1906, he resigned his commission and entered business to support his family. In 1907–08, he coached Harvard's backfield. He was recommissioned and returned as Army's head coach in 1913.

With scouting information that most of Notre Dame's offense relied on power plays, Army spent the entire week preparing to defend a running attack that relied on the surging force of the

The starting eleven of Notre Dame's 1913 football team. (*University of Notre Dame Archives*)

old wedge play to break through an opponent's line.[7] Little did West Point realize what was coming.

Meanwhile, back at Cartier Field, Harper was conducting secret practices to keep his aerial open-style attack under wraps until the unveiling on Saturday afternoon, November 1.

Notre Dame's campus buzzed with excitement as students and faculty anticipated the big showdown between the West and the East. The entire undergraduate student body had become so emotionally involved that many skipped afternoon classes to show support by watching their favorite Blue and Gold team prepare for Army.[8] The contest had grown out of proportion, and its importance was no longer a mere football game between Notre Dame and Army. This was "The Game" that everyone was talking about making or breaking Notre Dame's bid for national recognition and respect for its athletics program. The pressure was mounting.

Conducting closed secret practices was difficult to achieve with such overwhelming numbers of students crowding the field. Understanding the students' excitement, Harper allowed them to remain at practice to encourage their team onto victory. The enthusiastic roar provided Dorais an opportunity to practice directing the team under game-like conditions.

After two solid weeks of rehearsing offensive plays against every possible defensive front his team could possibly face, Dorais's arsenal was now ready for the tough but revered Cadets.

On Wednesday evening, the team members and support staff packed their bags. Because his limited budget only allowed for eighteen players to make the trip, Harper had no choice but to leave fourteen of his players behind.

Early on Thursday morning, every student and professor marched over a mile downtown to accompany the team to the railroad station for their 800-mile overnight trip to New York.[9] Even local townspeople joined in the festivities in sending off the team. After cheering and applauding each player as he boarded the Lakeshore Railroad train, the crowd began to sing the college fight song in tribute to their hometown heroes.[10]

Eighteen players, two coaches, and four administrators settled into the railroad coach for the day-long trip to Buffalo. With its limited $1,000-travel budget, the entourage brought along bags of sandwiches and apples packed with loving care by the ladies in the refectory.[11] Saving approximately $50 by not eating breakfast and lunch, dinner was only $1.50 per person.[12]

By the time the train reached Buffalo, darkness had set in. At approximately 11 p.m. they transferred trains and onto Pullman Cars with sleeping berth accommodations and steamed toward West Point.[13] This was the first time a Notre Dame team traveled on an overnight train. Rockne remembered the eleven starters being assigned to the lower bunks, and the subs the uppers. Even though Harper demanded they get a good night's sleep the night before a game, most of the players were too excited and remained awake all night.

Arriving at West Point around 1:30 p.m. Friday afternoon, the players scrambled off the train carrying their own personal bags and football equipment.[14] They loaded their belongings on an

Army truck's flatbed and were escorted to West Point's Cullum Hall for their overnight accommodations. Writing in advance on October 27, 1913, to Lt. Dan Sultan, Harper clarified most of the travel party members were Catholic and required either fish or eggs for their Friday evening meal. He also pointed out they were scheduled to depart for South Bend at 7:40 p.m. on Saturday.[15] As guests of West Point, they were also given freedom to frequent the Officer's Club.

West Point, the nation's oldest service academy, had operated since 1802 at the site of a military post set up by Benedict Arnold during the American Revolution. Its 16,000 acres were located on a scenic overlook on the Hudson River. The Academy's motto is "Duty, Honor, Country." Cadets also were required to adhere to the Cadet Honor Code, which states, "A cadet will not lie, cheat, steal, or tolerate those who do."[16] The Cadets displayed great hospitality and treated their midwestern visitors with respect and honor.

Saturday morning's New York Times headlines read, "Army Wants Big Score," while the subtitle stated, "Confident of Victory, but Notre Dame has team of Heavy Men."[17] The article continued, "The westerners arrived on Friday from South Bend and took up their abode in Cullum Hall adjoining the Army football field. In late afternoon they went out on the gridiron for a full hour's work. Their workout was in secret as was that of the Cadets taking the field after Notre Dame had retired. The westerners were expected to flash an open-field attack and the Cadets were wondering what it consisted of."[18]

Harper kept a lid on his offensive rehearsal. Dorais led his team through every phase of the offense except Notre Dame's passing game. The practice centered on movement and stretching out their legs as the long train ride prevented the team from working out on Thursday.

The Plains, West Point's home football field, was adjacent to Cullum Hall. It was a large grassy area primarily designed for the cadets' marching and routine military practice. The field was surrounded by sprawling wooden bleachers accommodating more than three-thousand spectators.

The long grey line of cadets held a dress parade on Saturday morning. West Point never charged for games, so many people made it a whole day's affair by joining the five-hundred cadets sitting in the western bleachers.[19] The crowd was expected to number well over capacity. Most had come to witness Army's easy victory as predicted by the New York newspapers.

As an extra incentive, Lieutenant Daly raised the corps of cadets' hopes by leading them to the first undefeated football season in West Point history. They had romped to four straight victories and were staring number five in the eye. Harper had elevated Notre Dame's pride by scheduling the toughest national opponents he could possibly find, and today Blue and Gold adrenaline was overflowing. Rockne later said, "Notre Dame's eighteen players not only saw the trip to West Point as Crusaders on a mission, but the team felt as if they represented the whole mid-west."[20]

On November 1, 1913, the two head coaches, Notre Dame's Jesse C. Harper, a University of Chicago graduate, and West Point's Lt. Charles Daly, a four-time All-American from Harvard, exchanged starting line-ups for Army's home game.[21]

POSITION	ARMY	NOTRE DAME
Left End	Jouette	Rockne
Left Tackle	Wynne	Jones
Left Guard	Meacham	Keefe

Center	McEwan	Feeney
Right Guard	Jones	Fitzgerald
Right Tackle	Weyand	Lathrop
Right End	Merillat	Gushurst
Quarterback	Pritchard	Dorais
Left Halfback	Hoge	Pliska
Right Halfback	Hobbs	Finnegan
Fullback	Hodgson	Eichenlaub

The team captains, Army's left halfback Benny Hoge and Notre Dame's left end Knute Rockne, shook hands at midfield. Referee William Morice from the University of Pennsylvania showed the two players each side of his half-dollar piece. Representing the visiting team, captain Rockne made the call while the referee flipped the coin. Looking on were umpire Bill Roper from Princeton and head linesman Fred Luehring from Northwestern University.[22] Notre Dame won the toss electing to receive. The ball was set on a mud tee at the Army 40-yard line, and plebe kicker Johnny McEwan, the center, signaled that he was ready.[23] Referee Morice waved his arm, blew his whistle, and signaled the game to start.

Army's McEwan kicked the ball high and deep to Notre Dame's Dorais positioned on the 5-yard line. Returning it to the 25-yard line, a horde of Cadets hit Dorais hard, knocking him to the ground. Feeney, Notre Dame's center, quickly assembled the team over the ball. Dorais called out the signals. Plunging into the defense, Eichenlaub was stopped abruptly for no gain and a second down. Dorais selected his bruising fullback again, but the ball was fumbled on the exchange and recovered by Army.[24] Notre Dame's body language was tense with emotion.

The confident Cadets were stopped short on three consecutive downs by the determined Blue and Gold. Army's Paul Hodgson punted, driving the ball to Notre Dame's 5-yard line. Fielding the ball cleanly, Dorais eluded Army tacklers for a 30-yard return. Lining up in the single-wing, right halfback Pliska received a direct snap and plunged through the line for a 5-yard gain. With second and 5, Dorais dropped back, noticed wide-open Rockne 30 yards downfield, and sailed the ball well over his outstretched arms. Army was caught flatfooted, but the ball fell harmlessly to the ground. After another failed running attempt, Notre Dame shifted into punt formation. Dorais hurried, and not ready, shanked the ball out-of-bounds at midfield.[25]

Unable to penetrate the determined Notre Dame defense, Army readied to punt again. Hodgson drove a short kick downfield where Dorais picked up the bounding ball and was hit head-on by an Army flanker resulting in another Notre Dame fumble. It was apparent that the Notre Dame players were keyed to a pitch and physically unable to control their emotions. Gaining possession, Army rushed the ball three straight times for short gains but was unable to make a first down. When tackling the hard-running Army backs, Notre Dame's defense refused to relinquish an extra yard. It was becoming clear to both sides they were in for a smashing physical game that might end up as a punting duel between Dorais and Hodgson.[26] Army looked to have the kicking advantage.

It was only the first period, but Army quickly realized they had scheduled a highly spirited little Indiana squad unwilling to quit. Gaining possession, Notre Dame's Finnegan and Eichenlaub ripped off valuable yardage behind excellent blocking and advanced the ball to Army's 35-yard line. Concerned and nervous, Daly paced the sideline behind the bench area where over thirty black-shirted Cadets observed their struggling teammates. Notre Dame aligned in a balanced-line single wing, but Dorais surprised Army by quickly shifting back under the center.

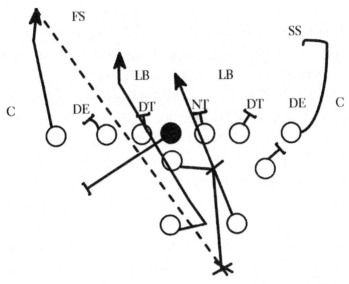

FIGURE 10.2 Harper's most successful play-action pass was a fake run into the line by the fullback and the quarterback dropping back to throw a pass to a wide open left end. This play scored the first touchdown against Army in 1913.

Receiving the snap from Feeney and dropping back, he passed the ball to Rockne sprinting downfield, but again the pass was thrown well over his head falling incomplete.[27] Dorais was now zero for two passing.

Army was not impressed with Notre Dame's self-destructing open-style offense. After an exchange of numerous punts, Notre Dame gained a first down on two surprising but successful running plays.

On the third play, Dorais decided to open up the offense. Not shaken from overthrowing earlier passes, the confident quarterback called for a play-action pass. Faking an assumed quick-hitting running play, Dorais completed a perfectly thrown 25-yard touchdown pass by hitting Rockne in stride and over the shoulder down the left side of the field (Figure 10.2). Never witnessing such a well-executed pass play before, a roar of surprise and appreciation came from the five-hundred strong cadet corps amassed in the west stands. Expecting their home team to bowl over this little college located somewhere west of the Appalachians, they couldn't believe their eyes.[28]

Surprised and knocked down, Army got back on its feet and retaliated with characteristic determination and fight. With Cadets Hodgson and Hobbs running behind their big tackles, and Hoge leading the way, Army battered into Notre Dame's territory. Not to be outdone, the Cadets unleashed their version of the passing game as quarterback Prichard connected with receiver Jouette. He successfully cradled in two button-hook passes while moving the ball down to Notre Dame's 15-yard line. After a succession of plunges into the line, fullback Hodgson scored by bulling over from the 1-yard line. The kick-after attempt was wide, leaving Notre Dame breathing a sigh of relief and holding onto a slim one-point lead.[29]

The quarter ended with three thousand bewildered fans scratching their heads. How could this be happening? People questioned the loss of cadet Dwight Eisenhower because of an injured knee and its impact on his teammates' morale. The potential All-American running back was suited up but held out of competition.

The teams exchanged punts following the kick-off, but Army regained possession after the Blue and Gold fumbled away their opportunity to move the ball. Trailing 7–6 and feeling the pressure mounting, Army drove the ball deep into Notre Dame's territory. Now with the ball on Notre Dame's 3-yard line and with the partisan crowd and teammates on the sidelines shouting their approval, Army had confidence it would score. Two running attempts were turned back for no gain, but a defensive holding call provided the Cadets another first down moving the ball nearer yet to the goal line.

Army again attempted three straight line smashes only to be thwarted and hurled back for no gain. On fourth and 3 inches to go, Prichard, the Cadet's quarterback, faked a wide lateral and on a delayed play carried the ball over for the touchdown.[30] The crowd relaxed and applauded as the point-after attempt was good providing Army an expected 13–7 lead late in the second quarter.

Harper and Dorais decided it was now time to turn up their game. Gaining possession by receiving the kickoff on its own 15, Notre Dame opened up the throttle. Dorais faked an end sweep, keeping the ball on a quarterback boot, and running for a 10-yard gain. On first and 10, Dorais hurled the ball to Rockne for a 25-yard gain to midfield. Faking a long throw to his well-covered left end, Dorais turned and dumped a short 10-yard pass to Pliska, who sprinted through the defense for a 35-yard gain. With the ball on Army's 15, a well-conceived completed pass to Finnegan, running a short crossing route, placed the ball on Army's 5-yard line with first and goal to go. The Cadets, concerned about their vulnerable porous pass defense, gave up a quick rushing touchdown. Pliska, following his interference, drove off-tackle for the score. The point-after attempt by Dorais was good giving Notre Dame a slim 14–13 lead.

In the second quarter, the Blue and Gold's quarterback baffled the Cadets' defense by completing five of six passes. His first-half stats were an impressive six completions of nine attempts for 95 yards and one touchdown.[31]

At halftime, the Notre Dame players sat in the end zone, covered their shoulders with blankets to preserve body heat, and listened intently to Harper's warnings about not letting down. The first 30 minutes were physically and emotionally intense for both teams, but Harper recognized Army's mental apprehension contending with the Blue and Gold's second-period passing attack. He talked about being ready for the unexpected, to be tough when things got tough, and to play with pride.

Frustrated about his defense allowing such an easy touchdown in the second period, Daly cleverly improvised at halftime to contend with Notre Dame's complex blend of passing and running. Deciding to move his defensive ends off the line like today's defensive corners, Daly was one of the first coaches to create a five-man defensive line (Figure 10.3).[32] Up to this day, no eastern football coach or team had experienced such a confusing offensive attack. Notre Dame's receivers seemed to appear from nowhere as the secondary reacted to the run, only to have it turn into a pass at the last moment. Catching the ball with their hands over their shoulder or in front of their body as they cut inside or out, Notre Dame's receivers were able to elude tacklers.

Army's innovative defensive adjustment in the third period initially disrupted Notre Dame's offense on their first drive. Stopped at midfield, Dorais attempted a 52-yard unsuccessful dropkick providing Army with possession on its own 45-yard line. Turning up their strong physical play, Army meticulously fought their way back yard by yard to Notre Dame's 15. A 3-yard plunge by substitute fullback Frank Milburn moved the ball to the 12. Three thousand fans were now on their feet cheering as the game now looked promising for their undefeated Cadet team.

Things were getting ugly for the Blue and Gold as they were flagged with a 10-yard penalty resulting in an Army first down on the 2-yard line. Notre Dame's eight-man goal-line defense tightened up by running a three-deep secondary stacked behind and breathing down the linemen's necks. On first down, Army's Hodgson was thrown for a loss by Rockne closing down hard from his outside end position. With second down and goal, Milburn received the handoff but was immediately smashed to the ground.

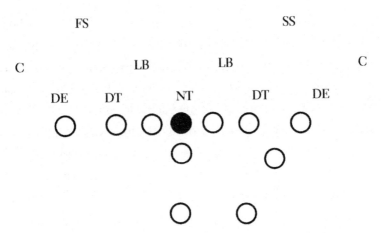

FIGURE 10.3 One of the first five-man defensive fronts employed in college football was designed by Army's head coach Lt. Charles Daly during halftime of the 1913 game against Notre Dame. Unable to stop the Blue and Gold passing game, Army responded by alternating five- and seven-man defensive fronts.

Third down and 3, Prichard, attempting to give Notre Dame a taste of its own aerial medicine, dropped back to the 10-yard line and lofted the ball to Merillat standing all alone just over the goal line. Reacting instinctively to the play, Dorais sprinted in front of the Army end waiting for the ball to arrive and with outstretched arms tipped the pass and intercepted it with his fingertips. Forward momentum carried him back across the goal line and out to Notre Dame's 10-yard line before being tackled. The Blue and Gold followed Harper's direct instructions of getting tougher. A great goal-line stand stopped Army's momentum, and the tide turned in Notre Dame's favor.[33]

The powerful undefeated Cadets and three thousand spectators stood in disbelief. Dazed and frustrated, Army moved in and out of their seven- and five-man fronts only to be at the mercy of Dorais's keen and well-trained football mind. Marching down the field successfully with each possession, Dorais attacked the five-man front with Eichenlaub slashing up the middle. The huge fullback continually bounced off Army's would-be tacklers for positive gains. With Army running the seven-man front to stop the bruising running game, Dorais completed pass after pass to his ends Rockne and Gushurst, as well as to halfbacks Pliska and Finnegan releasing out of the backfield. Alternating the run and the pass, Notre Dame's scoring machine was in high gear. The Blue and Gold scored three unanswered touchdowns and added three successful extra points to gain a 35–13 victory.

Although newspaper accounts vary on Dorais's exact statistics, studying 1913 play-by-play records indicate he completed all eight attempts in the second half for an additional 148 yards and one touchdown.[34] Eichenlaub scored two touchdowns, one by rushing for 1 yard and one for 8 yards.

Astounded and bewildered, Army was unable to fathom Notre Dame's offensive open-style attack because they had never contended with such advanced football tactics. Dorais and his adept receivers had achieved an unbelievable record of fourteen completions in seventeen attempts including a net gain of 243 yards and two touchdown passes with an unprecedented 80-percent completion rate. The people in attendance were not only amazed with Dorais's accuracy but were also stunned with the length of his completed passes while his receivers caught the ball in stride. Some of his spirals traveled 40 yards before being received, which was unheard of in the East, except for the feats of the highly successful forward-passing Carlisle Indians.

Newspaper reporters, three thousand fans, game officials, and Army walked away believing the old-style mass physical plays and side-arm passes to stationary receivers had become obsolete.

Football men in attendance marveled at Notre Dame's play. Bill Roper, former Princeton head coach and the game's umpire, said, "I always believed such open-style playing was possible under the new rules, but I had never witnessed the use of the forward pass developed to such a state of perfection."[35]

That night, unable to send his customary telegram, Harper made a long-distance call back home to give Melville and the school the incredible news of their victory.

Sunday's national newspaper accounts heralded Notre Dame's unorthodox open-style play. *The New York Times* headlines read, "Notre Dame Passes Rout Army 35–13. Dorais Unleashes Sensational Air Attack that Amazes East."[36] The story line account read, "The Westerners flashed the most sensational football that has been seen in the East this year, baffling the Cadets with a style of open-play and a perfectly developed forward pass. The yellow egg was in the air half the time with the Notre Dame receivers spread all over the field. The Army players were hopelessly confused and chagrined before Notre Dame's great playing and their old-fashioned style of close-line smashing play was no match for the spectacular and highly perfected attack of the Indiana collegians."[37]

The Times also added, "The Notre Dame eleven is coached by Jesse Harper, who used to play for Chicago. There are no doubt the teams from the mid-west making greater progress with the forward pass than eastern teams that focus on defense and have always viewed the pass as a risky plan of attack."[38]

The *New York Herald* said, "Many critics have been condemning the forward pass as a happy-go-lucky play at best. Well, along comes Notre Dame to open the eyes of football lovers here with a record of twelve successful forward passes out of fourteen attempts [incorrect statistics]. Nothing like that has ever been seen in an Eastern game of any importance, and it is doubtful if such a thing ever occurred in any game of east of the Alleghenies."[39] At the time, the East was unaware that Harper's teams and Stagg's Chicago Maroons had been playing open-style football for many years.

The *Chicago Record-Herald* stated, "The Catholic team traveled to Army's stronghold and bewildered, cuffed and kicked the Army into submission, 35–13, a score that is not only decisive, but stamps the Notre Dame men as a team of unusual strength. When it is taken into consideration Army beat Colgate 7–6, and Colgate humiliated Yale 16–6, the only deduction possible is that Notre Dame is far ahead of most eastern squads."[40]

The *New York Evening Telegram* reported "In all the years that 'new' football has been around, the possibilities of the game were never better exemplified than they were in the Army-Notre Dame game. It would not be surprising if the majority of college football teams adopted their wide-open style of attack by next season. Notre Dame, coached by Jesse C. Harper, displayed a versatile and dazzling attack that may revolutionize the style of offensive play throughout the country."[41]

One of the most common and inaccurate legends about the game is that this is where the forward pass was first introduced to football, which is not the case, of course. What this game did show is that on November 1, 1913, a run play-action passing team with multiple receivers and the open receiver catching the ball with his hands in stride was superior to a drop-back passer throwing the ball to a single stationary (cradle catching) receiver downfield and teams that relied mostly on a ground game. What surprised Army was the effectiveness of the play-action forward pass used in conjunction with a strong physical rushing game and not employed, as they had seen before, as a last ditch effort to score or to gain yards.

Even though the new open-style offense buried the old-fashioned mass plays that Saturday afternoon, Notre Dame's fullback was heralded as the key to their accomplished passing game because he successfully rushed for positive yardage all afternoon while scoring two rushing touchdowns. Army was unable to ascertain whether the rushing or passing game was next to strike their vulnerable defense.

The significance of Notre Dame's 35–13 victory over Army not only was one of exemplifying the unlimited possibilities of the forward pass to the nation's football coaches and fans but also introduced Notre Dame football to the nation. Notre Dame players were quickly heralded as among the best in the country. The *Chicago Evening Journal* reported, "Individually Notre Dame has some of the finest football material in the country. Eichenlaub and Dorais have no superiors in their positions and the team work and spirit of the school is excellent. The team is coached by Jesse Harper, who has shown himself a great football instructor."[42]

Similar accolades were recognized by the *Chicago Daily News* when saying, "Coach Harper has undoubtedly put together the best eleven to ever wear the Blue and Gold. The team was almost perfect in every detail of technical play, and in addition possesses two stars of first magnitude in fullback Eichenlaub and quarterback Gus Dorais."[43]

The *New York World* reported, "All of Notre Dame's touchdowns came as a result of their wonderful forward passing. Rockne, Pliska and Finnegan were all doing fine work receiving, while Gus Dorais was tossing the ball."[44] The *New York Press* went further by predicting, "If Dorais of Notre Dame is not an All-American quarterback, he comes pretty near being so by our judgment."[45] Joe Byrne wrote, "Every day impresses deeper into the Eastern football critics' minds the fact that Dorais is really a wonder. I hope they make the little quarterback an All-American."[46]

Two weeks later, on November 15, nearly twenty-five thousand spectators witnessed the University of Chicago earn football honors by winning the Western Intercollegiate Conference championship by defeating Minnesota 13–7 at Minneapolis. With an undefeated season on the line, the Maroons scored in the fourth quarter from 3 yards out as captain Norgren's two pile-driving smashes carried him in for the touchdown. The score was set up by two well-executed forward passes that moved the ball well over 40 yards down the field. Stagg's annual success with his pioneer open-style forward-passing offense continued to receive little national recognition for Chicago's unparalleled achievements. The Maroons just kept on quietly winning games as the eastern schools' football programs continued to gain the national attention.[47] Finally, the many silent years of the media was broken by this small, unheard-of midwestern university. Notre Dame's football program was now recognized as one of the elite programs in the country.

Jesse C. Harper's vision and goal of achieving a national presence for the Notre Dame football program had arrived. In a few short weeks, Harper accomplished what some professionals, like Stagg, had worked toward for a whole career. He had established six major goals for himself at Notre Dame, and number five was now chalked up and conquered. The only goal remaining to achieve was reestablishing Notre Dame's playing relationships with the eight boycotting Western Conference members.

Enjoying their two-day return trip home, Harper and the team stopped off and spent Sunday afternoon relaxing at Niagara Falls before boarding the train for the overnight trip back to South Bend. Arriving home on Monday and receiving a warm hero's welcome from the community, the team immediately began preparing for Penn State.

Although Penn State's contract called for a game scheduled for Saturday, November 8, the date was changed to Friday the 7th. Harper had only two days to prepare the team before getting back on the train for a repeat trip out East.

Monday, after their arrival back home, was a light rehearsal day with kicking. Harper was concerned about Notre Dame's three fumbles (one on a punt return) and their two short punts during the previous week's Army game. Tuesday was a full offensive and defensive day. The team had a short light workout on Wednesday morning before boarding the Lakeshore train at noon in South Bend headed to Pittsburgh.

Upon arrival, the travel party of twenty four would transfer onto the Bellefonte line, costing sixty cents per person, and head to State College, Pennsylvania, for an overnight before competing against the Nittany Lions on Friday afternoon.[48]

The game had a scoreless first period. Notre Dame's Rockne caught a touchdown pass in the second quarter, and with Dorais's successful PAT, provided the Blue and Gold a 7–0 halftime lead. Despite limited preparation and a quick turnaround by playing six days after defeating Army, Notre Dame prevailed 14–7. Notre Dame was on top of their open-style game with brilliant passes by Dorais and excellent receptions by the receivers. Eichenlaub again carried the rushing load while scoring a single touchdown. Their home field loss was the first one recorded at Penn State in five years, since their 12–5 defeat to the Carlisle Indians on October 5, 1908.[49]

The *Philadelphia Evening Bulletin* reporting the game said, "Billy Morice, the Army games referee and a spectator at Penn State, said the best quarterback in America is Dorais, the Notre Dame pilot. I officiate all over the country and I will say he is the king of them all. He not only is an outstanding passer, but also a great open-field runner and field general."[50]

Notre Dame was now sporting an undefeated 5–0 record and headed for a dual trip to play Christian Brothers College in St. Louis, scheduled for November 22, followed by a Thanksgiving Day game with Texas the following week.

After defeating Christian Brothers 20–7 to run their record to 6–0, the Blue and Gold party of twenty one boarded the Missouri Pacific Railroad in St. Louis and headed to Austin, Texas. The University of Texas Longhorns were undefeated with seven wins and a Southwest Conference championship having defeated Oklahoma, Kansas, and the Kansas Aggies. The Notre Dame team was scheduled to arrive in Austin on Monday evening, November 24, and stay at Saint Edward's College.[51]

The *Chicago Daily Tribune* gave the following game account against mighty Texas: "The undefeated Blue and Gold battered the Texas defensive line to establish the run and then opened up with a series of play-action passes and drop kicks that turned into a number of scores. The Notre Dame backs plunged into the Texas line seventy-seven times for 248 yards and passed twenty-one times, ten of which netted 200 yards for a game total of 448 yards. Notre Dame led 10-7 at halftime and then scored nineteen unanswered points in the second half. Seven thousand spectators were amazed at Notre Dame's well-coached team and their precision in offensive execution." The final score read Notre Dame 29, the University of Texas 7.[52]

Many of the nation's journalists caught Notre Dame fever. From writer Harvey T. Woodruff to the illustrated pen of Sydney Smith, articles were printed in newspapers across the country from the *Portland Oregonian* to the *Key West Sea Gulf* featuring Jesse Harper and his Notre Dame nomadic eleven.

Accolades were piling up for Harper as the 1913 season progressed and more battles were won. Woodruff reported, "From West Point to Austin Texas, was a considerable change of scenery for a football eleven quest of worthy opponents, but that was only part of the program which Coach Jesse Harper found necessary to secure for his Notre Dame Football team this fall. Visits to Penn State and St. Louis are sandwiched in between, and still the coach and his chargers are clamoring for more action. They have offered to play a post season contest with Nebraska, which has jumped into national prominence."[53] The Nebraska contest did not materialize, however, despite Harper's willingness to play another game.

The 1913 Blue and Gold were ranked as one of the premier college teams in the nation based on strength of schedule and by successfully playing to an undefeated season. Media and football experts were acclaiming Notre Dame's 1913 eleven as one of the top teams in the country.[54] The undefeated Harvard Crimson was considered as the strongest eastern team. The University of Chicago, undefeated in seven games, along with Army, Michigan, Colgate, Carlisle, Dartmouth, and Navy, all with only one loss, were recognized as being among the best. Washington & Jefferson, winner of ten while tying one, was also represented as one of the better eastern teams.

Individually, Notre Dame's outstanding senior passing quarterback Gus Dorais was selected as a first-team All-American, senior left end and captain Knute Rockne was selected as a third-team All-American, and junior fullback Ray Eichenlaub garnered a second-team All-American fullback's position.

The *Notre Dame Dome*, when highlighting the 1913 football season, reported, "Good leaders are necessary—coaches and captains. To the coach the team must look for perfection and finish; to the captain, for confidence, inspiration and example. Captain Rockne was a very important factor in our success. Coach Harper developed the team to perfection as no team could have worked with greater unison. They played with harmony, co-operation and not for individual, but for the team's success."[55]

Notre Dame's 1913 football season entered their sports history books as one of the finest ever played by the Blue and Gold. Not only were they undefeated, but also Notre Dame's open-style exciting football introduced the nation to a passing offense averaging between fifteen and twenty attempts per game while completing over 60 percent. Notre Dame gained more than 200 yards passing in every game, with the exceptions of Alma and St. Louis's Christian Brothers. The contest with Army awakened the East's media to modern football. Football competition between Notre Dame and Army in 1913 developed into a long-lasting rivalry between two great institutions.

The major Chicago papers were now comparing Notre Dame's superior playing ability to that of the leading teams in the country and particularly with the Western Conference champion, the University of Chicago. Professor Stagg and mentored pupil Harper had reached the same level of respect from the regional media and the midwestern public in one short, but highly successful football season.

Harper's professional innovative coaching of the forward pass, demonstrated against quality eastern teams, could not have influenced minds and changed archaic attitudes of college football coaches without the overwhelming positive reaction and swift reporting of the nation's powerful eastern media.

The sleeping giant was awakened. Less than one hundred years ago, Harper brought to Notre Dame, a refreshing change in football—a modern rushing and passing offense that was complementary in nature. His basic offensive football philosophy is still demonstrated by colleges across the country to this day.

The University of Chicago's pioneer open-style game developed by Stagg, which Harper fine-tuned and introduced at Notre

Dame, was a well-kept secret for years. Because the Western Conference presidents mandated a five-game season beginning in 1906, the teams' competition was relegated to regional or conference opponents, and even when the season was expanded to seven games in 1908, Illinois was the lone Western Conference member to compete with an eastern foe when it played Syracuse in 1909 and 1910. Illinois did not play another eastern team until 1916, when they lost to Colgate 15–3. Indiana, Iowa, Purdue, Wisconsin, Ohio State, Northwestern, and Chicago all scheduled no eastern opponents from 1906 to 1916, resulting in national media obscurity of their style of football.

Notre Dame's independent status allowed Harper to change the landscape from regional play to scheduling teams across the continent. His vision, willingness to take risks, and capacity to understand the technical application in coaching individual and team skills contributing to offensive success elevated Notre Dame's football program into the national limelight.

Melville Harper, Jesse Harper's widow, and son James, right, accepting his football Hall of Fame plaque from Notre Dame Athletic Director Moose Krause during a game in 1971. (*James Harper*)

The Legacy

IN JANUARY, 1918, HARPER RECEIVED THE NEWS OF HIS FATHER-in-law's serious illness and departed for Kansas with his wife Melville to be with her family. The Campbell family owned and operated a 20,000-acre cattle ranch that required immediate management. After deep thought and discussions with his wife and her family, Harper made the decision to resign from Notre Dame and return to Kansas with Melville and their two children to operate the Campbell family ranch.

Harper was honored the next month in the February issue of the *Notre Dame Scholastic,*

> Jesse C. Harper, maker of Notre Dame History and recognized as one of the great coaches, severs his connection with the university next June. Leaving on his own volition and amid great regret, Coach Harper will devote his entire time to 'coaching' steers on the large cattle ranch in western Kansas. From a chaotic state of athletics, Harper uplifted the Blue and Gold to a plane of equality with the best schools in the East and the West. Business ability, strategic football wizardry, exceptional

knowledge of the minor sports, coupled with dogged persistency, has accomplished an outstanding record in Notre Dame Sports' annals.[1]

Leading Notre Dame's football program from 1913 to 1917, Harper's teams won 34, lost 5, and tied 1 for an incredible .863 winning percentage.[2] Eighteen of Harper's scheduled football games were against major national opponents, whereas fifteen were played on the road. His overall winning percentage currently ranks second among all of Notre Dame's past head mentors with five or more years of experience. Only Knute Rockne's thirteen-year record at Notre Dame of 105 wins, twelve losses, and five ties for a lifetime winning percentage of .881 is better.[3]

Because of his coaching methods, Harper was referred to as the "wonder man" of the West. Notre Dame's student paper reported, "Harper has demonstrated his coaching ability. He has won by sheer merit a position in the foremost ranks of the country's great mentors. Possessing a commanding personality, sterling integrity, and unwavering directorship, he is respected and honored by the whole Notre Dame community. An examination of his schedules bears testimony to the high esteem with which he is recognized in both the East and West. He has produced great teams, and in doing so has won everyone's admiration by the absolute integrity of his methods."[4]

Harper was not only successful on the field but also established unique and successful athletics procedures unheard of in his time. He developed a policy of scheduling games years in advance instead of annually like most college programs. He scheduled Wisconsin in 1917 and in 1918 secured Purdue as an annual opponent for many future years. His goal of reestablishing Notre Dame's playing relationships with the eight boycotting Western Conference members was finally accomplished.

Harper was one of the first college athletic directors to recommend stringent academic standards for student-athlete's eligibility and to have the Board of Controls adopt his proposals. Balancing the athletics budget was also a primary goal. He demanded athletics to pay its own way. Harper balanced the football budget every year by securing lucrative travel guarantees and spending with frugality despite scheduling competition requiring long overnight trips.

An avid nationwide recruiter, Harper developed a network from Notre Dame's graduates and his current athletes for identifying potential student-athletes. He encouraged their enrollment by sending them personal letters relating a warm, honest, and sincere desire to have them join his Notre Dame teams. Making no promises other than to be fair in judgment, he emphasized their need to earn a position through hard work and dedication. Work-study positions were available for student-athletes enrolling to help pay for their tuition, books, and room and board.

Team leaders Rockne and Dorais were searching for head college football coaching positions, and Harper was committed to helping them get placed. An opening occurred at Columbus (now Loras) College in Iowa, and Harper was asked to recommend a candidate for the position. The story goes that a flip of the coin determined whether Rockne or Dorais would accept the head football position. Dorais won the toss and became Loras's head football coach from 1914 through 1917. Returning to Notre Dame, Dorais spent two years as an assistant coach until he left in 1920 to further his football coaching career at Gonzaga University. In 1925, he accepted the athletic directorship and head football job at the University of Detroit and completed a career with an overall head coaching record of 150 wins, seventy losses, and thirteen ties. From 1943 to 1947, Dorais led the professional National Football League's Detroit Lions. He was inducted into the National College Hall of Fame in 1954.

Rockne, on the other hand, was offered a graduate assistantship teaching chemistry at Notre Dame's prep school along with an assistant football position and the head track coaching job. Working together as peers, Harper and Rockne developed a deep brotherly relationship while together mentoring and coaching the Notre Dame student-athletes.

For the 1916-17 academic year, Harper recruited George Gipp for baseball and football. Originally from Northern Michigan, Gipp attended Notre Dame in 1917 and played football for Harper as a freshman.[5]

Commitment to and respect for his close friend Knute Rockne resulted in Harper's recommendation for "Rock" to inherit the Notre Dame Head football and athletic directorship positions. Unwilling to back down on his 1916 promise to his close friend Rockne, that on his resignation the job was his, Harper supported his stand with Notre Dame's president Father Cavanaugh. When the good father inquired about another potential coach to fill the vacated football position, Harper replied by saying, "He's a good coach, but Rockne's better."[6] After several visits, Father Cavanaugh finally broke down and respectfully fulfilled Harper's request by hiring Knute Rockne to fill his shoes in 1918. In 1920, Gipp, playing for Rockne, was named as a First-Team All-American halfback.

Despite the long-distance relationship, Rockne and Harper remained close friends until Rockne's tragic death in the crash of TWA Flight 599 in 1931. Harper's youngest son James "Jim" Harper recalled,

Uncle Rock and Dad had a mind set that just ran parallel. Rock always called Dad 'coach.' They were on the phone a lot and maintained a strong writing connection as he at times sought Dad's advice on various college issues. The last time I saw Uncle Rock was in 1928, but our families were very close. I have a picture of them standing in our ranch's front yard. He always stopped to see Dad and our family when traveling by plane to Southern California. When Uncle Rock had his tragic life-ending plane crash in Bazaar, Kansas in 1931, he was only 125 miles from the ranch. Dad drove there, identified his body, and accompanied Uncle Rock by train to South Bend. Dad was one of the pall bearers at his funeral.[7]

Knute Rockne, a close personal friend and mentored football pupil of Jesse Harper's, was inducted into the National College Football Foundation's Hall of Fame in 1951 as the greatest football coach in the history of the game. Rockne's career winning percentage is superior to the entire nation's college head football coaches' records for the past one hundred years as he stands at the top of the list of numerous football coaching giants.[8]

When at the height of his career, Rockne was questioned about his successful Notre Dame team's offense, he gave praises on his close friend Jesse Harper. Rockne acknowledged that the football system he coached at Notre Dame was pioneered by Chicago's Alonzo Stagg but honed and fine-tuned by his coach, Jesse Claire Harper, who introduced it to Notre Dame when Rockne was a player in 1913.[9] He mastered the offense while an assistant to Harper until 1917 and subsequently changed the game of football forever.

Notes

CHAPTER 1: BEFORE THE FORWARD PASS

1. Michael MacCambridge and Dan Jenkins. *ESPN College Football Encyclopedia* (New York: ESPN Publishing, 2005), 501.
2. Ibid., 501.
3. Allison Danzig. *The History of American Football* (Englewood Cliffs, N.J.: Prentice Hall), 485.
4. Mac Cambridge and Jenkins, *ESPN College Football Encyclopedia*, 348.
5. *The New York Times*, "Chicago's Notable Victory, Michigan's First Defeat," December 1, 1905, 10.
6. Ibid., 10.
7. Mac Cambridge and Jenkins, *ESPN College Football Encyclopedia*, 1079–80.
8. *The New York Times*, "Penn's Scant Victory over Cornell's Team," December 1, 1905, 10.
9. Ibid., 10.
10. *The New York Times*, "Penn's Scant Victory over Cornell's Team," December 1, 1905, 10.
11. Percy D. Haughton, *Football and How to Watch It* (Boston: Little, Brown and Company, 1924), 78.
12. Yost, *Football for Player and Spectator*, 264–68.
13. Ibid., 264–68.
14. Ibid., 264–68.
15. John W. Heisman, *Principles of Football* (St. Louis, Mo.: Sports Publishing Bureau, 1922), 131–32.
16. Yost, *Football for Player and Spectator*, 176–82.
17. A. A. Stagg and W. W. Stout, *Touchdown* (New York: Longmans, Green & Co., 1927), PAGE
18. Yost, *Football for Player and Spectator.*, 273–303.
19. *The New York Times*, "West Point - 6; Annapolis, 6," December 2, 1905, 10.
20. College Football, http://www.phys.utk.edu/sorensen, 1–3.
21. Ibid., 2.
22. *The New York Times*, "'Football Unfit for College Use,' President Eliot Talks in His Report on Harvard for 1893-94," January 31, 1895, 6.

23. *Chicago Tribune*, "Fatalities and Casualties," December 1906. Amos Alonzo Stagg's papers, Box 154, Folder 54, Special Collections Research Center, University of Chicago.

24. *The New York Times*, "Football Conference at the White House," December 5, 1905, 11.

25. *The New York Times*, "President's Football Reform Plan Started," November 27, 1905, 5.

26. *The New York Times*, "Abolition of Football or Immediate Reforms," 28 November, 1905, 11.

27. *The New York Times*, "Football Conference Will Convene Today," December 8, 1905, 9.

28. Ibid., 9.

29. Ibid., 9.

30. Ibid., 9.

31. Ibid., 9.

32. National Collegiate Athletic Association, www.ncaa.org.

33. *Minutes of the American Intercollegiate Football Rules Committee*, December 29, 1905, 1–5. Amos Alonzo Stagg's Papers, Box 50, Special Collections Research Center, University of Chicago.

34. Ibid., 1–5.

35. *The New York Times*, "Ten Yard Rule a Failure," December 26, 1905, 8.

CHAPTER 2: A BOLD CONCEPT

1. DR. L. H. Baker, *Football: Facts and Figures* (New York: Farrar & Rinehart, 1945), 35.

2. Ibid., 35.

3. A. A. Stagg and W. W. Stout, *Touchdown* (New York: Longmans, Green & Co., 1927), 69.

4. Baker, *Football: Facts and Figures*, 36.

5. Ibid., 36.

6. *Minutes of the American Intercollegiate Football Rules Committee*, December 29, 1905, 3. Amos Alonzo Stagg's Papers, Box 50, Special Collections Research Center, the University of Chicago.

7. *Minutes of the American Intercollegiate Football Rules Committee*, January 12, 1906, 4. Amos Alonzo Stagg's Papers. Box 50.

8. *Minutes of the American Intercollegiate Football Rules Committee*, January 12, 1906, 4. Amos Alonzo Stagg's Papers. Box 50.

9. *Minutes of the American Intercollegiate Football Rules Committee*, February 10, 1906, 1. Amos Alonzo Stagg's Papers, Box 50.

10. *Minutes of the American Intercollegiate Football Rules Committee*, January 12, 1906, 4. Amos Alonzo Stagg's Papers, Box 50.

11. *Minutes of the American Intercollegiate Football Rules Committee*, March 30, 1906, 1–8. Amos Alonzo Stagg's Papers, Box 50.

12. "Forward Pass Rules," December 1927, 17–24. Amos Alonzo Stagg's Papers, Box 54, Folder 27, Special Collections Research Center, University of Chicago.

13. Ibid., 17–24.

14. *The New York Times*, "New Style Football will be Spectacular," August 26, 1906.

15. *The New York Times*, "West Point's Spring Practice," August 28, 1906, 1.

16. Fielding Harris Yost, *Football for Player and Spectator* (Ann Arbor, Mich.: University Publishing Company, 1905), 81.

17. *The New York Times*, "Football Committee Suggests New Rules; Forward Pass Proposed," December 10, 1905, 2.

CHAPTER 3: THE MENTOR

1. Edwin Pope, *Football's Greatest Coaches* (Atlanta, Ga.: Tupper and Love, Inc.), 236.

2. Allison Danzig, *The History of American Football* (Englewood Cliffs, N.J.: Prentice Hall, 1956), 173.

3. Ibid., 173–74.

4. Pope, *Football's Greatest Coaches*, 231–32.

5. Tim Cohane, *Great College Coaches of the Twenties and Thirties* (New Rochelle, N.Y.: Arlington House Publishing, 1973), 195.

6. Ibid., 195.

7. The Amos Alonzo Stagg Award presented by the American Football Coaches Association (AFCA) annually honors Stagg's life's passions, coaching football, living an exemplary lifestyle, and mentoring young men. "Its purpose was to perpetuate the example and influence of Amos Alonzo Stagg. Stagg was instrumental in founding the AFCA in the 1920s. He was considered one of the great innovators and motivating forces in the early development of the game of football."

8. A. A. Stagg and W. W. Stout, *Touchdown* (New York: Longmans, Green & Co., 1927), 276–67.

9. Allison Danzig, *Oh, How They Played the Game* (New York: Macmillan, 1971), 52–53.

10. Ibid., 52–53.

11. Pope, *Football's Greatest Coaches*, 245.

12. Stagg and Stout, *Touchdown*, 138.

13. Danzig, *The History of American Football*, 22–23.

14. www.phys.utk.edu/sorensen/cfr/Output/1891CF_1891_T.... 1.

15. Danzig, *The History of American Football*, 22–23.

16. Ibid., 23–24.

17. Pope, *Football's Greatest Coaches*, 238.

18. *History of Morgan Park*, 2006, Morgan Park Academy.org, 1–2.

19. Ibid., 1.

20. DR. L. H. Baker, *Football: Facts and Figures* (New York: Farrar & Rinehart, 1945), 563.

21. Danzig, *The History of American Football*, 23–24.

22. Ibid., 24–34.

23. Stagg and Stout, *Touchdown*, 189.

24. Danzig, *The History of American Football*, 106.

25. Ibid., 106.

26. Western Conference's presidents restrictions effective 1906 season.

27. Michael Mac Cambridge and Dan Jenkins, *ESPN College Football Encyclopedia* (New York: ESPN Publishing, 2005), 501.

28. *Chicago Daily Tribune*, "Stagg Stops the Football Work. - Orders Maroon Candidates Off Marshall Field Until School Opens," September 25, 1906, 8.

29. Ibid.

30. *Forward Pass Plays Devised by Stagg*, September 20, 1906, 1–13. Amos Alonzo Stagg's Papers, Box 30, Special Collections Research Center, University of Chicago.

31. Ibid., 13.

32. Ibid., 11.

33. Ibid., 11.

34. Ibid., 2.

35. Ibid., 7.

36. Ibid., 5.

37. Ibid., 1–13.

38. *Forward Pass Plays Devised by Stagg*, October 29, 1906, 9.

39. *Forward Pass Plays Devised by Stagg*, September 20, 1906, 5.

40. Ibid., 1.

41. Ibid., 6.

42. Ibid., 4.

43. Danzig, *The History of American Football*, 39.

44. Ibid., 39.

45. Stagg and Stout, *Touchdown*, 136.

CHAPTER 4: A PERFECT SPIRAL

1. *The New York Times*, "New Football a Chaos, the Experts Declare-Ground Gaining by Carrying the Ball made Impossible," October 20, 1906, 10.

2. *New York Times*, "First Real Football Tests the New Rules," October 27, 1906, 3.

3. Ibid., 3.

4. Ibid., 3.

5. *The New York Times*, "Football Differences Prolong Big Meeting – Many Discrepancies arise in Council of Experts," October 29, 1906, 4.

6. *The New York Times*, "New Football a Chaos, the Experts Declare-Ground Gaining by Carrying the Ball made Impossible," 10. College Football 1906 Ranking of Teams Within College Conference, http://www.phys.utk.edu/ sorensen/cfr/cfr/Output/1906/CF_1906_Conferences.html.

7. Michael Mac Cambridge and Dan Jenkins, *ESPN College Football Encyclopedia* (New York: ESPN Publishing, 2005), 1098.

8. Ibid., 1098.

9. The Official Website of Badger Athletics, Hall of Famers, http://www.uwbadgers.com/hall_of_fame/year.aspx?HOFID=

10. Philip A. Dynan, *"The First Forward Pass,"* 1955, 1. St. Louis University Archives, Athletic Public Relations.

11. Ibid., 2.

12. Mac Cambridge and Jenkins, *ESPN College Football Encyclopedia*, 320.

13. Allison Danzig, *The History of American Football* (Englewood, N.J.: Prentice Hall, 1956), 33–34.

14. Dynan, *"The First Forward Pass,"* 2.

15. Ibid., 2, 3.

16. Danzig, *The History of American Football*, 35.

17. Ibid.

18. Danzig, *The History of American Football*, 34–35.

19. Dynan, *"The First Forward Pass,"* 2.

20. Ibid., 3.

21. *The Echo (Carroll College Pioneers Student Newspaper)*, October 1906.

22. *Waukesha Freeman Newspaper (Wisconsin)*, "Portrait of the Past," June 8, 1985, 1.

23. Brian Kunderman, "Football's Forward Pass Turns 100 Years Old," September 1, 2006, www.slu.edu/readstory/more/7166.

24. Dynan, *"The First Forward Pass,"* 4.

25. Kunderman, "Football's Forward Pass Turns 100 Years Old."

26. Dynan, *"The First Forward Pass,"* 4.

27. Ibid., 6.

28. Ibid., 6–7.

29. Danzig, *The History of American Football*, 35.

30. Ibid., 495.

31. Kunderman, "Football's Forward Pass Turns 100 Years Old."

32. Amos Alonzo Stagg, *Touchdown* (New York: Longmans, Green & Co., 1927), 304.

33. Danzig, *The History of American Football*, 36.

34. Ibid., 35.

35. Ibid., 36.

36. Ibid., 36.

37. Ibid., 44.

38. *Chicago Daily Tribune*, "Test New Rules in Actual Play," September 30, 1906, A1.

39. Ibid., A1.

40. Ibid., A1.

41. *Chicago Daily Tribune*, "Yale Plays Well Under New Rules. Roome Star of the Game," October 4, 1906, 10.

42. *The New York Times*, "Tigers Score Only Once-Forward Pass Tallies," October 6, 1906, 13.

43. *Chicago Daily Tribune*, "Harvard Beats Bowdoin, 10 - 0, forward passes not attempted until Last Minute of Play," October 4, 1906, 10.

44. *Chicago Daily Tribune*, "Harvard defeats Maine Team," October 7, 1906, A3.

45. *Chicago Daily Tribune*, "Whirlwind Game at Hanover," October 7, 1906, A3.

46. *New York Times*, "Tricks Score on Harvard; Quarterback Kick, Followed by Forward Pass, Yields Touchdown," October 11, 1906, 7.

47. *Chicago Daily Tribune*, "Michigan loses to Penn 17 – 0," November 18, 1906, A1.

48. *Chicago Daily Tribune*, "Camp on Princeton Game," November 18, 1906, A2.

49. *Chicago Daily Tribune*, "Navy in Triumph over Army," December 2, 1906, A1.

50. *New York Times*, "'Football Unfit for College Use,' President Eliot Talks in a Report on Harvard for 1893-94," January 31, 1895, 6.

51. *Chicago Journal*, "President Eliot Approves of New Game," November 2, 1906, 46. Amos Alonzo Stagg's Papers, Box 154, Folder 54.

52. *Collier's*, "Final Stage of the Football Season," November 24, 1906, 21. Amos Alonzo Stagg's Papers, Box 154, Folder 54.

53. *Chicago Daily Tribune*, "Casualties of the Football Season of 1906," December, 1906, 9. Amos Alonzo Stagg's Papers, Box 154, Folder 54.

54. Ibid., 9.

CHAPTER 5: A ROOKIE COACH

1. *Chicago Daily Tribune*, "Jesse C. Harper, Coach, Trainer, and Athletic 'Pooh-Bah' at Notre Dame," November 16, 1913, Amos Alonzo Stagg's papers.

2. James Harper (son of Jesse Harper), Interview in South Bend, at College Football's Hall of Fame, August 14, 2006.

3. *Chicago Daily Tribune*, "Jesse C. Harper, Coach, Trainer, and Athletic 'Pooh-Bah' at Notre Dame."

4. *Chicago Daily Tribune*, "Chicago Defeats Iowa - 42 - 0." October 8, 1905, 1.

5. *Cap and Gown* (University of Chicago Maroons Yearbooks 1904-1907), "Baseball Report." Special Collections Research Center, University of Chicago.

6. *1906-07 Alma College Academic Catalog*, "Calendar Section." Alma College Library Archives.

7. A. A. Stagg letter of reference to H. B. Patton, February 1908. Amos Alonzo Stagg's papers, Box 14, Folder 3.

8. *1906-07 Alma College Academic Catalog*, "Calendar Section."

9. *Almanian* VIII, No. 3, 1906, 12. Alma College Library Archives.

10. Ibid., 12.

11. Ibid., 12.

12. Leather helmets were available from sporting goods companies such as Wilson and Rawlings and were optional to wear until being required in the 1930s. The early 1900s helmet was constructed of layers of leather sewn together with ear flaps dangling from each side. They were either flat tops or skull caps but offered little protection for the head. Most teams between 1890 and 1915 played without helmets, but the Alma College players all wore leather helmets in 1906–07.

13. Mac Cambridge and Jenkins, *ESPN College Football Encyclopedia*, 512.

14. *Almanian* VIII, No. 3, 1906, 12.

15. Ibid., 12–13.

16. Ibid., 13.

17. Ibid., 13.

18. Gordon Beld, "Scores from Yester Years," *Alma College Football Fact Book*, 1972 ( ), 38.

19. *Almanian*, VIII, No. 3, 1906, 14.

20. Ibid., 15.

21. Ibid., 15.

22. Beld, "Scores from Yester Years," 38.

23. *Almanian* VIII, No. 2, "Around the Campus," November 1906, 12.

24. James "Jim" Harper (son of Jesse Harper), interview with Phil and Rose Brooks at Marriott Hotel by South Bend's College Football's Hall of Fame, August 14, 2006.

25. Letter of reference to H. B. Patton, February 1908. Amos Alonzo Stagg's papers, Box 14, Folder 3.

26. *South Bend Tribune*, "Harper Brought Fiscal Sense to N.D. Football," September 24, 1987, D-3. Jesse C. Harper's Papers, Wabash College Archives, Robert T. Ramsey, Jr. Library Archival Center.

27. Beld, "Scores from Yester Years," 38.

28. *Almanian (Alma College Student Newspaper)*, "He's Still Smiling," September 1907, 1.

29. *Alma Record (Alma, Mich.)*, "Harper is Pleased," September 14, 1907, 2.Alma Public Library Archives.

30. *Weekly Almanian*, "He's Still Smiling," September 1907, 1.

31. *Alma Record (Alma, Mich.)*, "Harper is Pleased."

32. *Weekly Almanian*, "The First Victory," October 8, 1907, 1.

33. *Weekly Almanian*, "The Second Victory," October 15, 1907, 1.

34. *Weekly Almanian*, "Scored on by Ferris Institute, October 22, 1907, 1.

35. Ibid., 2.

36. Beld, "Scores from Yester Years," 38.

37. *Weekly Almanian*, "The Olivet Game," November 5, 1907, 1.

38. Ibid., 1.

39. *Alma Record*, "The Olivet Game," November 6, 1907, 1.

40. *Weekly Almanian*, "Defeats Mt. Pleasant," November 19, 1907, 1.

41. Ibid., 1.

42. *Alma Record*, "M.A.C. Out of MIAA," November 13, 1907, 1.

43. Michigan Intercollegiate Athletic Association (MIAA) All-Time Football Conference Champions, www.miaa.org.

44. *Weekly Almanian*, "Alma Wins Again," November 19, 1907, 1.

45. Michael Mac Cambridge and Dan Jenkins, *ESPN College Football Encyclopedia* (New York: ESPN Publishing, 2005), 512.

46. Ibid., 501.

47. Beld, "Scores from Yester Years," 38.

48. *Weekly Almanian*, "M.A.C. - 0, Alma - 0," December 30, 1907, 1.

49. Ibid., 1.

50. *Alma Record (Alma, Mich.)*, "Football Season ends with splendid game followed by Reception," November 27, 1907, 1.

51. Beld, "Scores from Yester Years," 38.

Chapter 6: South to Wabash

1. James Harper (son of Jesse Harper), Interview at College Football's Hall of Fame, in South Bend, August 14, 2006.

2. Harper's Letter of Reference to Professor Patton from Stagg, Colorado School of Mines, March 16, 1909. Amos Alonzo Stagg's Papers, Box 14, Folder 3, Special Collections Research Center, University of Chicago.

3. Ibid.

4. Harper's Letter of Reference to President Hardy from Stagg, Mississippi Agriculture College, January 8, 1906. Amos Alonzo Stagg's Papers, Box 14, Folder 3.

5. Harper's Letter of Reference to Professor Patton from Stagg, Colorado School of Mines, February 1908, Amos Alonzo Stagg's Papers, Box 14, Folder 3.

6. Harper's Letter of Reference to Professor Patton from Stagg, Colorado School of Mines, March 16, 1909. Amos Alonzo Stagg's Papers, Box 14, Folder 3.

7. *The Bachelor (Wabash College Newspaper)*, "Harper, Chicago '06 to Coach Football Men," May 6, 1909, 1. Wabash College, Robert T. Ramsey, Jr. Library Archival Center.

8. Ibid., 1, 3.

9. Ibid., 3.

10. *The Bachelor*, "Harper, Chicago '06 to Coach Football Men," 3.

11. *The Bachelor*, "College Is Open For Seventy-Eighth Year," September 23, 1909, 1.

12. *The Bachelor*, "Scarlet Football Prospects Look Good," September 23, 1909, 1.

13. Ibid., 1.

14. *The Bachelor*, "Eller Schedules Game for Saturday," September 27, 1909, 1.

15. *The Bachelor*, "Wabash Calendar," September 23, 1909, 1.

16. *The Bachelor*, "Roger Wilson is New Captain," September 30, 1909, 1.

17. *The Bachelor*, "Scarlet Football Prospects Look Good," September 23, 1909, 1.

18. *The Bachelor*, "Wabash Defeats Illinois Eleven 27 to 0," October 4, 1909, 1.

19. Ibid., 1.

20. Ibid., 1–3.

21. *The Bachelor*, "Scarlet's Opponents Commence the Season," October 4, 1909, 1.

22. *The Bachelor*, "DePauw's Dream of 20 – 0 rudely Shattered," October 11, 1909, 1.

23. Ibid., 3.

24. Ibid., 1.

25. Michael Mac Cambridge and Dan Jenkins, *ESPN College Football Encyclopedia* (New York: ESPN Publishing, 2005), 512.

26. Mac Cambridge and Jenkins, *ESPN College Football Encyclopedia*, 512.

27. *The Bachelor*, "Scarlet Eleven Meets St. Louis Saturday," October 21, 1909, 1.

28. Ibid., 1.

29. *The Bachelor*, "St. Louis U. in a 14 to 0 Victory," October 25, 1909, 1.

30. *The Bachelor*, "Hanover Swamped by End Runs of Wabash," November 1, 1909, 1–3.

31. Ibid., 1.

32. Letter from S. T. Henry, secretary-treasurer, Intercollegiate Conference Athletic Association, Chicago, May 12, 1913. Jesse C. Harper correspondence, File DC920q, Wabash College, Robert T. Ramsey, Jr. Library Archival Center.

33. *The Bachelor*, "Hanover Swamped by End Runs of Wabash," November 1, 1909, 1–3.

34. *The Bachelor*, "Scarlet in Readiness for Big Purdue Game," November 4, 1909, 1–3.

35. *The Bachelor*, "Scarlet's Win a Wonderful Victory Over the Old Gold and Black Eleven Saturday," November 8, 1909, 1.

36. Ibid., 1.

37. Ibid., 1.

38. Ibid., 1.

39. Ibid., 1.

40. Ibid., 1.

41. Mac Cambridge and Jenkins, *ESPN College Football Encyclopedia*, 642.

42. *The Bachelor*, "Wabash Prepares for Strong Catholic Eleven," November 18, 1909, 1.

43. Ibid., 1.

44. Mac Cambridge and Jenkins, *ESPN College Football Encyclopedia*, 501.

45. *The Bachelor*, "Wabash Prepares for Strong Catholic Eleven," 3.

46. *The Bachelor*, "Wabash Bows to the Western Champions," November 23, 1909, 1.

47. *The Bachelor*, "King Football 'Exits' Until Next September," December 2, 1909, 1.

48. *The Bachelor*, "Coach Jesse Harper Signs Long Contract," November 18, 1909, 3.

49. *Vanderbilt Journal of Entertainment and Technology Law* 8, No. 2, spring 2006, "The Age of Innocence: The First 25 Years of the NCAA, 1906 – 1931," 239. http://law.vanderbilt.edu/journals/jetl/articles/vol8no2/Carter.pdf

50. *The Bachelor*, "As to Football," November 6, 1909, 3.

51. Ibid.

52. John S. Watterson, "Inventing Modern Football," *American Heritage Magazine*, September/October 1988, 7. [says 10 deaths others 11]

53. *Cavalier Daily (Charlottesville, Va.)*, "What's inside this Chapel may surprise you," March 4, 2004, 1–2.

54. *The Bachelor*, "Movement to Reform Football," January 10, 1910, 3.

55. Forward Pass Rules, Football Rules Guide 1910, 170–77. Amos Alonzo Stagg's Papers, Box 54, Special Collections Research Center, University of Chicago Archives.

56. Ibid., 17–24.

57. *The Bachelor*, "Coach Harper to Return First of Winter Term," December 20, 1909, 1.

58. *The Bachelor*, "Coach Harper Explicit in New Football Rules," March 10, 1910, 1–4.

59. *The Bachelor*, "Wilson Gives Life in Wabash Service," October 29, 1910, 1–2.

60. Ibid., 1.

61. Ibid., 1.

62. Ibid., 1.

63. *The Bachelor*, "Question of Football's Future Now Open," November 2, 1910, 1–2.

64. *The Wabash (Wabash College Magazine)*, "Tribute to Ralph Wilson," November 1910, 18. Wabash College, Robert T. Ramsey, Jr. Library.

65. *The Wabash*, "Athletics – Football," April 1911, 134–35.

66. *The Wabash*, "Athletics – Football," November 1911, 45–47.

Chapter 7: A Change of Plans

1. Allison Danzig, *Oh, How They Play the Game* (New York: MacMillan, 1971), 190.

2. *The Wabash (Wabash College Magazine)*, "Tribute to 1911 Athletics," December 1911, 124–27. Wabash College, Robert T. Ramsey, Jr. Library.

3. *Notre Dame Scholastic*, "Athletics," November 25, 1911, 158–59. Archives of the University of Notre Dame (UNDA).

4. Ibid., 159.

5. Ibid., 159.

6. Ibid., 159.

7. Danzig, *Oh, How They Play the Game*, 190.

8. *The Wabash*, "Tribute to 1911 Athletics," June 1912, 363.

9. Tim Cohane, *Great College Football Coaches of the Twenties and Thirties* (New Rochelle, N.Y.: Arlington House, 1973), 23.

10. Anthony J. Lisska, "A Backward Glance at the Forward Pass," *Historical Times* XVI, Issue 1, Fall 2002, 1–7.

11. Ibid., 3.

12. Ibid., 4.

13. Ibid., 4.

14. Ibid., 5.

15. Ibid., 5, 6.

16. *Notre Dame Scholastic*, "Champion of Indiana," November 2, 1912, 110–11. UNDA.

17. *Notre Dame Scholastic*, "Champion of Indiana," 110.

18. Michael Mac Cambridge and Dan Jenkins, *ESPN College Football Encyclopedia* (New York: ESPN Publishing, 2005), 642.

19. James Harper (son of Jesse Harper), Interview with Phil and Rose Brooks, Marriott Hotel, South Bend, Indiana, August 14, 2006.

20. James Harper (son of Jesse Harper), Interviews with Phil & Rose Brooks, August 14, 2006.

21. James Harper (son of Jesse Harper), Interview with Phil and Rose Brooks, August 14, 2006.

22. *The Bachelor (Wabash College Newspaper)*, "Daughter Arrived," November 20, 1912, 3. Wabash College, Robert T. Ramsey, Jr. Library Archival Center.

23. *The Bachelor*, "Twenty Men Aspire to Scarlet Quintet," November 20, 1912, 1.

24. *The Bachelor*, "Harper Accepts Offer as Notre Dame Coach," December 14, 1912, 3.

25. *The Bachelor*, "A Debt of Gratitude," December 14, 1912, 3. , 3.

CHAPTER 8: BLUE AND GOLD

1. William Cotter letter from to Jesse C. Harper, December 16, 1912., University of Notre Dame Athletic Director's Records (hereafter cited as UADR) 2/122, Archives of the University of Notre Dame (hereafter cited as UNDA).

2. Ibid., 2.

3. Ibid., 2.

4. Jesse C. Harper letter to William Cotter, December 17, 1912. UADR 2/122, UNDA.

5. *Notre Dame Magazine*, "The Man Who Set the Table," 1988, 8–9.

6. Ibid., 8.

7. Ibid., 9.

8. Jesse C. Harper communication to University of Texas athletics manager, January 1, 1913. UADR 3/82, UNDA.

9. St. Louis – Texas Trip's Expense Account, December 12, 1913. UADR 3/17, UNDA.

10. Penn State University's athletics manager communication to Jesse C. Harper, January 21, 1913. UADR 3/64, UNDA.

11. Michael Mac Cambridge and Dan Jenkins, *ESPN College Football Encyclopedia* (New York: ESPN Publishing, 2005), 706.

12. Ibid., 122.

13. James Beach and Daniel Moore, *The Big Game* (New York: Random House, 1948), xii. UADR/160, UNDA.

14. Ibid., xii.

15. Gene Schoor, "ND's Biggest Game," *100 Years of Notre Dame Football* (New York: William Morrow, 1987), 15. UADR/160, UNDA.

16. Ibid., 15.

17. Cadet Hal Loomis letter to Jesse Harper, January 1913. UADR 3/21, UNDA.

18. Jesse C. Harper letter to West Point's football manager, January 18, 1913. UADR 3/21, UNDA.

19. Harold Loomis's Western Union telegram to Jesse C. Harper, April 8, 1913. UADR 3/21, UNDA.

20. Beach and Moore, *The Big Game*, xii.

21. Mac Cambridge and Jenkins, *ESPN College Football Encyclopedia*, 102, 706, 853.

22. Ibid., 642.

23. Jesse C. Harper communication to Ohio Northern athletics manager, December 21, 1912. UADR 3/60, UNDA.

24. Jesse C. Harper to professor James Mitchell, Alma College athletics manager, January 19, 1913. UADR 3/19, UNDA.

25. Gordon Beld, "Scores from Yester Years," *Alma College 1972 Football Fact Book*, 39. Alma College Archives.

26. Professor James Mitchell communication to Jesse C. Harper, January 23, 1913. UADR 3/19, UNDA.

27. Jesse C. Harper communication to professor James Mitchell, Alma College athletics manager, January 29, 1913. UADR 3/19, UNDA.

28. *Notre Dame Scholastic*, "Athletic Notes," September 27, 1913, 1, 14. UNDA.

29. South Dakota All-Time Football Scores, www.usdcoyotes.com/sports/football/alltimescores.pdf, 1.

30. Jesse C. Harper communication to professor James Mitchell, Alma College athletics manager, March 19, 1913. UADR 3/19, UNDA.

31. Jesse C. Harper communication to South Dakota's athletics manager, January 11, 1913. UADR 3/78, UNDA.

32. *The Bachelor (Wabash College Newspaper)*, "Notre Dame Football Schedule is Completed," March 22, 1913, 3. Wabash College, Robert T. Ramsey, Jr. Library Archival Center.

33. Mac Cambridge and Jenkins, *ESPN College Football Encyclopedia*, 642.

34. *Gridiron Generals Journal* XVIII, No. 9, "John L. Marks 1911-12," 26. PATH – 112.

35. *1914 Dome*, "Monogram Men," Notre Dame Publishing. 148.

36. *Notre Dame Scholastic Weekly*, June 14, 1913. Volume XLVI, No. 36 page 580.

37. Gene Schoor, "A Treasury of Notre Dame Football," *Collier's Magazine* Reprint by Knute Rockne. "From Norway to Notre Dame," 5 October, 1930. Funk & Wagnalls Company. New York: 1962. 33.

38. Ibid., 33–34.
39. Ibid., 38.
40. Ibid., 41.
41. Gene Schoor, *A Treasury of Notre Dame Football* (New York: Funk & Wagnalls, 1962), 9.
42. *Gridiron Generals Journal*, "John L. Marks 1911-12," 27.
43. Gene Schoor, "A Treasury of Notre Dame Football," *Esquire Magazine* Reprint by Dale Stafford, "Dorais the Mighty Mite," October, 1945. Funk & Wagnalls Company. New York: 1962. 25.

CHAPTER 9: CREATING A MODERN GAME

1. John D. Kerezy (1977 graduate), "Harper and Milstead Represent Wabash in Football Hall of Fame," Wabash College article, spring, 1979, 21. Wabash College, Robert T. Ramsey, Jr. Library Archival Center.
2. *Gridiron Generals Journal* XVIII, No. 9, 27. UADR/112, Archives of the University of Notre Dame (UNDA).
3. *Kansas City Star*, "Jess Harper Again Takes Up Battle He Left for Rock," August 26, 1931, 2.
4. Charles (Gus) E. Dorais, *Forward Pass* (Chicago, Ill.: Athletic Book Company Publishers, 1927), 14.
5. Steele, *Knute Rockne: A Bio-Bibliography*, 13.
6. http://home.no.net/blrgerro/cdpoint.htm, Cedar Point. 1913. 2
7. Rules Changes throughout the History of College Football: The Ball, http://homepages.cae.wisc.edu/~dwilson/rsfc/RuleChanges.txt, 1
8. Dorais, *Forward Pass*, 42.
9. Allison Danzig, *Oh, How They Played the Game* (New York: MacMillan, 1971), 233.
10. http://home.no.net/blrgerro/cdpoint.htm, Cedar Point. 1913. 2.
11. Steele, *Knute Rockne: A Bio-Bibliography*, 195.
12. *Forward Pass Plays Devised by Stagg*, September 20, 1906, 1–13. Amos Alonzo Stagg's Papers, Box 30, Special Collections Research Center, University of Chicago.
13. Dorais, *Forward Pass*, 16.
14. Ibid., 22.
15. http://home.no.net/blrgerro/cdpoint.htm, Cedar Point. 1913. 2.
16. Gus Dorais Collegiate Career, http://wikipedia.org/wiki/Gus_Dorais.
17. Dorais, *Forward Pass*, 52.
18. *Forward Pass Plays Devised by Stagg*, 1–13.
19. Dorais, *Forward Pass*, 50.
20. http://home.no.net/blrgerro/cdpoint.htm, Cedar Point. 1913. 2.
21. *Notre Dame 1915 Dome*, "The Season," 138.

22. *Notre Dame Scholastic*, "Athletic Notes," October 4, 1913, 31. Archives of the University of Notre Dame.

23. Ibid., 31.

24. Ibid., 47.

25. Ibid., 47.

26. *Notre Dame Scholastic* "Athletic Notes," 48.

27. *Notre Dame Scholastic*, "Athletic Notes," 77–78.

28. Ibid., 78.

29. Ibid., 78.

30. Michael Mac Cambridge and Dan Jenkins, *ESPN College Football Encyclopedia* (New York: ESPN Publishing, 2005), 642.

31. Ibid., 122.

32. Ibid., 122.

CHAPTER 10: THE REBIRTH OF INTERCOLLEGIATE FOOTBALL

1. *Notre Dame Scholastic*, "Athletic Notes," October 18, 1913, 78. Archives of the University of Notre Dame. (UNDA)

2. (Gus) E. Dorais, *Forward Pass* (Chicago, Ill.: Athletic Book Company Publishers, 1927), 36.

3. Ibid., 25.

4. *Notre Dame Scholastic*, "Athletic Notes," 78–79.

5. Notre Dame Football Web-site, Football Archives, History, Notre Dame's All-Time Football Lineups, http://und.cstv.com/sports/m-footbl/archive/nd-m-footbl-archive.html, 73.

6. James Beach and Daniel Moore, *The Big Game* (New York: Random House, 1948), xii. UADR/160, UNDA.

7. Ibid., 3.

8. Gene Schoor, "ND's Biggest Game," *100 Years of Notre Dame Football* (New York: William Morrow, 1987), 17. UADR/160, UNDA.

9. Ibid., 17.

10. Schoor, "ND's Biggest Game," 17.

11. Ibid., 17.

12. Jesse C. Harper's Penn State Expense Sheet, November 14, 1913, UADR 3/64, UNDA.

13. Allison Danzig, "The First Army-Notre Dame Game," *The History of American Football* (Englewood Cliffs, N.J.: Prentice-Hall, 1956), 195.

14. Jesse C. Harper communication to West Point's Lt. Dan Sultan, October 27, 1913, UADR 3/21, UNDA.

15. Ibid., 27.

16. United States Military Academy at West Point, www.usma.edu/about.asp

17. *The New York Times*, "Army Wants Big Score," November 1, 1913, 12.
18. Ibid., 12.
19. Schoor, "ND's Biggest Game," 18.
20. Michael R. Steele, *Knute Rockne: A Bio-Bibliography* (Westport, Conn.: Greenwood Press, 1983), 214.
21. *Notre Dame Scholastic*, "Brilliant Forward Passes Overwhelm the Army," November 8, 1913, 109. *New York Times*, 1 November reprint. UNDA.
22. Ibid., 109.
23. Ibid., 107.
24. Ibid., 108
25. Ibid., 108.
26. Ibid., 108.
27. Harry Cronin, "Notre Dame Passes Rout Army – 35 – 13," *Notre Dame 1887-1923 Scrapbook*, November 1, 1913. UNDA.
28. Ibid., 107.
29. Ibid., 107.
30. *Notre Dame Scholastic*, "Brilliant Forward Passes Overwhelm the Army," 108.
31. Ibid., 108.
32. Schoor, "ND's Biggest Game," 20.
33. *Notre Dame Scholastic*, "Brilliant Forward Passes Overwhelm the Army," 109.
34. Ibid., 109.
35. Ibid., 107.
36. *The New York Times*, "Notre Dame Passes Rout Army 35 – 13," November 1, 1913, 12.
37. Ibid., 12.
38. Ibid., 12.
39. *Notre Dame Scholastic*, "Brilliant Forward Passes Overwhelm the Army," 110. *New York Herald*, 1 November reprint. UNDA.
40. *Notre Dame Scholastic*, "Brilliant Forward Passes Overwhelm the Army," *Chicago Record-Herald*, 1 November reprint. UNDA.
41. *Notre Dame Scholastic*, "Brilliant Forward Passes Overwhelm the Army," 110. *New York Evening Telegram*, 1 November reprint. UNDA.
42. *Notre Dame Scholastic*, "Brilliant Forward Passes Overwhelm the Army," 111. *Chicago Evening Journal*, 1 November 1913 reprint. UNDA.
43. *Notre Dame Scholastic*, "Brilliant Forward Passes Overwhelm the Army," 110. *Chicago Daily News*, 1 November reprint. UNDA.
44. *Notre Dame Scholastic*, "Brilliant Forward Passes Overwhelm the Army," 112. *New York World*, 1 November reprint. UNDA.
45. *Notre Dame Scholastic*, "Brilliant Forward Passes Overwhelm the Army," 112. *New York Press*, 1 November reprint. UNDA.

46. *Notre Dame Scholastic*, "Brilliant Forward Passes Overwhelm the Army,"
112. Quote Joe Byrne. UNDA.

47. *Chicago Daily Tribune*, "Chicago is Champion," 15 November, 1.

48. Jesse C. Harper's Penn State Game Expense Sheet, November 14, 1913,
UADR 3/64, UNDA.

49. *The New York Times*, "State's First Defeat at Home," November 8, 1913,
12.

50. *Notre Dame Scholastic*, "Brilliant Forward Passes Overwhelm the Army,"
126. *Philadelphia Evening Bulletin*, 8 November reprint. UNDA.

51. *Notre Dame Scholastic*, "Athletic Notes," November 29, 1913, 158.
UNDA.

52. Ibid. Reprinted from the *Chicago Daily Tribune*.

53. *Notre Dame Scholastic*, "The Team Leaves for South," 22 November
1913. UNDA.

54. *Notre Dame Scholastic*, "Athletic Notes," *Chicago Herald*, 22 November
1913 reprint. UNDA.

55. *The Dome (1914)*, "1913 Football," Notre Dame Publishing, 151.

The Legacy

1. *Notre Dame Scholastic*, "Athletic Notes," February 16, 1918, 281. UNDA.

2. Michael Mac Cambridge and Dan Jenkins. *ESPN College Football
Encyclopedia* (New York: ESPN Publishing, 2005), 642.

3. Knute Rockne's career record, "Career Winning Percentages," College
Football History – Leading College Coaches, www.hickoksports.com/.

4. *Notre Dame Scholastic*, "Athletic Notes," February 16, 1918, 281. UNDA.

5. George Gipp, National Football Foundation College Football Hall of
Fame, www.collegefootball.org.

6. James Harper (son of Jesse Harper), interview with Phil & Rose Brooks at
Marriott Hotel by South Bend's College Football's Hall of Fame, August 14,
2006.

7. Ibid., August 14, 2006, interview.

8. Knute Rockne's career record, "Career Winning Percentages," College
Football History – Leading College Coaches, www.hickoksports.com/.

9. Allison Danzig. *The History of American Football* (Englewood Cliffs, N.J.:
Prentice Hall), 222.

Bibliography

ARCHIVES

Alma College Library Archives, Alma, Mich.
Alma Public Library Archives, Alma, Mich.
Denison University Archives, Granville, Ohio
St. Louis University Archives, St. Louis, Mo.
University of Chicago Special Collections Research Center, Chicago, Ill.
    Amos Alonzo Stagg Papers
University of Notre Dame Archives, Notre Dame, Ind.
University of Notre Dame Athletic Director's Records, Notre Dame, Ind.
Wabash College, Robert T. Ramsey, Jr. Library Archival Center, Crawfordsville, Ind.
    Jesse C. Harper Papers

PRIMARY SOURCES

Alma College Academic Catalog
The Alma Record (Alma, Mich.)
The Almanian
The Bachelor (Wabash College Newspaper)
Cap and Gown
The Cavalier Daily (Charlottesville, Va.)
Chicago Daily Tribune
The Dome (University of Notre Dame)
The Echo
Kansas City Star
The New York Times
The Notre Dame Magazine

The Notre Dame Scholastic (magazine)
The South Bend Tribune (newspaper)
The Wabash (Wabash College Magazine)
The Waukesha Freeman Newspaper (Wisconsin)
The Weekly Almanian (Alma College Student Newspaper)
Vanderbilt Journal of Entertainment and Technology Law

BOOKS

Alma College 1972 Football Fact Book

Baker, DR. L. H. *Football: Facts and Figures.* New York: Farrar & Rinehart, Inc., 1945.

Beach, James, and Daniel Moore. *The Big Game.* New York: Random House. 1948.

Beld, Gordon. "Scores from Yester Years." *Alma College 1972 Football Fact Book.* St. Alma, MI: Alma College Archives, 1973.

Cohane, Tim. *Great College Football Coaches of the Twenties and Thirties.* New Rochelle, N.Y.: Arlington House Publishing, 1973.

Danzig, Allison. *The History of American Football.* Englewood Cliffs, N.J.: Prentice Hall, 1956.

Danzig, Allison. *Oh, How They Played the Game.* New York: Macmillan, 1971.

Dorais, Charles (Gus) E. *Forward Pass.* Chicago, Ill.: Athletic Book Company Publishers, 1927.

Haughton, Percy D. *Football and How to Watch It.* Boston: Little, Brown, 1924.

Heisman, John W. *Principles of Football.* St. Louis, Mo.: Sports Publishing Bureau, 1922.

Mac Cambridge, Michael, and Dan Jenkins. *ESPN College Football Encyclopedia.* New York: ESPN Publishing, 2005.

Pope, Edwin. *Football's Greatest Coaches.* Atlanta, Ga.: Tupper and Love, 1955.

Schoor, Gene. "ND's Biggest Game." *100 Years of Notre Dame Football.* New York: William Morrow, 1987.

Schoor, Gene. *A Treasury of Notre Dame Football.* New York: Funk & Wagnalls Company, 1962.

Stagg, Amos Alonzo, and Wesley Winans Stout. *Touchdown.* New York: Longmans, Green & Co., 1927.

Steele, Michael R. *Knute Rockne: A Bio-Bibliography.* Westport, Conn.: Greenwood Press, 1983.

Yost, Fielding Harris. *Football for Player and Spectator*. Ann Arbor, Mich.: University Publishing Company, 1905.

PUBLISHED SOURCES

"Abolition of Football or Immediate Reforms." *The New York Times*, November 28, 1905.

"Alma Wins Again." *The Weekly Almanian*, November 19, 1907.

Almanian, VIII, No. 3, 1906.

"Army Wants Big Score." *The New York Times*, November 1, 1913.

"Around the Campus." *Almanian* VIII, No. 2, November 1906.

"As to Football." *The Bachelor*, November 6, 1909.

"Athletic Notes." *The Notre Dame Scholastic*, September 27, 1913.

"Athletic Notes." *The Notre Dame Scholastic*, October 4, 1913.

"Athletic Notes." *The Notre Dame Scholastic*, November 22, 1913.

"Athletic Notes." *The Notre Dame Scholastic*, November 29, 1913.

"Athletic Notes." *The Notre Dame Scholastic*, February 16, 1918.

"Athletics." *The Notre Dame Scholastic*, November 25, 1911.

"Athletics - Football." *The Wabash*, April 1911.

"Athletics - Football." *The Wabash*, November 1911.

"Baseball Report." *Cap and Gown*, 1904-1907.

Beld, Gordon. "Scores from Yester Years." *Alma College 1972 Football Fact Book*. St. Alma, MI: Alma College Archives, 1972.

"Brilliant Forward Passes Overwhelm the Army." *The Notre Dame Scholastic*, November 8, 1913.

"Camp on Princeton Game." *Chicago Daily Tribune*, November 18, 1906.

"Career Winning Percentages." *College Football History – Leading College Coaches*, www.hickoksports.com/

"Champion of Indiana." *Notre Dame Scholastic*, November 2, 1912.

"Chicago Defeats Iowa - 42 - 0." *Chicago Daily Tribune*, October 8, 1905.

"Chicago is Champion." *Chicago Daily Tribune*, November 1, .

"Chicago's Notable Victory, Michigan's First Defeat." *The New York Times*, December 1, 1905.

"Coach Harper Explicit in New Football Rules." *The Bachelor*, March 10, 1910.

"Coach Harper to Return First of Winter Term." *The Bachelor*, December 20, 1909.

"Coach Jesse Harper Signs Long Contract." *The Bachelor*, November 18, 1909.

College Football 1906 Ranking of Teams Within College Conference, http://www.phys.utk.edu/sorensen/cfr/cfr/Output/1906/CF_1906_Conferences.html.

"College Is Open For Seventy-Eighth Year." *The Bachelor*, September 23, 1909.

Cronin, Harry. "Notre Dame Passes Rout Army – 35 – 13." *Notre Dame 1887-1923 Scrapbook*, November 1, 1913.

"Daughter Arrived," *The Bachelor*, November 20, 1912.

"Defeats Mt. Pleasant." *The Weekly Almanian*, November 19, 1907.

"DePauw's Dream of 20 – 0 rudely Shattered." *The Bachelor*, October 11, 1909.

Dynan, Philip A. *"The First Forward Pass,"* athletic public relations article, St. Louis University Archives, 1955.

The Echo. October, 1906

"Eller Schedules Game for Saturday." *The Bachelor*, September 27, 1909.

"First Real Football Tests the New Rules." *The New York Times*, October 27, 1906.

"Football Committee Suggests New Rules; Forward Pass Proposed." *The New York Times*, December 10, 1905.

"Football Conference at the White House." *The New York Times*, December 5, 1905.

"Football Conference Will Convene Today." *The New York Times*, December 8, 1905.

"Football Differences Prolong Big Meeting – Many Discrepancies arise in Council of Experts." *The New York Times*, October 29, 1906.

"Football Season ends with splendid game followed by Reception." *The Alma Record*, November 27, 1907.

"Football Unfit for College Use," President Eliot Talks in His Report on Harvard for 1893-94." *The New York Times*, January 31, 1895.

Football's Forward Pass Turns 100 Years, www.slu.edu/readstory/more/7166.

Gipp, George. National Football Foundation College Football Hall of Fame, www.collegefootball.org.

Gus Dorais, http://wikipedia.org/wiki/Gus_Dorais.

Hall of Fame Members, http://www.uwbadgers.com/hall_of_fame/year.aspx?HOFID=.

"Hanover Swamped by End Runs of Wabash." *The Bachelor*, November 1, 1909.

"Harper Accepts Offer as Notre Dame Coach." *The Bachelor*, December 14, 1912.

"Harper Brought Fiscal Sense to N.D. Football." *The South Bend Tribune (Ind.)*, September 24, 1987.

"Harper is Pleased." *The Alma Record*, September 14, 1907.

"Harper, Chicago '06 to Coach Football Men." *The Bachelor*, May 6, 1909.

"Harvard Beats Bowdoin, 10 - 0, forward passes not attempted until Last Minute of Play." *Chicago Daily Tribune*, October 4, 1906.

"Harvard defeats Maine Team." *Chicago Daily Tribune*, October 7, 1906.

"He's Still Smiling." *The Weekly Almanian*, September, 1907.

History of Morgan Park. 2006. Morgan Park Academy.org.

http://home.no.net/blrgerro/cdpoint.htm, Cedar Point. 1913.

"Jess Harper – Again Takes up Battle He left for Rock." *Kansas City Star*, August 26, 1931.

"John L. Marks 1911-12." *Gridiron Generals Journal* XVIII, No. 9.

Kerezy, John D. "Harper and Milstead Represent Wabash in Football Hall of Fame." Wabash College article, spring 1979.

"King Football 'Exits' Until Next September." *The Bachelor*, December 2, 1909.

Lisska, Anthony J. "A Backward Glance at the Forward Pass." *The Historical Times* XVI, Issue 1 (Fall 2002): 1–7.

"M.A.C. - 0, Alma - 0." *The Weekly Almanian* , December 30, 1907.

"M.A.C. Out of MIAA." *The Alma Record (Alma, Mich.)*, November 13, 1907.

Michigan Intercollegiate Athletic Association, www.miaa.org.

"Michigan loses to Penn 17–0." *Chicago Daily Tribune*, November 18, 1906

"Monogram Men." *The 1914 Dome*, Notre Dame Publishing. 148.

"Movement to Reform Football." *The Bachelor*, January 10, 1910.

National Collegiate Athletic Association, www.ncaa.org.

"Navy in Triumph over Army." *Chicago Daily Tribune*, December 2, 1906.

"New Football a Chaos, the Experts Declare-Ground Gaining by Carrying the Ball made Impossible." *The New York Times*, October 20, 1906.

"New Football a Chaos, the Experts Declare-Ground Gaining by Carrying the Ball made Impossible." *The New York Times*, October 30, 1906.

"New Style Football will be Spectacular." *The New York Times*, August 26, 1906.

"Notre Dame Football Schedule is Completed." *The Bachelor*, March 22, 1913.

"Notre Dame Passes Rout Army 35 – 13." *The New York Times*, November 1, 1913.

The Notre Dame Scholastic, November 8, 1913. Reprint, *Chicago Record-Herald*. Reprint, *New York World*, Reprint, *New York Press*, Reprint, *Philadelphia Evening Bulletin*, Reprint, *Chicago Daily News*, Reprint, *New York Herald*, Reprint, *New York Evening Telegram*.

Notre Dame's All-Time Football Lineups, http://und.cstv.com/sports/m-footbl/archive/nd-m-footbl-archive.html.

"Penn's Scant Victory over Cornell's Team." *The New York Times*, December 1, 1905.

"Portrait of the Past." *The Waukesha Freeman Newspaper (Wisconsin)*, June 8, 1985.

"President's Football Reform Plan Started." *The New York Times*, November 27, 1905.

"Question of Football's Future Now Open." *The Bachelor*, November 2, 1910.

"Roger Wilson is New Captain." *The Bachelor*, September 30, 1909.

Rules Changes Throughout the History of College Football: The Ball, http://homepages.cae.wisc.edu/~dwilson/rsfc/RuleChanges.txt.

"Scarlet Eleven Meets St. Louis Saturday." *The Bachelor*, October 21, 1909.

"Scarlet Football Prospects Look Good." *The Bachelor*, September 23, 1909.

"Scarlet in Readiness for Big Purdue Game." *The Bachelor*, November 4, 1909.

"Scarlet's Opponents Commence the Season." *The Bachelor*, October 4, 1909.

"Scarlet's Win a Wonderful Victory Over the Old Gold and Black Eleven Saturday." *The Bachelor*, November 8, 1909.

Schoor, Gene. "ND's Biggest Game." *100 Years of Notre Dame Football*. New York: William Morrow. 1987.

Schoor, Gene. "A Treasury of Notre Dame Football." *Collier's Magazine* Reprint by Knute Rockne. "From Norway to Notre Dame," 5 October, 1930. Funk & Wagnalls Company. New York: 1962. 33.

Schoor, Gene. "A Treasury of Notre Dame Football." *Esquire Magazine* Reprint by Dale Stafford, "Dorais the Mighty Mite," October, 1945. Funk & Wagnalls Company. New York: 1962. 25.

"Scored on by Ferris Institute." *The Weekly Almanian*, October 22, 1907.

South Dakota All-Time Football Scores, www.usdcoyotes.com/sports/football/alltimescores.pdf.

"St. Louis U. in a 14 to 0 Victory." *The Bachelor*, October 25, 1909.

"Stagg Stops the Football Work.—Orders Maroon Candidates Off Marshall Field Until School Opens." *Chicago Daily Tribune*, September 25, 1906.

"State's First Defeat at Home." *The New York Times*, November 8, 1913.

"Test New Rules in Actual Play." *Chicago Daily Tribune*, September 30, 1906.

"The Age of Innocence: The First 25 Years of the NCAA, 1906–1931." *Vanderbilt Journal of Entertainment and Technology Law* 8, No. 2, spring 2006.

"The First Victory." *The Weekly Almanian*, October 8, 1907.

"The Man Who Set the Table." *The Notre Dame Magazine*, 1988.

"The Olivet Game." *The Alma Record (Alma, Mich.)*, November 6, 1907.

"The Olivet Game." *The Weekly Almanian*, November 5, 1907.

"The Season." *The Notre Dame Dome (1915)*.

"The Second Victory." *The Weekly Almanian*, October 15, 1907.

"Tigers Score Only Once-Forward Pass Tallies." *The New York Times*, October 6, 1906.

"Tribute to 1911 Athletics." *The Wabash*, December 1911.

"Tribute to 1911 Athletics." *The Wabash*, June 1912.

"Tribute to Ralph Wilson." *The Wabash*, November 1910.

"Tricks Score on Harvard; Quarterback Kick, Followed by Forward Pass, Yields Touchdown." *The New York Times*, October 11, 1906.

"Twenty Men Aspire to Scarlet Quintet." *The Bachelor*, November 20, 1912.

United States Military Academy at West Point, www.usma.edu/about.asp.

"Wabash Bows to the Western Champions." *The Bachelor*, November 23, 1909.

"Wabash Calendar." *The Bachelor*, September 23, 1909.

"Wabash Defeats Illinois Eleven 27 to 0." *The Bachelor*, October 4, 1909.

"Wabash Prepares for Strong Catholic Eleven." *The Bachelor*, November 18, 1909.

"West Point - 6; Annapolis, 6." *The New York Times*, December 2, 1905.

"West Point's Spring Practice." *The New York Times*, August 28, 1906.

"What's inside this Chapel may surprise you." *The Cavalier Daily* (*Charlottesville, Va.*), March 4, 2004.

"Whirlwind Game at Hanover." *Chicago Daily Tribune*, October 7, 1906.

"Wilson Gives Life in Wabash Service." *The Bachelor*, October 29, 1910.

"Yale Plays Well Under New Rules. Roome Star of the Game." *Chicago Daily Tribune*, October 4, 1906.

Watterson, John S. "Inventing Modern Football." *American Heritage Magazine*, September/October 1988.

Index

abolishment of football, 16, 17
Adrian College, 148
Albion College, 95, 97, 98, 107
Albright College, 66
Alma College, 46, 87–91, 94–109, 111–115, 118, 160–162, 187, 188
American Football Rules Committee (AFRC), 25, 47
Amherst College, 16
Arizona State University, 15
University of Arkansas, 143
Army, *see* United States Military Academy
Army–Navy game, 12, 79, 127, 136
Auburn University, 23

backfield shift, 36, 41, 48
Bangs, Francis, 17
baseball skills, 46, 48, 86, 99
Bates University, 79
Baylor University, 16
Bell, John C., 23, 24
Berger, Al, 141, 164, 184
Bezdek, Hugo, 143
blocking, 10, 14, 25, 26, 36, 38, 39, 45, 48, 50, 58, 72, 82, 91, 92, 96, 117, 119, 127, 140, 183, 186, 200; cross-blocking, 55
blocking rules, 48
bootleg pass, 53, 55
Boston College, 15
Bowdoin College, 78

Brooklyn Poly Prep, 165
Bruske, August, F., 87, 98
Butler University, 116, 120, 125, 126, 131
button-hook, 173, 202

Camp, Walter, 16, 19, 21, 23, 24, 35, 41, 65, 79, 80
Canton Bulldogs, 145
Carlisle Indian School, 64, 65, 76, 79, 80, 154, 206, 211, 213
Carroll College, 67, 71–73, 75
Cartier Field, 146, 182–186, 195
Cavanaugh, John W., 149, 220
Cedar Point, Ohio, 172, 174–176, 182
Central Michigan, 16, 106
choice pass, 138, 139, 176, 180
Christian Brothers College, 156, 162, 212, 214
Clemson University, 68
Cochems, Edward B., 61, 67–74, 83, 143, 191
Colgate University, 77, 188, 208, 213, 215
college administrators, 12, 14–16, 19, 47
College of Pacific, 36
Columbia University, 15–17, 67, 129
Columbia East, 67
Cornell University, 3–5, 12, 24, 77
Cotter, William, 153–155
cradle catch, 31, 32, 45, 48, 139, 172, 178
crossing pattern, 56
curl pattern, 45

Daly, Charles D., 24, 29, 158, 194, 198, 200, 204, 205

Dartmouth College, 15, 24, 65, 66, 77, 78, 147, 166, 213

Dashiell, Paul, 23, 24

deaths, football related, 1, 11, 14, 26, 82, 83, 127, 129, 132–134, 137, 217, 220

defensive adjustment, 61, 204

defensive backs, 182, 192

defensive corners, 56, 204

defensive scheme, 60, 72

Denison University, 143–145, 174

DePauw University, 116–118, 120, 134

Detroit Lions, 220

Dorais, Gus, 141, 164, 167, 168, 170, 172–176, 179, 180, 182–186, 190, 192–197, 199–201, 203–207, 209, 211, 213, 219, 220

downs, four for a first down adopted, 142; three for a first down, 19

dropkick, 108, 204

Duke University, 15

Earlham College, 134

eastern football, 12, 204, 207, 209

Eckersall, Walter, 3, 11, 49, 51, 87, 100, 143, 146, 165, 166, 167

Eichenlaub, Ray, 140, 141, 164, 183, 184, 186, 192, 199, 200, 205, 206, 209, 211, 213

Eisenhower, Dwight D., 202

eligibility rules, 14

eligible receiver, 60

Eliot, Charles, 16, 80, 81

end sweep, 6, 41, 42, 82, 96, 115, 141, 186

end zone, 4, 9, 96, 203

equipment, players', 9

experimental game, 19

Fairmount College, 19

fake kick, 36, 57

fake punt, 57, 59

fatalities in football, see deaths

Feeney, Al, 183, 199, 201

Ferris Institute, 94, 96, 105

Fine, J. B., 24, 29

Folsom, Bob, 58, 65, 78

football, shape of, 32, 69, 174

Fordham University, 16

forward pass, first, 21; first official, 73

forward pass, first legalized, 25

forward pass, first plays designed for, 32

forward pass, limited in length, 28

forward-pass plays 33, 44, 60, 139, 172, 175, 182; see also passing patterns/routes

forward-pass rules, 25–29, 44, 45, 51, 66, 77, 140

Franklin College, 67

Franklin Field, 3

fullback, 22, 41, 52, 77, 80, 92, 96, 104, 119, 122, 140, 166, 183, 184, 186, 189, 199, 201, 202, 204, 206, 208, 209, 213

Georgetown University, 15, 128, 131

Georgia Tech, 68

Gipp, George, 220

goal line, 2–6, 7, 9, 19, 22, 27, 77, 80, 81, 105, 123, 125, 131, 143, 202, 205

Gonzaga University, 219

guarantee, 153, 155–162

Hackett, H. B., 74, 76

halfback, 3, 14, 22, 28, 41, 42, 51–53, 55–57, 67, 71, 72, 92, 102, 112, 119, 121, 128, 131, 140, 144, 145, 166, 183, 184, 187, 199, 200, 220

Hamilton College, 16

Harper, James "Jim," son, 220

Harper, Jesse Clair, 46, 49, 84–86, 88,
    89, 90, 92–94, 96, 99, 100–102, 104,
    109, 111–116, 118, 120, 121, 123–127, 131,
    132, 134, 137–140, 142, 147–151, 154,
    156, 157, 159, 160, 162–164, 167, 168,
    172–174, 176–182, 184, 185, 192–194,
    198, 201, 203, 205, 207, 209, 210,
    212–214, 216, 218, 220, 221
Harper, Katherine, daughter, 150, 171
Harper, Melville Campbell, wife, 112,
    114, 130, 137, 138, 146, 149, 150, 171,
    207, 216, 217
Harper, William Rainey, 39
Harvard University, 11, 12, 15, 16, 17, 23,
    24, 39, 55, 66, 76, 77–80, 127, 146, 158,
    194, 198, 213
hash marks, 9
Haverford College, 16, 24
Heisman, John, 7, 22, 23, 26, 61, 68, 191
Hillsdale College, 96, 104
Holy Cross, College of the, 66, 67, 78
huddle, 8, 35, 36, 92, 177
Hyde Park High School, 165

incomplete pass, 27, 64, 103, 130, 141, 142
injuries, football related, 8, 9–11, 14, 18,
    26, 27, 30, 41, 71, 80, 82, 83, 120,
    125–127, 129, 132, 183, 185
intentional grounding, 140
Intercollegiate Athletic Association of
    the United States (IAAUS), 16–18
Intercollegiate Football Association
    (IFA), 13
Intercollegiate   Football   Rules
    Committee (IFRC), 6, 13, 17, 18, 23,
    24, 44
interference, 10, 30, 38, 40–43, 48, 52,
    55, 56, 82, 91, 92, 101, 102, 118, 131, 203

Kalamazoo College, 97, 101, 104
kickoff, 43, 64, 68, 93, 106, 117, 122, 123,
    125, 203
Knute Rockne All American, 175

Lafayette College, 3, 16, 116, 120, 122
Lambert, Kent "Skeet," 119, 121,
    139–142, 146
Lambert, Ward "Piggy," 121–124
lateral, 21, 22, 28, 31, 32, 36, 38, 39,
    43–45, 203
Lawrence College, 73
Lebanon Valley College, 66
Lehigh University, 66, 157
line of scrimmage, 6, 8, 25, 27, 28, 35, 38,
    39, 41, 43, 58, 74, 82, 128, 129, 138, 140,
    142, 144, 177, 186, 191, 193
linebackers, 53, 54, 56, 60, 61, 103, 191
Longman, Frank "Shorty," 166, 167

man-to-man defense, 61, 192, 193
Marks, John, 147, 148, 151, 164, 166
Marquette University, 74, 125, 134, 140,
    142, 148
Marshall Field, 1, 49, 62, 86
mass interference, 10, 40, 41, 43, 82
McCracken, Henry M., 16, 17
McEwan, Johnny, 199
Menomonee Falls High School, 72
Merillat, L. A., 188, 199, 205
Miami of Ohio, 124, 145
Michigan State University (Michigan
    Agricultural), 95, 96, 97, 107, 108, 114,
    116, 118, 124, 126, 134, 140, 146, 154,
    160
Michigan Intercollegiate Athletic
    Association (MIAA), 95, 97, 105, 107,
    108, 160
misdirection play, 38, 44, 55, 56, 60, 92,
    103, 115, 121, 122

MIT, 15

model game, 19

Morgan Park Academy, 39, 40, 85, 99, 112

Morris Harvey College, 148

multiple formations, 50, 51, 115

Muskegon High School, 58

National Collegiate Athletic Association (NCAA), 18

Navy, see United States Naval Academy

neutral zone, 25, 82, 119

New York University, 14, 16

Northwestern University, 16, 199, 215

Norwich College, 66, 77

O'Connell, John F., 162

Oak Park High School, 58, 59

Oberlin College, 2, 23, 24

off-tackle plays, 51, 82

offensive football philosophy, 38, 214

offensive formations, 72

Ohio Northern University, 153, 160, 162, 183, 184

Ohio State University, 125, 157, 215

Ohio University, 67

Ohio Wesleyan, 145

Olivet College, 95, 97, 105–108, 124

onside kick, 4, 25, 28, 66, 78, 79, 83

open-style football, 19, 44, 48, 74, 76, 79, 82, 83, 90, 142, 167, 172, 193, 201, 208

Otterbein College, 144

out of bounds, 8, 9, 27

out-of-bound rule, 9

overshifted formation, 51

pass patterns/routes, 26, 31, 44, 45, 48, 139, 173, 174, 175, 182; see also, bootleg pass, button-hook, choice pass, crossing pattern, curl pattern, play-action pass, screen pass

pass-play book, 50

passing, techniques, 32; overhead spiral, 48, 69, 71, 72

passing tree, 139

Penn State University, 66, 146, 154, 157, 159, 162, 164, 182, 210, 211, 213

play-action pass, 52, 56, 57, 58, 60, 74, 93, 103, 115, 138, 177, 179, 180, 192, 201, 208, 212

Pliska, Joe, 141, 184, 185, 187, 199, 200, 203, 206, 209

Princeton University, 12, 16, 21, 22, 24, 77–79, 199, 206

punts, 3–5, 8, 19, 31, 80, 94, 122, 201, 202, 211; frequency, 8

punt-out, 4

Purdue University, 51, 67, 76, 86, 116, 118, 120–126, 131, 134, 140, 147, 148, 171, 215, 218

quarterback, 3, 5–8, 11, 22, 28, 29–33, 35, 38, 41, 43, 45, 48–57, 67, 77–81, 83, 85, 87, 92, 93, 94, 100–102, 104, 112, 115, 117, 119, 121–123, 125, 127, 138–140, 142–144, 146, 158, 164, 165, 167, 170, 173, 176, 177, 179, 181, 188–190, 192–194, 199, 201–203, 209, 211, 213

red zone, 6, 7

Reid, William, Jr., 15, 17, 23, 24

Robinson, Bradbury, 70– 75, 174

Rockefeller, John D., 39

Rockne, Knute, 140, 152, 164–168, 170, 172–176, 178–180, 182, 184–187, 196, 198–201, 203, 204, 206, 209, 211, 213, 218–221

Roosevelt, Theodore, 12, 15, 194

Roudebush, George, 144, 145, 174
Marshall, Roy, 96, 104
rugby, 15, 35, 63, 174
rules, 1906 changes, 25
rules committee, 13–15, 17–19, 23–26, 29, 36, 44, 47, 65, 97, 103, 128, 129, 142, 224, 225; *see also* Intercollegiate Football Rules Committee
running back, 52, 53, 87, 101, 130, 202
running game, 5, 44, 49, 60, 65, 68, 72, 74, 75, 81, 104, 107, 179, 180, 183, 188, 192, 194, 206
Rutgers University, 16, 188

safety, of football, 82
San Jose State University, 16
Savage, C. W., 24, 29
Schneider, Jack, 70, 71, 73, 75
scoring, change in, 143
screen pass, 58, 59, 60
secondary coverage, 60
sideline coaching, 104
sleeper play, 59
Southwestern Louisiana, 16
Springfield College, 38, 40, 67
sprint-out play, 51, 52
St. John's Military Academy, 73
St. Louis University, 67–75, 83, 116, 119, 131, 143
Stagg, Amos Alonzo, 2, 8, 20, 22–24, 34–61, 64, 69, 76, 86–88, 90, 91–94, 97, 100, 101, 108, 112, 113, 143, 166, 167, 172, 181, 191, 208, 210, 214, 221
Stanford University, 5, 12, 15, 42
Starbuck, Sam, 122
State University of New York at Brockport, 15
student-athletes, 13, 169, 172, 185, 219, 220

substitution rule, 9, 10
Susquehanna College, 37
Swarthmore College, 14
Syracuse University, 16, 67, 125, 154, 215

T-formation, 36, 38, 92, 102
tackle-back formation, 41, 43, 82
tackles-back formation, 41, 42
tackling, 1, 10, 14, 35, 36, 45, 64, 96, 117, 118, 127, 131, 183, 200
Temple University, 15
Thorpe, Jim, 145
touchdown pass, 59, 186, 201, 211
Trinity College, 15, 16
Tufts University, 77, 188

unbalanced formation, 51, 72
Union College, 14, 15
United States Military Academy, 12, 73, 77, 79, 80, 119, 127, 136, 157–159, 162, 164, 176, 182, 188, 189, 193–195, 197, 198–209, 211, 213, 214
United States Naval Academy, 12, 23, 24, 79, 80, 127, 136, 188, 213, 229, 248
University of Akron, 23
University of Arizona, 15
University of California, 15
University of Chicago, 1, 2, 11, 23, 24, 34, 36, 39, 41, 42, 46, 61, 62, 84, 86, 89, 98, 99, 112, 146, 166, 167, 198, 208, 210, 213, 214
University of Cincinnati, 16, 144, 145
University of Colorado, 12
University of Detroit, 118, 160, 219
University of Georgia, 22, 23, 57
University of Illinois, 3, 58, 59, 62, 76, 85, 86, 116, 120, 121, 148, 158, 215
University of Iowa, 72, 74, 85, 86, 87, 99, 215, 219

University of Kansas, 12, 74, 75
University of Kentucky, 154
University of Michigan, 2, 5, 47, 79, 108, 125, 160, 161
University of Minnesota, 2, 24, 76, 79, 86, 125, 161, 210
University of Nebraska, 11, 12, 24, 154, 156, 213
University of North Carolina, 22, 23, 57
University of North Dakota, 68, 154
University of Notre Dame, 66, 108, 116, 125, 140–142, 146–164, 166–173, 176, 182, 184–188, 190–195, 197–214, 217–220
University of Oklahoma, 156, 212
University of Pennsylvania, 3–5, 12, 23, 24, 44, 79, 199
University of Pittsburgh, 120, 124, 148, 154, 211
University of Rochester, 16
University of South Dakota, 161, 162, 185–187, 190–194
University of Texas, 24, 154–157, 159, 162, 164, 212
University of Tulsa, 16
University of Virginia, 15, 128
University of Wisconsin, 67, 68
Vanderbilt University, 12, 233, 244, 250
Villanova University, 64, 65, 127
Virginia Tech, 13
Wabash College, 110–128, 130–134, 137, 138, 140–142, 146–151, 160, 162, 163, 165, 167, 171
Wake Forest University, 16
Walsh, M. J., 149, 163
Warner, Glenn "Pop," 22, 61, 77
Washburn College, 19
Washington & Jefferson College, 58, 77, 78, 213

Wesleyan College, 77
Wesleyan University, 66, 67
West Virginia University, 146
West Virginia Wesleyan, 145, 146
Western Conference, 2, 47, 49, 67, 120, 140, 147, 148, 154, 155, 161, 169, 185, 210, 214, 215, 218
Williams College, 66
Williams, Henry L., 24
Wilson, Ralph, 130–133, 137
Wilson, Roger, 116, 117
Wooster College, 144

Yale University, 12, 16, 21, 22, 24, 35, 38, 39, 41, 67, 76, 77, 79, 119, 154, 157, 158, 188, 208
Yost, Fielding, 2, 4–7, 31, 108, 166

Zuppke, Robert, 58, 59, 76

Acknowledgments

Coaching football for more than four decades at the college and high school levels has provided me the opportunity to work with thousands of young men and coaches. I want to thank every young man competing under my guidance and every associate coach working on my staff over the years for their tireless preparation, commitment to excellence, and ability to succeed. I am privileged to have coached young men from the Michigan high schools of Corunna, Lansing Resurrection, Lansing Monsignor Gabriels, East Lansing, and St. Joseph Lake Michigan Catholic, and at Alma College and Eastern Michigan University.

Special thanks go to my close friend Jim O'Malley for encouragement and critiquing the manuscript at various stages and our friend John Rubleske for editing the original manuscript. Thanks to John Madill for his professional photography of former Lake Michigan Catholic football players reenacting old formations.

Guidance from professional writers Gordon Beld and Pen Campbell, along with prolific author Jill Culby, was greatly appreciated. While researching, I met so many wonderful people willing to help. I would like to recognize special university staff including: Jennifer Starkey, Alma College Librarian; Elizabeth Swift, Wabash Archivist, and Johanna Herring, retired

Wabash Archivist; Daniel Meyer, Associate Director and University Archivist at the University of Chicago's Special Collections Research Center, Assistant Director, Julia Gardner and her associates at the University of Chicago's Special Collections Research Center; Brian Kunderman, Information Director, St. Louis University, John Waide, St. Louis University Archivist; Katie Sanders, Carroll College Archivist and Rick Mobley, Sports Information Director, Carroll College; Craig Hicks, Denison University and Anthony J. Lisska, Granville Historical Society, Denison University; Sharon Sumpter, Assistant Archivist, Elizabeth Hogan, Photo Archivist, the Archives University of Notre Dame, and Charles Lamb Photograph Curator, the Archives University of Notre Dame.

Thanks also go to Frank Maggio at Hinshaw & Culbertson LLP Firm in Rockford, Illinois, for introducing me to James "Jim" Harper, born December 4, 1918. Jim has become a great friend and an invaluable resource. I am proud to honor and credit his dad, Jesse Clair Harper, for his role and impact on intercollegiate football.

I offer all my love and appreciation to our children Mike, Julie, Patti, and Therese, their spouses Wendy, Dave, and David, our eight grandchildren Tiffany, Bonnie, Philip, James, Jodie, Angie, Jennifer, and Jacqulyn for their love, support and sacrifice. My deepest love and indebtedness go to my wife Rose. Her unending support, lifetime commitment, and unconditional love will always be cherished.

I also wish to thank the staff of Westholme Publishing and its publisher, Bruce H. Franklin, for his insight and enthusiastic interest in this story.

CPSIA information can be obtained
at www.ICGtesting.com
Printed in the USA
BVOW08s0903191216

471220BV00002B/384/P